A SHORT HISTORY OF ENGLAND

He that will trow it, trow it;
he that will not, lefe.

Adjuration of the Saxon Historian

A SHORT HISTORY OF
ENGLAND

BY

R.J.WHITE

*Fellow of Downing College, Lecturer in History
at the University of Cambridge*

CAMBRIDGE
AT THE UNIVERSITY PRESS
1967

Published by the Syndics of the Cambridge University Press
Bentley House, 200 Euston Road, London, N.W. 1
American Branch: 32 East 57th Street, New York, N.Y. 10022

© Cambridge University Press 1967

Library of Congress Catalogue Card Number: 67–11531

Printed in Great Britain
at the University Printing House, Cambridge
(Brooke Crutchley, University Printer)

Preface

'Anyone who undertakes to write a history of England down the ages', G. M. Trevelyan once said, 'must needs be out of his depth in one part or another of the course, and must make good as best he may by lusty swimming.' That was in the 1920s. A lesser mortal undertaking the task in the 1960s must accumulate what Thomas Carlyle called 'a formidable apparatus...swim-bladders...life preservers...and other precautionary and vehicu-latory gear...' To label my own swim-bladders would be to retail the names and titles of a host of scholars, many of whom, I fear, would not wish to be associated with a work like the present; and some of whom, I apprehend, will think that I have been unduly sparing in the use of quotation marks. Perhaps I may be allowed simply, but without any claim to originality, to write here the single word *majoribus*.

In acknowledgement of personal and private indebtedness I must thank my wife for serving me with infinite patience as both life-preserver and vehicular gear, and in especial for her contribution to the first two chapters, among whose waters I should otherwise have sunk like a stone. Hers also were the labours of the index.

R. J. W.

Cambridge 1967

Contents

vii

Introduction

On the Character of English History

Boswell: The History of England is so strange, that, if it were not so well vouched as it is, it would hardly be credible.

Johnson: Sir, if it were told as shortly...as the History of the Jewish Kings, it would be equally liable to objections of improbability.

Dr Johnson gave as an example of the strangeness of English history Charles I's concessions to Parliament. 'Related nakedly,' he said, 'without detail of circumstances, they would not have been believed.' Anyone can test this for himself by reading the naked narration in Thomas Hobbes's *Behemoth*. What is wanted is not simply 'corroborative detail' but what the Doctor called 'preparation for introducing the different events': in other words, time, and space, and big books. 'Short Histories', more especially when they are intended to serve as text-books, produce incredulity. Brevity may be the soul of wit, but it is the enemy of historical truth, and—as Johnson concluded: 'Truth, sir, is of the greatest value in these things.'

A Frenchman has described the history of England as one of mankind's outstanding successes. If only for that reason it is peculiarly ill adapted to the demands of brevity. Success takes a lot of explaining and, perhaps, when it is over, excusing. Unless, of course, it be simply accounted to providential favour, which is a form of cheating on a scarcely less enormous scale than those ancient alibis which relied upon Divine chastisement for the destruction of empires from St Augustine to Bossuet. Not that the English have noticeably denied themselves such short-cuts to truth. From Burke to Butterfield they have been taught, both mystically and critically, to take notice of the providential element in their history. Quite apart from politicians and historians, they have taken it for granted in their conversation, and more especially in their songs. When Mr Podsnap in *Our Mutual Friend* told the foreign gentleman: 'This island was Blest, sir, to the Direct Exclusion of such Other Countries as—as there may happen to be,' the foreign gentleman laughed politely and said that 'it was a little particular of Providence, for the frontier is not large'. And we are meant to laugh, too. Mr Podsnap was putting into prose what his countrymen had been singing since James Thomson and Dr Arne gave them *Rule Britannia*, the song that was to become their second national anthem, investing their imaginations with the vision of an autochthonous race no less separately and especially 'blest' than the ancient Greeks or the modern Japanese. 'When Britain first at Heaven's command arose from out the azure main...' evokes the vision of a sacred land mass rising out of the sea at a Divine fiat, a vision which looks back to the gleam of Shakespeare's 'precious stone set in the silver sea', and forward to Kipling's *Recessional* and Elgar's *Pomp and Circumstance* number 2. Surely such a people might be excused from troubling about historical explanation!

'It has been the misfortune of this age,' Edmund Burke once complained, 'that everything is to be discussed.' He was writing at the outbreak of the French Revolution, when an old world was going down in ruin and a new world was struggling to be born. It is at such times that everything comes into debate, even Providence, and such a time is now. The British, the people of providential favour have lost, or given up, an empire. Their part in the world in terms of wealth and power is passing into other hands. They are accustomed to reminders that they are no longer a first-class power. The next History of Great Britain will probably be called the History of England, and its author will be a man called Heap. But even Uriah Heap's History of England will be required to go behind Providence in seeking to explain the success that crowned the British nation before it shrank to be England and learnt to be 'umble. And it will need to be elaborate, detailed, and long. For nothing exceeds like success.

What, apart from its notorious success, are the characteristics of English history? Were it not for our modern distrust of 'real Essences' we should be inclined to say that it has a 'character', like a person, a balance of dispositions which constitute an identity. We detect this 'character' in action from age to age, and more especially in times of crisis. It is not the same thing as 'the national character', which may or may not exist, and certainly undergoes changes with the passage of time. Rather it is to be discerned in certain patterns of collective behaviour, a number of perennially operative forces which are for the most part traceable to material circumstances such as racial composition, geographical configuration, and climate. There is nothing mysterious, let alone mystical, about such factors, although there is a certain mystery about the way the inhabitants of these islands have used them or been affected by them. Racial, geographical, climatic determinism is a blind alley, leading to nothing, explaining nothing. It is what a people do with their geography, their geology, their climate, that matters. Climate is a mediator rather than a master. Some people learn toleration from being shut up indoors or compelled to share tiny patches of shade with their fellows. Others develop a burning hatred of the very sight of their fellow men, and run into blood feuds, mayhem, or homicidal mania. To live in a country where for a great part of the year one needs hardly any clothes and can survive on a handful of figs may produce either the high-tension politics of the Greek city state or the inertia of the great tropical despotisms. There are physical circumstances, as Montesquieu put it, in which 'it is for the legislator to make civil laws which determine the nature of the climate...' The climatic interpretation of the 'moderation' of the English, of which they are immoderately proud, and which is said to have made parliamentary government possible, has been exploded like the myth of their temperate climate, the myth of the nineteenth-century tourist agency, with the setting in of the Little Ice Age in the twentieth. The happy notion that the British achievement of a workable system of parliamentary democracy was the offspring of open-air assemblies under oak-trees has gone the same way as 'our liberty-loving Anglo-Saxon ancestors' of the Teutonic historians.

The two facts worthy of consideration in respect of physical environment are the highly variegated stock of the people who populated the island and the early stage at which their homeland acquired a considerable degree of insularity. Not only were the components of the stock Celtic, Saxon, Danish and Norman, but each component brought with it a fringe of unidentifiable folk, slaves, camp-followers, or hangers-on drawn from the most diverse origins. Those who arrived with the Roman conquest came from every far-flung region of the empire, while the Normans of the Conquest were a positive league of nations. To call the one 'Roman' and the other 'Norman' tells us next to nothing about them. The British Isles were populated for much more than a thousand years by the mixed and mongrel peoples of a Europe in the process of what used to be known as *die Völkerwanderung*. No great nation of Europe was ever a pure stock, and if there is one thing that can be confidently said about the putative nation that became known as the 'British' it is that it was less pure than any other. Here again the perpetration of myths and legends by popular songs and patriotic verse has done its worst for us. 'Saxon and Norman and Dane are we,' sang Alfred Tennyson, a bearded Celt from the Danelaw, greeting the Princess Alexandra in 1863. And what of the Celt? asked Matthew Arnold, for without the Celt we should have been mere puddings, offspring of what Thomas Carlyle called 'a gluttonous race of Jutes and Angles, lumbering about in pot-bellied equanimity'. Without the Normans, we should be without Brooks of Sheffield, that notoriously sharp gentleman whose everlasting memorial is to be found in Domesday Book.[1] And who knows where we should be without the Danes? Nor should we ever underrate the fact that the Roman spirit presided over us for a period nearly as long as that which divides us at the present day from the reign of Elizabeth I. 'The very habit of blending together things so diverse as the Celtic spirit and the Roman, the medieval and Renaissance, the feudal and the democratic, has constantly produced new forms of life and thought which Britain has given back to the Continent as her own peculiar contribution to the life and thought of Europe,'

[1] For Brooks of Sheffield, see chapter 2 of *David Copperfield*. It is noteworthy that when the French translate an English comedy of north-country manners, they make the man from the north a Norman.

4

wrote R. G. Collingwood in 1936.[1] Thus 'Britain has given to Europe the Irish and Anglo-Saxon scholarship and art of the dark ages, the empirical philosophy of the school of Locke, the principles of parliamentary government, and the fruits of the industrial revolution'.

As for the insularity of the island, how many—or how few—thousands of years ago it happened no one knows. Certain it is that Britain was for many thousands a part of the mainland, 'a refuse-heap on the edge of the ocean into which are swept the outworn relics of ethnic migrations and spiritual fermentations'.[2] The mere fact of the sea having marked off the island from the continental land mass, thus constituting the famous 'moat' to which the British have been adjured so often to look, matters little. For many centuries before the final conquest of 1066, peoples in tribes and families had been crossing over in boats no bigger than dug-out canoes and wicker-woven coracles. At no time has the moat proved impassable. At its most formidable, the barrier has served to delay rather than to impede, and whether it can do as much as that in an age of jet-propelled transport aircraft is still a matter for speculation. Yet 'Britannia, the pride of the ocean,' seated on her sand-bank, complete with helmet, shield and trident, and with a lighthouse at her back, still looks out from the penny-piece of Queen Elizabeth II, and there are still no wings in the sky above the sea.

As a controlling factor in the history of England, physical insularity has been of greater psychological than material force. It has helped to procreate what the French know less happily as 'Maginot-mindedness', a sense of security, of final invincibility. There was built up a historic memory of successful exclusion, and with it an assumption of ineffable superiority, sufficiently infuriating to what Kipling called 'lesser breeds without the law', but enormously effective in times of emergency for closing mind and imagination against the possibility of defeat. Perhaps it was the routine ebullience of an elderly lady facing the

[1] R. G. Collingwood and J. N. L. Myres, *Oxford History of England*, vol. I, *Roman Britain and the English Settlements*, 3rd edition (Oxford, 1937), p. 5.
[2] The words are those of R. G. Collingwood.

commandos of Boer farmers that caused Queen Victoria to tell Mr Balfour: 'Please understand that there is no one depressed in *this* house; we are not interested in the possibilities of defeat; they do not exist.' But it was the assurance of a historic people that caused the message to be inscribed on cards in every public-house in the summer of 1940. The shared experience of memories of successful repudiation, achieved at a high price in blood and sweat and tears, may surpass even the welding-power of a common stock and a common language. The admixture of an unspoken sense of moral rightness, likewise derived from historic memory, can make such a people literally invincible long after geographical immunity from catastrophe has ceased to be a reality. 'A war fought for our own self-preservation has been nearly always (not, I say, in every case) a war for the liberation of Europe...a war in which world opinion will be mainly on our side,' wrote Sir Llewellyn Woodward in 1942.[1] He thought it was his knowledge of English history that enabled him to understand why the English people could feel sure that no enemy would break through their gates. 'Since the sixteenth century we have never had to admit that continental defeat meant total defeat in a great war. Why should we ever make such an admission?'

Geography, too, gave England the forests, the fens, the heath and the moorland, many thousands of acres unsown for centuries, providing the slack which goes with a hinterland, 'free' land to be taken up at need. The frontier has been a famous factor in the history of Russia and the United States. The late B. S. Sumner, discussing Russia as a land of colonization,[2] reminded us that 'for many centuries the frontier played the same part in the history of western Europe, but owing to its diminutive size internal colonization for the most part ceased to be a dominating theme after the later Middle Ages; overseas colonization took its place, and the peoples of Europe struggled with new frontier conditions in new worlds'. The same theme was developed in American historical writing by F. J. Turner in his classic study.[3]

[1] Sir Llewellyn Woodward, *Short Journey*, pp. 244–6.
[2] *Survey of Russian History* (London, 1944), p. 9.
[3] *The Frontier in American History* (New York, 1921).

It is easy to forget that frontier conditions have played a prolonged and important part also in the history of the small island
of Britain. The fen-and-forest frontier was real enough from
very early times. The Devil's Dyke and the Fleam Dyke, east
and south-east of Cambridge, served to close the gap between
the natural barriers of the fenland and Epping Forest against
East Anglian invasion of Mercia. It was a sound instinct that
led Lady Callcott to open *Little Arthur's History of England* with
the statement that, 'a very long time ago, Britain was so full of
trees, that there was very little room for houses...' At much
the same time, Sir Walter Scott opened his *Ivanhoe*, the book
from which many English men and women for long gained
their earliest impression of medieval England, with Gurth the
swineherd and Wamba the jester tending pigs in a glade of
Sherwood Forest. In 1945 the late Oliver Onions began his
finest historical novel[1] with a boy trudging along the dikes of
Holderness at dusk to meet the terrifying figure of a fenman on
stilts.

For long ages, forest and fen and wilderness outpaced the
strip cultivation of the village fields. Beyond 'some strip of
herbage strown that just divides the desert from the sown', lay
the hinterland where the name of lord and bondman, like the
name of slave and sultan in the waste-lands of Omar's Persia,
'scarce was known'. There, under the greenwood tree or beside
the marsh, haunted the outlaw and the dispossessed, from
Hereward the Wake at Ely to Robin, Earl of Huntingdon, in
Sherwood, from the exiled Duke in Arden to the numberless
hordes of poor men who came out to swell the Pilgrimage of
Grace in 1536, Kett's rebellion in 1549, and many another rabble-
ment. Here was land to be had for the man who would go to it,
from the younger sons of poor men for whom there lacked
holdings in the village fields to the northern farmer who 'stubb'd
Thurnaby waäste' for greed. And here, with 'free' land, there
might be liberty, opportunity, a chance to get foot-loose from the
grinding custom of lordship or manor. The frontier, restricted
though it was in England, still had its part to play in the making

[1] *The Story of Ragged Robyn.*

of what the Americans were to call 'rugged individualism'. John Locke was to declare, as late as 1690, that whatsoever a man 'removed out of the state that Nature hath provided and left it in, he hath mixed his labour with it, and joined to it something that is his own, and thereby makes it his property...' and that 'the same measure may be allowed still, without prejudice to anybody, full as the world seems'. If anyone complained that there was no longer room enough Locke retorted 'let him plant in some vacant places in America', for 'in the beginning all the world was America...' At that time such easy advices were not unnatural, for even at home less than half the land was cultivated by 1650, although the draining and enclosure of the fenland was the great enterprise of reclamation of the seventeenth century.

The forest and woodland which had covered so much of England in medieval times shrank rather for the service of iron-smelting and the building of 'the wooden walls of England' in the shape of the great men-of-war of the seventeenth and eighteenth centuries than for the extension of arable farming, for which few of these areas were suited. As they fell to the axe they were lamented by the poet as well as by the shipwright, the patriot and the arborealogist.[1] Much of the devastation coincided with the Romantic Revival in poetry, and a minor poetess like the Victorian Mary Howitt, who spent her girlhood years on the edge of Needwood Forest, was torn between lamentation for the death of so much natural beauty and satisfaction that her father, the land-surveyor of Uttoxeter, was launched upon nine years of prosperity in the employment of the Crown Commission. In the reign of George III Dr Darwin and Thomas Gisborne, and many another gentleman poetizer of the neighbourhood, published his lament, too. And somehow, despite the savage forest-laws which had been such a bitter cause of protest all through the centuries when the forests were hunting and gaming preserves under the royal prerogative, the forests were supposed

---

[1] It is said that Cuthbert Collingwood, Nelson's vice-admiral at Trafalgar, when he was an old man in retirement, never went for a walk without a pocketful of acorns with which to replenish the nurseries of his country's hearts of oak.

to have been the favourite haunts of liberty. *Ce beau système,* wrote Montesquieu of the origins of free institutions in England, *a été trouvé dans les bois.* It was, however, the existence of 'waste' in the form of heath and moorland which is more likely to have had a healthy influence upon English life, and that rather material than moral. In feudal times *assarts,* or *intakes,* patches of land taken in from the waste, were generally held at a money-rent, and this probably had some influence upon the progress of commutation or the replacement of service-rent by money-rent in general. Villeinage, which means serfdom, became extinct in Elizabethan times, the last recorded case in the courts belonging to the year 1618. At the same time, Puritan England took a poor view of the moral influence of commons. 'The two great nurseries of Idleness and Beggary etc. are Ale-houses and Commons.' There children are brought up 'as ignorant of God or of any civil course of life as the very savages'. So wrote a Puritan in 1652.

The confidence of the English in the continuity of their history; their scepticism about sudden breaks, or the need for revolutionary change; their faith in freedom slowly broadening down from precedent to precedent; these things, too, were largely the offspring of geography. The island's immunity for nine centuries from invasion: the comparative peace and security within which its institutions have had the chance to develop; the early stage at which a single sovereign authority was able to exercise almost unchallenged sway over the national territory; and not least the fortunate chance by which the principal problems of constitutional moment were set to rest before the onset of the problems of industrial revolution: all these things counted for much in the achievement of a habit of continuity. Whether we call it the Whig genius for co-operation with Providence or with history[1] or, as Burke liked to call it, 'the happy effect of following nature, which is wisdom without reflection and above it..., preserving the method of nature in the conduct of the state...by the spirit of philosophic analogy', it has certainly meant that when a cleavage occurs, as it did in 1688, 'we actually build bridges in our rear, we seek to join up again, as though it

[1] H. Butterfield, *The Englishman and his History* (Cambridge, 1944), pp. 96–7.

mattered to us to maintain the contact with the past',[1] so that the debate goes on, and the pace of progress, while it may be impeded by procrastination, is never wrecked upon the rocks of revolutionary cataclysm or wrenched in the embittering rapids of civil war. One of the consequences of the habitual conservatism of the English style in politics—a style which informs all parties alike when they exchange opposition for authority—is the happy absence of irreconcilables. As long ago as the mid-eighteenth century, English Tories learnt in the hard school of experience that the cost of Jacobitism was political futility. By the mid-twentieth century they have learnt the same lesson about opposition to planning and the Welfare State. 'It is seldom the case that the measures of one party (when it has its turn in office) are reversed because a general election produces a change of government.'[2]

Perhaps all this is another way of saying that one of the leading characteristics of English history is not simply the presiding spirit of compromise but the comparative insignificance of dogma, indeed a generally wholesome indifference to ideas. The greatest English man of genius is a poet, not a philosopher. The most influential English philosopher opened his masterpiece with an almost off-hand repudiation of innate ideas, and gave the rest of it to a philosophy of experience. Indeed, John Locke's *Essay concerning Human Understanding* is really an essay on the limits of human understanding. An English Descartes or Kant is inconceivable. The English mind is not like that, or so the English are inclined to say with perhaps unwarranted pride, while other peoples go on to ask whether, in that case, the English can be said to have a mind at all. Perhaps the English leave the fatigue of 'having a mind' to the British, and particularly to the Scots, while they get on with their success story.

[1] H. Butterfield, *The Englishman and his History* (Cambridge, 1944), p. 101.
[2] *Ibid.* p. 101.

1

Roman Britain

The Roman invasion was the first of Britain's historically recorded invasions: Julius Caesar himself wrote a laconic and somewhat ambiguous account of his two campaigns of 55 and 54 B.C. But this well-publicized invasion was only one of many unrecorded sporadic incursions into southern Britain, which had by that time been completely overrun by tribes coming from the Continent. Archaeological evidence has now revealed the long painful periods of the Iron Ages known as A, B and C,[1] when southern Britain with her small but effective barrier of the Channel and its dangerous tides became the refuge of many warring groups of Brythonic-speaking Celts coming in small groups from places between Normandy and the Rhine-mouth in Iron Age A; to be displaced by warriors of 'La Tène' culture, who built most of the great hill-forts in their struggle to dominate the lowland zone of Britain; they in turn clashed and merged with Belgic tribes driven from the area now known as Belgium, in about 75 B.C., to conquer the fertile corn-growing areas of Hertford-shire and Essex. The Belgae became known as the Catuvel-launi, with their prosperous new capital at Camulodunum (Colchester); their aggression against the older Trinobantes of Essex touched off the invasion of the great Julius Caesar, or so he said.

Thus, when the outraged Trinobantes appealed to Caesar in his Gallic camp, they were the last of the billiard-ball succession of many displaced persons of Britain. This almost legendary island, noted for its tin, lead and silver mines, and as a rich source of iron, hides, slaves and hunting-dogs, all highly prized by the Romans, proved to be not only very rich but dangerously disunited. Had not the Catuvellauni founded the first British coinage, issuing fine coins decorated with the symbolic ear of

[1] Extending from *c.* 400 to 100 B.C.

corn? And were they not known to be actively helping their continental relatives in their fight against Rome?

Thus the logic of Caesar's conquest of Gaul led to his first invasion of Britain: Britain was too close to the mainland to be ignored. The historic decision was made, and Britain's destiny was to become a frontier province of an empire based on the Mediterranean. The great experiment of 'continentalization' which was to last for over four hundred years had started.

The average Roman soldier thought of Britain as a misty island full of woad-painted savages. One legion threatened to mutiny when ordered to embark for the white cliffs of Dover. They hesitated again when they saw British charioteers awaiting their disembarkation, until shamed into action by a heroic standard-bearer. Caesar should have known more about the treacherous tides of the Channel as well as of British skill with chariots. Both had been noted three centuries before his time by a Greek merchant from Marseilles called Pytheas. But the Romans could not possibly have appreciated the great strides the Britons had made in the last two thousand years, emerging from the Stone Age culture of the peoples who had built Stonehenge and the primitive barbarism of the folk who worshipped the little chalk idols found in the Yorkshire barrow at Folkton, to become the Belgic farmers who ploughed the great cornlands of South Britain, created fine wrought-iron work for domestic and agricultural uses, and imported large quantities of Roman silver wine-cups and wine-jars. They were now about to receive much more than luxury goods from Rome; they were to be hammered into greater unity and forced to receive imperial ideas of government and religion. In his first campaign Caesar advanced on Wheathampstead (near St Albans), captured it, and made the Catuvellauni sue for peace and pay tribute to Rome. It is not for nothing that Roman helmets and Roman shields have been found in the Thames, marking the passage of that river by the most celebrated soldiers of the known world, and the later foundation of Londinium (London) at the first fordable and navigable point where they could make a bridge-head for their orderly descent upon the whole of Britain.

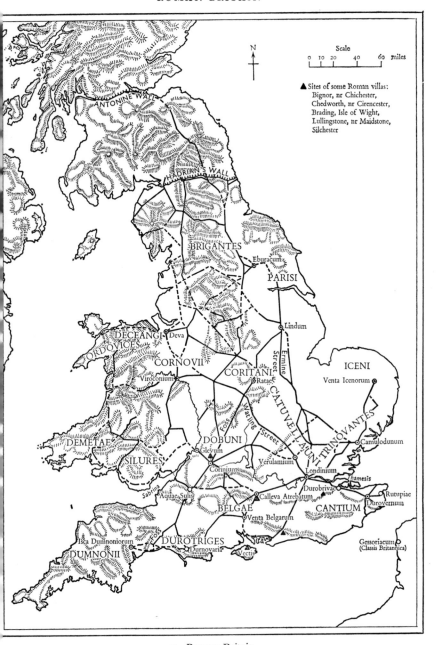

Scale
0 10 20 40 60 miles

▲ Sites of some Roman villas:
Bignor, nr Chichester,
Chedworth, nr Cirencester,
Brading, Isle of Wight,
Lullingstone, nr Maidstone,
Silchester

N

ANTONINE WALL

HADRIAN'S WALL

BRIGANTES

Eburacum

PARISI

DECEANGI
ORDOVICES
Deva

CORNOVII

Viroconium

Lindum

CORITANI

Ratae

ICENI

Venta Icenorum

CATUVELLAUNI

TRINOVANTES

Camulodunum

DEMETAE

SILURES

DOBUNI

Glevum

Corinium

Verulamium

Londinium

Durobrivae

Thamesis

Rutupiae

Durovernum

CANTIUM

Sabrina

Aquae Sulis

Calleva Atrebatum

BELGAE

Venta Belgarum

Isca Dumnoniorum

DUROTRIGES

Durnovaria

Vectis

DUMNONII

Gessoriacum
(Classis Britannica)

Fosse

Watling Street

Ermine Street

1 Roman Britain

13

Caesar's destiny recalled him to Rome and the fatal Ides of March, and while the young Octavian waged war with Antony and Cleopatra for the mastery of the Roman world, the Belgic Britons took advantage of this distraction to increase their continental trade and forget to pay the Roman tribute. Thus the Catuvellaunian disobedience forced the Emperor Claudius, now secure in Rome, to deal with them and gain an easy foreign victory. In A.D. 43 the Roman army landed at Rutupiae (Richborough) in Kent. The large-eared and slightly ridiculous Emperor Claudius himself spent sixteen days in this island, receiving the hastily remembered tribute from the overwhelmed Catuvellauni, while the future Emperor Vespasian advanced with his crack legions and subdued the south-west and the Isle of Wight. The great Iron-Age stronghold of Maiden Castle faced its final assault, and there is vivid archaeological evidence of final surrender to the discipline of the legionaries: skulls pierced by Roman spears and arrows, and skeletons with hands clutching joints of meat, eloquent testimony of sudden disaster. The new city of Durnovaria (Dorchester) was built below the dismantled fortress. The White Horse of the Atrebates no longer flourished in native freedom under Uffington Castle, and Hod Hill became a new legionary fortress to overawe the farmers of Cranborne Chase. Within a few years of the Claudian conquest military engineers and forced native labour had built a network of roads, the first British roads, radiating from the south-east into the west and the midlands. We only know of these great events from the Roman historians' point of view, but the British resentment at their swift subjugation to superior technical forces can be gauged from the sudden frenzy of the revolt of the Iceni under their famous Queen Boadicea or Boudicca (A.D. 61). There was no doubt that Roman legionaries in their new legionary town at Colchester had behaved with insolence towards the dispossessed Catuvellauni and that the native aristocracy had reason to fear the long memory of the unscrupulous Roman tax-gatherers.

The outraged and warlike Boudicca is the first British woman to emerge from prehistoric obscurity into the light of history.

The flames of the Roman cities of Colchester, Verulamium (St Albans) and London bathe her in garish light, and their inhabitants butchered by her followers or falling beneath her scythed chariot-wheels substantiate her claims to be the first British fury. It is not known whether she was acting in concert with the Druids whose religious centre on Mona (Anglesey) was about to be attacked by the Roman legionaries, who would tolerate all religions save those which offered human sacrifices and which acquired political power based on copper-mines or other large financial assets. No doubt Boudicca was an ardent Druid and would have gone to her death like the women of Anglesey recorded by Tacitus, whose flowing dishevelled hair and bloodcurdling cries momentarily terrified the legionaries when about to attack the Druids' stronghold. Through a mixture of headstrong rashness and stupidity, Boudicca, her daughters and followers met their end somewhere in Suffolk at the hands of the great Suetonius Paulinus, a hardened veteran from North Africa. Their line of retreat before the steady advance of the Roman veterans was blocked by the wagons of local British onlookers, mostly women, who had flocked thither to witness the victory of their Queen. So Boudicca perished, an awful warning to lowland Britons, who never presumed to fight Rome again. In their rout they left behind them in the river Alde the hacked bronze head, torn from its great torso, of the Emperor Claudius, a statue freshly erected in Colchester to mark the centre of the worship of the divine emperor and the Roman state. The Britons, having worked off their spleen, now settled down to enjoy the *Pax Romana* and sample the novel pleasures of town life in the new and once again rebuilt cities of London, St Albans, Colchester, and above all Aquae Sulis (Bath).

Agricola, the famous Roman governor, blessed with great abilities and a son-in-law (Tacitus) who was to record them for all posterity, inaugurated this first great experiment in urbanizing the British people. Tacitus records admiringly that triumphal arches rose in the forums while British chieftains assumed the toga and took to club-life, dinner-parties and the public baths. 'Agricola left the province at peace in itself and secure from danger.' This, no doubt, must be taken with the customary grain of salt. Certainly the great governor inflicted a salutary chastisement on the northern barbarians at Mons Graupius, but the fort of Inchtuthil had soon to be dismantled, and the southern Highlands were gradually abandoned. It would perhaps be true to say that in these barbaric northern regions he made a desert and called it peace; but there is little doubt that South Britain flourished under Roman protection, and that the aristocratic Britons soon acquired a veneer of Romanization, while even their slaves and workmen picked up some pidgin Latin, or so we judge from scraps of inscriptions left on tiles, for example 'satis' (Roman for 'knocked off'?). However, the imagination boggles at the notion of British aristocrats lounging in the open courts and chilly porticos of Bath or St Albans, and we know for a fact that 'British warms', or woollen hooded cloaks became popular wear. A Roman governor in Britain could find no better way of rewarding an efficient secretary than by giving him 'a woollen wrap of Canusine wool, a gold brooch, two thick rugs, a British "tossia" or cloak, and a sealskin'. Wine in fine red Samian ware was imported in large quantities, as we can see from the wreckage off Puddingpan Rock, near Whitstable, while British oysters became the fish-and-chips of the Romano-British world. The Romanized Britons seem to have continued to drink their barley-beer as well, and to have preferred butter-cooking to olive oil. They picked up sufficient Latin to chaffer in the market-place and to understand what went on in the law courts. At home and in the family they continued to talk their Celtic tongues. They employed Gallic tutors for their children, but we know of no British writers or universities until Christian times. If, as Trevelyan says, the Romans dropped new towns as they marched over Britain by road and navigable river, towns like hygienic grid-irons, or chessboards, full of temples, baths and shops, these creations were tender southern plants, apt to be nipped by the chill northern airs. There must have been a certain thinness of texture, for example at Silchester, where the planned town area was far larger than the acreage ever covered by houses or shops. Roman plays were never performed in any of the town amphitheatres, where the gravel still lies as mute witness of animal displays and contests watched by the gambling, heavily muffled citizens and soldiers. In fact the Romano-British town never 'took', save for Londinium, which seems to have been a cosmopolitan mart and a law unto itself. British villas and British temples soon evolved on lines similar to those of the Rhine frontier. In Gaul and even Germania a winged-corridor villa was evolved to meet the needs of Romans facing the rigours of the north.

Although over 600 villas have been excavated so far, no more than about 75 are of the luxurious type associated with the eighteenth century's idea of the great country-house. Most Romano-British villas are to be found in the south and south-west; west Kent, Surrey, Sussex (round Chichester, where very recently a large palace has been discovered, possibly used for governmental purposes), areas round Venta Belgarum (Winchester) and so on in the shelter of the Downs to Bath. It seems that there existed alongside these large estates with their well-cultivated farms a large number of small, impoverished farms and villages, as in Cranborne Chase and at Little Woodbury, working in Iron-Age squalor, where fields were ploughed and cropped in much the same way as those of the villas, but the Roman invention of hypocausts was used not to warm the houses but to dry off the perennially wet harvests. It was once thought that the primitive Britons lived in these grain-pits, so it is reassuring to know that there was some progress, however slight. The inhabitants of Park Street and Lockleys in Hertfordshire built their original small farms in Belgic times. Then, about A.D. 65, a new house was built on a rectangular plan with five rooms and a cellar over the original hutments. Windows were glazed and walls plastered, but it was not until A.D. 150 that more additions were made and there was more rebuilding. The big villa at Lullingstone started in much the same humble way in the prosperous Darent valley of Kent. Here a further rebuilding about A.D. 330 was on a luxurious scale, with bath-houses, a dining-room with splendid mosaic floors, over an elaborate system of hypocausts, and even Christian wall-frescoes on what must have been a private Christian chapel. Even more

17

magnificence was to be found at Brading in the much-favoured Isle of Wight (whence came Kipling's genial Roman legionary who recounted the tale of his own happy childhood in *Puck of Pook's Hill*), where there must have been a big estate worked by large numbers of slaves, a large courtyard very like the real ones found in Rome, and mosaic floors depicting the Eleusinian Mysteries. Was the original owner of this property an educated Romano-British aristocrat who had possibly visited Rome, and even Greece, or was he a retired Roman official coming directly from the Mediterranean world?

It is a strange thing that although we know how well heated, drained, and 'modern' these villas were, we do not know what they were called or what were the names of their owners. No written records survive to tell us whether the slaves who worked the land lived in the big barns that often enclosed the further ends of the courtyards, or whether they lived like the later serfs with their families in wooden hutments on the estate. But we do know that the Romano–British villa-owners possessed orchards of apples, plums and pears, and even tried to cultivate vines. They kept much poultry and herds of swine which grazed on the mast of the woods under the Downs. They grew cabbages and onions and beans in their vegetable-gardens, and roses were trained over pergolas in their pleasure-gardens and courtyards, and they planted avenues and plantations of beeches and sweet-chestnuts. We may also be sure that their walls and floors were warmer than most today by virtue of ingenious systems of ventilation and hot-air ducts; the hypocausts were stoked day and night by special stoker slaves with stacks of wood, so that it is true to say that the inhabitants of these villas enjoyed much more comfort in their dining-rooms and more frequent hot baths than the Victorian gentlemen who began excavating villa remains in their parks. Yet we do not know how long after A.D. 400 this kind of life was possible in Britain, or when it was that the last faithful slaves lighted the last fires for the hypocausts, or even whether most of these slaves ran away or murdered their masters, as happened most frequently in Gaul, or whether it was they or the Germanic invaders who lighted primitive fires on the priceless mosaic floors of the dining-rooms. All we can safely say is that a very civilized way of life, not possible again until the eighteenth century, was possible for the favoured British few from the first century A.D. and continued for over three hundred years; that the pleasant villa at Chedworth in the Cotswolds had time to grow and see families come and go for generations, and finally evolve into a semi-industrialized establishment where wool-dyeing and fulling were carried on— whether as a means of gaining self-sufficiency in a semi-feudalized way, or as a sort of state factory producing cloaks or uniforms for military purposes, we do not know. 'The Roman and his trouble are ashes under Uricon'; 'then 'twas the Roman, now 'tis I,' said Housman, not neglecting to add that the wind still blows through woods and hangers planted by these self-same vanished nameless men.

We do know that these villas belonged to an aristocracy who owned town houses, who regularly sold their surplus produce in local towns, and rode into their local tribal capital to administer justice in the forum. We even know how Britain was administered as one of the most important imperial provinces (Britain acted as a protective breakwater to both Gaul and Germania, and an important recruiting-ground and military depot). She was placed directly under the emperor, who always sent an important man as his *legatus Augusti pro praetore*, responsible for both army and law like the British viceroys in India. Only finance was exempted from his care and for that again the *procurator Augusti* was responsible directly to the emperor, who expected the island to prove a sound economic investment. From London the procurator administered the complex finances of land, poll and corn taxes, with customs duties and the produce of imperial estates. From the first, Britain was divided into two zones—the civil zone, or Britannia Superior, and the military zone, or Britannia Inferior, centred on York and Lincoln. When it was divided into four parts after the reorganization carried out by Diocletian, with a Vicarius of the Diocese of Britain under the Praetorian Prefect of the Gauls (whose main seat was at Trier), London was probably the main centre of the Vicar, his numerous officials, and the mint. From London a splendid system of roads radiated in all directions; from Richborough via London it was 350 miles to Hadrian's Wall; a general postal system was maintained by the government for governmental purposes, with rest-houses and state inns on the main posting-roads. Administrative as well as military and commercial purposes were thus served, for the various *coloniae* and *municipia*, or towns which governed the system of cantons, were thus linked together. These cantons were mainly old tribal areas where the local British aristocrats served as magistrates in their local 'senates'. Britain thus achieved an administrative unity it had never known before, and which it took the Saxons 500 years to achieve. A polyglot and cosmopolitan crowd of merchants, tradespeople, and slaves must have lived in these towns under an aristocracy of retired Roman officials and Celtic nobility. The facts recorded in stone that a Palmyrene trader married a South Shields woman and settled with her on the Tyne, that at Winchester an altar-stone was dedicated by a soldier, one Antonius Lucretianus, to 'the Italian, German, Gallic, and British mothers' speak volumes. All these varying peoples, if free, were Roman citizens after the famous decree of the Emperor Caracalla in A.D. 212, and pursued their lawful occasions and profits in these open unwalled towns from the Tyne to Southampton Water under the *Pax Romana*.

Villas and towns were much rarer in the military zones of the north and west. The Brigantes of Yorkshire never became romanized, and the Picts of the northern Highlands were generally hostile. Ireland remained untouched, although the *classis Britannica* (the Roman fleet patrolling the waters around Britain) did circumnavigate the British Isles for the great Governor Agricola. Setbacks were always to be expected from the treacherous barbarians of the hills and moors, and for this reason the Emperor Hadrian decided to build the great Wall in the north as a fortified belt seventy miles long, dividing the barbarians from the Romans. It was really a part of the great north-west frontier of an empire stretching from Syria and the Black Sea to the Rhine, and Hadrian's experiences of warfare on the Danube and Rhine served him in good stead. The Wall was started 122–123, and finally stretched from Wallsend in the east to Bowness-on-Solway in the west. In its final version it was a continuous stone wall from eight to ten feet thick, sixteen feet high, with a *vallum*, or parallel wide ditch, sixteen forts, and innumerable turrets and mile castles. All the work was done by the legionaries with forced native labour, and completed in ten years. This is rightly counted as one of the wonders of the Roman world.

The later Antonine Wall from the Firth of Forth to the Clyde was considerably inferior, with only a turf rampart ten feet high, and it was not long maintained. But the Romans preserved Hadrian's Wall with amazing pertinacity for over 250 years in the face of many invasions. At least five Roman emperors came to Britain to maintain or rebuild the Wall, and when it was finally breached it meant the end of Britain as an imperial province. Kipling was instinctively right in his picture of the awe experienced by the young legionary officer, Parnesius, in *Puck of Pook's Hill.* 'Old men who have followed the Eagles since boyhood say nothing in the Empire is more wonderful than the first sight of the Wall.' In his racy description of the well-known legionary route from Anderida through the Weald, up the Great North Road to York, and so to the Wall, Parnesius says:

Rome's race—Roman's pace, as the proverb says: twenty-four miles in eight hours, neither more nor less. Head and spear up, shield on your back...that's how you take the Eagles through Britain. There were no 'adventures' South of the Wall, but beyond the Wall was the twilight world of the Picts, or painted people, of hunting in the heather, and the eternal vigilance of the slingers and archers manning the great catapults on the Wall. No two Towers spoke the same tongue or worshipped the same gods.

This, like Kipling's picture of the Wall as 'one continuous town', is poetic exaggeration. No doubt there were swarms of merchants and camp-followers squatting by all the great gateways, and a number of small towns round the main forts, but we now know a great deal more about the archaeology of the Wall than in

Kipling's day (c. 1906). Although legions and emperors came and went, the Wall was manned mainly by Spanish and Gaulish auxiliaries; the *cohors Nerviorum* was housed in the lesser Forts, used its own native bows and slings, but drilled under Latin words of command. We know from inscriptions that Syrian archers served on both the Hadrian and the Antonine Walls, while a British cohort served on the Danube in Pannonia; no doubt they spoke their own language to one another, but on the parade-ground, in the markets and at the public baths they spoke or roared in pidgin Latin as a common tongue, just as they were paid in fine Roman coins minted both at Trier and at London, and in turn they paid their respects to the great statues of Roma Dea and the sacred Roman emperors. Having offered their respects to the state, they could also worship the Celtic gods of Britain's woods and rivers, as well as Mithras, the soldiers' god, or, later, the God of the Christians adopted by the Emperor Constantine. Altars were erected to Mars Camulus—a hybrid Roman-Celtic god of war; the Roman Minerva was identified with a Celtic Sulis at Bath, and numerous inscriptions were made to the *veteres* or 'old ones', both Celtic-Roman and foreign. The three mother-goddesses depicted on a Roman altar at Cirencester look peculiarly stolid and British, with laden baskets on their knees; and Brigantia, the guardian goddess of Yorkshire, is shown as a hefty northern female complete with wings, crown, gorgon's head and globe. But Kipling was probably right in describing the officers of an important legion as devout worshippers of Mithras. This was the most deeply felt religion of the soldiers of the empire; on the Wall and in Colchester, and more recently on the Wallbrook in London, strong evidences have survived of this powerful and esoteric cult. It was the only serious rival of Christianity, but it did not cater for women, or slaves, or the weak.

Britain must formally have become Christian after the Emperor Constantine's conversion and concordat with the Church in 313. He was most probably, however, still a sun-worshipper when hailed as emperor by his father's soldiers in York. His father, Constantius Chlorus ('palefaced'), a fine general, had done much to restore Britain after the troubles of the mid-third century. He had rebuilt much of the Wall and started work on the fortification of the 'Saxon shore'. Of his wife, Helena, we know little except that this mother of Constantine the Great was probably not his wife, and certainly not aristocratic or British. The official basilican Christian churches which now sprang up all over the empire had few counterparts in Britain. A small church has been discovered in Silchester (Calleva); Canterbury (Durovernum) possessed one; and there is evidence of a chapel in the villa at Lullingstone. This may be due to a British tenacity of pagan faith, as there is interesting evidence at Lydney in Gloucestershire of the erection of a big theurapeutic centre dedicated to the gods of the river Severn in later Roman times.

The first Briton to emerge from obscurity and speak for himself is a British monk, called Pelagius (about 400), who is the first British writer and controversialist. He seems to have come from western, or possibly northern, stock. He is described as 'bull-necked, full-faced, broad-shouldered, corpulent, and slow-moving like a tortoise, weighed down with porridge'. Such is the first Briton, seen through the embittered eyes of friends of his great adversary, St Augustine of Hippo. Nevertheless even they had to admit that his Greek was better than St Augustine's although it seems there were no universities in Britain. Yet the education he received must have been a very complete one. This surprisingly un-British trait is more than compensated by the peculiarly dogged mixture of obstinacy and sensible moderation in Pelagius' flat and courageous denial of St Augustine's exaggerated conception of Original Sin and the total depravity of the human race. Apparently Pelagius had experienced no such strange lusts and passions in London or Bath as St Augustine had in Carthage. Possibly St Augustine might have 'burned' less if he had experienced the cool daily rain of the West Country! Pelagius maintained to the end, while managing to avoid a heretic's fate, the heretical view that men can possibly be saved by their natural goodness and their own efforts. The Augustinians felt that his mind resembled the famous British mists, and that he had the ambiguity of their parti-coloured plaids, the famous cloaks known for their rain-resisting qualities throughout the empire.

In addition to the pig-headed Pelagius and the horsy Boudicca, we meet Carausius (*c.* A.D. 286), rival to the Emperor Constantine, the first British admiral and pirate, who may have been Menapian or Dutch in origin, but had the Drake-like characteristic of skipping from land to sea, combining dexterity as a pilot with great military ability and a great commercial flair. Carausius tried to set up a sea-empire based on the Channel and the North Sea, and had the temerity to issue large numbers of solid gold and silver coins from his newly established mints at London and Colchester depicting himself as a bull-necked Caesar. But he was defeated and finally murdered. Nevertheless, there was no lack of British 'usurpers', who emerged frequently before and after the final recall of the legions from Britain and the famous Rescript of the Emperor Honorius in A.D. 410 instructing them to take up arms to defend themselves against invading Saxons, Scots and Picts.

2

Saxon England

How did this peculiar but important part of the Prefecture of
the Gauls turn into Saxon England? The gloomy cataclysmic
view of a violent debacle in the early fifth century is no longer
held. It is known that by the end of the reign of Honorius
(A.D. 423) Britain's revenues had been lost to the empire for ever.
Honorius, when he recalled the last legions to help save Rome
from the onslaughts of Alaric the Goth, had told the British
towns after their pitiful appeal that 'they must look after their
own defences', and had probably meant to return as former
emperors had done. But the defence of the western empire never
allowed time or men to recover the lost territory. What sort of
fight the British put up when left as a civilian population, and
attacked not only by Saxon pirates from the North Sea, but
overrun by Picts and Scots who had finally breached the Wall,
is still a matter for violent controversy. The discovery in the
1940s of the Mildenhall Treasure—a magnificent dinner-set in
fine silver and pewter, depicting the triumph of Bacchus—would
seem to prove that a prosperous Roman villa-owner, now left
defenceless, with slaves in flight to join the Saxons, did what
many Greeks and Italians did in 1940: buried his most valuable
and heavy treasure and took to flight, first to the hills of the
west country, where opposition continued longest, and then to
Brittany, where the population was definitely altered by a large-
scale emigration from Britain. The celebrated last message[1] of
the Britons to Aetius in Gaul lamenting their fate, caught between
the barbarians and the cruel seas, would seem to support the
Victorian theory that the native British soon succumbed before
the victorious and manly Anglo-Saxons. But today evidence is

---

[1] See: Gildas, *De Excidio et Conquestu Brittaniae* (Concerning the ruin and conquest of Britain), *c.* A.D. 550. It may be read in translation, edited by Hugh
Williams (1899–1901).

coming to light (mainly from Celtic scholars), to prove that the British fought longer and better than was supposed. We have reason to understand the difficulties and the courage of underground resistance. We also know that there were many Germanic settlers in Britain before 400, put there, particularly in the eastern areas, to fight their marauding kinsfolk. By A.D. 500 the area of Britain physically controlled by Angles, Saxons, Jutes and Frisians amounted to less than a quarter of the British Isles. Detailed investigation of towns like Silchester, St Albans and Canterbury hints at a continuous urban life well on into the fifth century. Silver and copper coins ceased to circulate properly, but some kind of market-life may well have continued. Those who saw the shanties built in the ruins of Coventry in the 1940s may well understand this. Dr J. N. L. Myres, who once thought that 'the whole structure of rural society was shattered and re-formed by the English conquest', now thinks that 'post-Roman pottery reflects in varying degrees the survival of native populations in different communities'. Dr T. C. Lethbridge claims that the early Anglo-Saxons were mainly half-breeds and octoroons of mixed Teutonic and British blood as a result of the constant intermingling of the foederate Saxons imported from early times to man the Saxon Shore.

The traditional stories of monastic historians such as Gildas and Bede are too simple, too moralistic, to be quite true. Vortigern, a Romano-British nobleman (about 450) now become a 'tyrant', may well have invited more foederate Germans such as Hengist and Horsa to defend the unprotected shore of Kent; but it is much more likely that these defenders turned against their master, not because of his sexual crimes, but because the all-important supply of money and corn ran out. It may well be that Vortigern's chief 'crime' was that he favoured the Pelagian heresy. It is hard luck for the Romano-Britons that they cannot speak for themselves; later Saxon church-historians are our sole guide, along with Celtic myths round the shadowy figure of the last Roman, Ambrosianus, and his even more shadowy successor, Arthur. There may well have been a 'Roman' victory at Mount Badon which stemmed the German advance into the south-west,

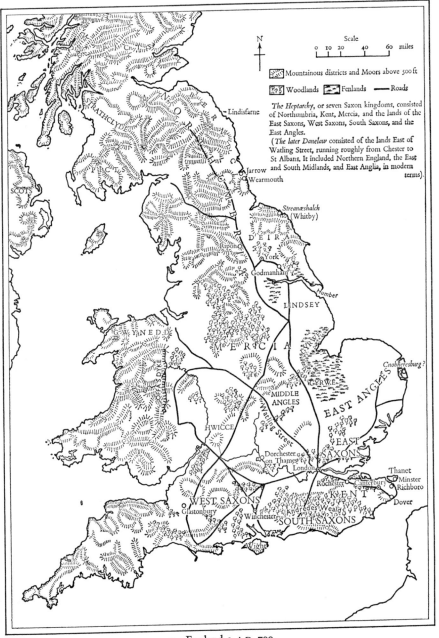

The Heptarchy, or seven Saxon kingdoms, consisted of Northumbria, Kent, Mercia, and the lands of the East Saxons, West Saxons, South Saxons, and the East Angles.

(The later Danelaw consisted of the lands East of Watling Street, running roughly from Chester to St Albans. It included Northern England, the East and South Midlands, and East Anglia, in modern terms).

2   England c. A.D. 700

but where it took place is lost in accretions of myth and legend. All we can safely say is that a twilight sub-Roman period set in for about 200 years, when, instead of the splendid coinage of the Roman period when Constantius Chlorus could strike a fine gold coin depicting himself welcomed as 'Restorer of the Eternal Light' by the goddess of the City of London, we find the sordid *minimi* and even the miserable *minimissimi* coins with their make-shift flans, crude design, and obvious tail-clipping of the Lydney hoard. By 600 these sub-Romans must have virtually given up town life through lack of technical skill and inability to repair walls and drains. The magnificent city of Bath became a ruin, with wild birds nesting in the great Roman baths. It was not sacked, but lamented and admired by the Saxon poets as the work of bygone giants. The south-west Britons lived on in their re-furbished and squalid Iron-Age forts, and the Anglo-Saxons advancing up the rivers from the east tended to build their timber halls in the river valleys, avoiding the decaying towns and villas because they had no technology to work them, and no administrative class, such as the Goths found in Gaul, to raise taxes and run the offices. Nevertheless a large number of Celtic-speaking natives, shepherds, smiths and ploughmen must have gone on tending the fields of the old Roman villas and producing the corn and, above all, the wool for which Britain had been famous. But no one in the British Isles lived in a properly run town or villa; the daily bath, good plumbing, and central heating had disappeared along with the habit of paying taxes and keeping accurate written records.

Whether or not the open-field system,[1] along with the village and the idea of kingship, came into Britain with the Saxon invaders, one thing is certain. There was no 'entirely fresh start', and a predominantly civilian society did not suddenly become a barbarian society based on war. The Romano-Britons had long withdrawn from town life into country life, while many Angles, Saxons and especially Jutes had grown to admire and copy

---

[1] Two or three large unfenced fields where the villagers tilled scattered strips, using communal plough teams. One field was allowed to lie fallow in rotation to enable the soil to recuperate.

Roman techniques, particularly the crafts of iron, silver and gold. The disappearance of the old Romano-Celtic names of places, rivers and towns, and of the old British tongue, is a stumbling-block to those, like Frederic Seebohm, who believed in the underground continuity of villas and villages. But the fact is that the English village emerged so triumphantly in the end that it virtually blotted out all that had gone before. The Saxon work of land settlement was so well done that at the present day in the village of Wilbraham in Cambridgeshire, and in many others, the village and its agriculture still work and cover up all traces of what went before.

It was a slow process of incorporation and adaptation in what proved a congenial environment. The deep plough used in Romano-British times was still used, and sheep-rearing went on as before; but more and more woods and forests were cut down by land-hungry settlers used to wielding the great German axe. The Anglo-Saxons could draw on continental experience as clearers of forest and marsh. The new land so won was kept arable by a two-field system, with one field left fallow while the other grew crops of spring and winter corn to feed the community of the tribal leader, his family and followers. Wheat, oats, barley and rye were all grown, although barley may well have become more important: the common word *bere-wick*, for an outlying farm, indicates the importance of the drink-crop. There is no reason to suppose that these farmers relished rye bread or black bread any more than their nineteenth-century descendants; the wheaten loaf, was highly prized. Oxen continued to plough the arable fields, and the basis of the share-out of land among the warriors may well have been the number of plough-beasts each contributed to the team of the community. Corn continued to be grown, but more on the valley bottoms where the ancient oak-trees receded before the axe. Sheep continued to be reared for wool and mutton, but the wool was now woven in individual households and by women rather than by slaves in the villas, and barley-drink or beer became the staple drink. Honey was still the main source of sweetening, and fruit, vegetables and pigs were still the main supply of food for the village. The basic huts of the village were of wattle and daub; the hall or *heorot* of the lord would be made of wood and carved in the fashion of all Scandinavian long-houses. The early Saxon cottage unearthed at Cardyke in Cambridgeshire had an earthen floor used as a midden, with broken bones, potsherds, and even a dead dog. The inhabitants were so primitive that they boiled their water by throwing heated pebbles into the pot; nevertheless, the Saxon women used ivory and silver ornamented work-boxes and bronze needles for their sewing. Their men were now called *ceorls* or *weocemen*.[1] They still ploughed and dug laboriously as before, but there were two important differences. They had to possess spears and swords and be prepared to fight and defend their homes; in return they paid no taxes to the government or anyone else, although they must still do a certain amount of work for their lord. Possibly they had a greater share in the land and its crops than before; certainly they must risk their lives to maintain them. It is not surprising that the theme of death and insecurity, particularly the horror of the kinless man, figures largely in their gloomy literature.

Ridding our minds of any idealistic pictures of free tribesmen working harmoniously together at the plough, we must look upon the estate as a basic institution before and after the Saxon conquest. Freedom is not to be found among these newcomers from the German forests. A large number of petty chieftains and their followers won the land by hard fighting, and took their reward in the land and labour of the conquered and their own weaker followers and their slaves. 'Lordship' became the basis of the community; 'kingship' was here to stay. Although the notion of kindred was strong, it had suffered some natural diminution in the sea-migration from Germany, when war-leaders attracted hardy seafarers from all parts. These war-leaders became the great objects of loyalty. 'Glory to the Prince, and Rewards to his followers,' was the main theme of heroic Saxon poetry typified by the words of Brightwold, the follower of Brihtnoth, the Ealdorman slain at the battle of Maldon, in

---

[1] Status names for agricultural workers who were neither noblemen nor slaves.

991, who decided to die fighting by his lord's side: 'I am old in years; I will not turn hence; but I by the side of my lord, by so dear a man, think to lie.' This quality of loyalty combined with courage and resolution was the hallmark of the fighting pagan society from the early migrations to the wars against the Danes. The most resolute war-leader became the king; most of the early kings were adventurers who relied upon their *comitatus* or followers, and their swords; their little kingdoms corresponded roughly to the old administrative cantons of Roman Britain because of geographical barriers. The Heptarchy consisted roughly of seven kingdoms, of which Kent, Northumbria, Mercia or the middle kingdom, and finally Wessex were the most important. Their kings, once established, all claimed descent from the gods and dwelt in great wooden halls, like that recently excavated at Old Yeavering in Northumbria, drinking and eating the plenty provided by their followers during the long winter months, armed with splendid swords and knives from which they derived their name 'Saxon' (*seax*), above all loving gold and fine jewelry and the sea-ships which had brought them their loot. They worshipped the old northern gods, Thor and Odin, who kept constant watch over this troubled enclosure of the earth or middle-garth; after all their adventures and trials these northern seamen heard at the last the boom of the surges of chaos breaking on the dykes of the world. The gods were doomed to disappear finally, when chaos would resume its sway. 'Few men can see further than the day when Odin shall meet the Wolf.' It is no great wonder that even the pagan priests, as well as their kings, welcomed the 'good news' of the Roman missionaries when they landed in Kent in 597, and brought England again into contact with the Christian hope and the ordered discipline of the Mediterranean world.

Significantly enough the Roman missionary, St Augustine of Canterbury, together with forty Italian monks, landed on the island of Thanet, possibly at or near the port of Richborough, not far from the scene of Caesar's invasion. There was now little trade with the Continent except a flourishing slave-trade as a result of constant warfare between the various kingdoms of the

Heptarchy; thus it was that Pope Gregory saw the fair-haired boys from Deira, or Yorkshire, exposed for sale, and decided to regain the old heritage of the Roman Church. Kent had more continental connections than the others, and her king, Æthelbert, had already married the Christian daughter of a Merovingian king. So the way was clear with royal patronage; the old church of St Martin in Canterbury was offered to these newcomers as a centre for their mission. Thus the pattern of royal and aristocratic patronage was set, and within the short lifetime in Britain of St Augustine (597–609) three sees were 'created' at Canterbury, Rochester and London. Within seventy years or so the whole of England became a practising and devout part of the Roman Church. The marriage of Æthelbert's daughter to the powerful Edwin, King of Northumbria, led Paulinus to the first northern bishopric; the defeat of Edwin by Mercia led to the conversion of the 'middle kingdom', and of the subordinate kingdom of East Anglia. There was a short period of fluctuating loyalties when an East Anglian king could erect a Christian altar alongside his old altar to the northern gods, but this aberration was soon wiped out by mass conversions conducted by St Felix and St Fursa, who created a monastery in the deserted Roman fort of Burgh Castle. So Roman forts and Roman towns became the centres of the new Roman order culminating in the late seventh century in the creation by Theodore of Tarsus (Archbishop of Canterbury) of fifteen dioceses. Thus the coming of Christianity not only increased the movement of consolidation within the island, but it led directly to the conversion of Germany and the north of Europe. The Saxons wished to bring their continental kinsfolk into the fold. St Boniface, born as the aristocratic Saxon, Wynfrid, at Crediton in Devon, became the apostle to the Germans, founding the great monastery of Fulda where he lies buried after his martyrdom by the Frisians. Thus the northern conversions to the Roman faith offset the great losses in the Mediterranean world, which was now partially overrun by the victorious armies of Islam. England had triumphantly vindicated her return to Europe and her Roman past.

The work of the English missionaries had a deep and lasting

influence on the Continent, comparable only to the influence of English ideas on France and Germany in the eighteenth century. St Boniface, Willibrord, and others converted not only the Rhineland and the 'old' Saxons, but virtually the whole of modern Germany. So the dark world of the northern forests which the Roman legions never penetrated found a new unity stemming from the Mediterranean world of the Roman Church. Stone abbeys and churches were built by Benedictine monks, and housed increasing numbers of illuminated MSS. and parchments. Libraries and *scriptoria* for the priceless work of copying manuscripts left by the Ancient World, along with carefully cultivated gardens and herbs, were to be found bearing testimony to the *Opus Dei* in Jarrow, York, Sherborne, Fulda, and Echternach. The first written laws and charters as a 'new and better form of testimony', came to England in the decrees of St Augustine's first convert, King Æthelbert of Kent. 'The theft of God's property in the Church will be compensated twelvefold', and *wergilds* (fines) were fixed for breaking the peace of the Church. Kings found they needed the power of the Church as much as the Church needed them. Ecgfrith, King of Mercia, was crowned according to the coronation rites as we know them today; he was consecrated by the special oil and unction at the hands of the Church. The Church took an increasingly large share of the government. Bishop Wulfstan's *Homilies* show obedience to the king as a Christian duty, and divide society into the famous threefold order of *Oratores*, *Laboratores*, and *Bellatores* (those who pray, those who work, and those who fight). Henceforth the Christian king was to rule as a pattern of good morality, good learning and good government. This was publicly demonstrated when the fall of the Mercian kingdom heralded the rise of the royal house of Wessex, and through Wessex there emerged 'England's darling', King Alfred, the finest flower of the early English state.

For it was the most recently created kingdom of Wessex which emerged as the final unifier of England. The early kingdoms of Kent and Northumbria had been subdued by the great pagan fighter Penda of Mercia (632–55), who ruled the 'middle

33

kingdom'. Offa's Dyke had been built by another great Mercian king as a boundary to Wales; the Wansdyke was erected as another boundary between Mercia and the West Saxons. The origins of their kingdom were as obscure as the background of their first king, or chief, Cerdic or Cynric, the Germanic war-leader with a Celtic name, who had landed from Southampton Water in the late fifth century and welded together a nucleus of what had been the richest and most fiercely held possessions of the Romano-British, including the realm of the shadowy King Arthur. His descendants forced their way slowly and painfully westwards; Devon was not gained until well into the seventh century, and Cornwall was still British in the eighth. But the West Saxon advance was inexorable, Somerset became much more Saxon than Celtic, the old Roman capital of Venta became Winchester, seat of their dynasty, which had by now received Christianity and increased its power at the expense of Mercia. Finally King Æthelwulf sent his youngest son to Rome to receive and exchange Papal gifts, and in the fullness of time and after the death of no less than three elder brothers, this Atheling or prince of royal blood blest by the Pope became Alfred, King of Wessex, and acknowledged leader of the English in their fight against the new wave of pagan invaders from the north, the dreaded Danes, or Vikings.

Although Alfred's reign (871–899) seems today to have been the prologue to the final union of the English kingdom and the ultimate defeat of the Danes, to his contemporaries and often to himself he must have looked like the last of the old Saxon kings. Northumbria had declined and was now practically a Danish kingdom; Mercia was hopelessly divided; and now Wessex, once recognized as paramount under the victorious Egbert, was in danger from many sides. Although the first attack of the Vikings was as early as 789, they had only become a serious menace by the middle of the ninth century. In 878, according to the Anglo-Saxon Chronicle, the Danish host occupied Chippenham in the heart of Wessex, 'and drove a great part of the inhabitants overseas, and reduced the greater part of the rest, except Alfred the king; he, with a small company, moved under difficulties through woods and into inaccessible places in marshes'.

Thus we come to the celebrated tale of the refugee king in hiding in the marshes of Athelney. The no less celebrated story of the burning of the cakes does not appear in Asser's life of Alfred, a contemporary biography by a bishop and personal friend. This story belongs to the post-conquest world of Norman England, and may well be a myth: the myth of the conquered English, just as Arthur embodies the myth of the conquered Britons. But the misfortunes of Alfred were real enough, and so was his matchless resolution. Although he became the embodiment of the Hero-King fighting to preserve the values of civilization, he only stemmed the tide of this first Viking invasion for a time; he had to allow a division of England, with the Danelaw (Danish-occupied area) running east from Watling Street. None the less, by his great victory, when he led the national *fyrd*, or army, of Somerset, Wiltshire and Hampshire at the battle of Edington, and by his brilliant improvisation of a navy to watch the Channel, he built up the first real English unity; and by the conversion and baptism of Guthrum, King of the Danes, and the subsequent Treaty of Wedmore he ensured the subsequent civilization of the Danes. His son, Edward the Elder, and his war-like daughter, the 'Lady of the Mercians', beat back the Danish menace and built up the *burgh* system of defence, of which War-wick is but one example. It was not their fault that a second wave of Danish invasion flooded England in the eleventh century and overwhelmed their descendant, branded for all time as Ethelred the 'Unready'.

In the temporary peace gained by his victory and wise treaty, Alfred was able to legislate for his united English people and to make his court at Winchester the centre of good learning and Christian scholarship. 'I, King Alfred, collected these together, and ordered to be written...those which I liked. I showed these to my councillors and they said they were all pleased to observe them.' These were the first English laws to be consciously enacted; informal, gathered from many sources, but with general consent; they included the earlier laws of Æthelbert of Kent, Ine of

Wessex and Offa of Mercia, along with the Mosaic Law and the Acts of the Apostles. 'Judge thou very fairly. Do not judge one judgement for the rich and another for the poor; nor one for the one more dear, and one for the one more hateful.' Thus the voice of Alfred, the wise judge as well as the creator of English resistance and the navy. 'Alfred had me made' is as true of English law and scholarship as of the beautiful jewel which he had engraved with these words for all to see (now in the Ashmolean at Oxford).

For Alfred wished not only to be just, but also to be a scholar. In a celebrated passage in his introduction to his translation into English of Pope Gregory's *Pastoral Care* he lamented the decline of learning in his time. At his accession he could not remember a single man south of the Thames capable of comprehending the Services of the Church or of translating a letter from Latin into English. Now he wished 'all the youth now in England, born of free men, who have the means they can apply to it, to be devoted to learning'. So he planned the education of his nobility and Church, much as Charlemagne had done. This most noble and thoughtful of the early English kings wanted above all to advance the life of the mind, and it grieved him 'to think that Englishmen who wanted such things must now seek them abroad, when once men had come to England in search of learning and wisdom'.

In spite of his heroic efforts, time (and Alfred invented a water-clock) was against him. The golden days of Saxon learning were over. They had enjoyed an early summer of great brilliance soon after the Conversion. Schools had been set up again in places like Canterbury (to this day, King's School, Canterbury lays claim to 604 as its foundation date, and in 1965 received a generous benefaction from an old scholar and man of letters, Somerset Maugham, which would have pleased King Alfred himself). Libraries had been carefully collected together. Perhaps the work of Benedict Biscop, a Northumbrian nobleman with a passion, and the means, for collecting valuable manuscripts for his monastic foundation at Jarrow and Wearmouth, did more than anything else to bring about the 'Northumbrian renaissance' (*c.* 670–735). Bede, the first English historian, was its finest flower, and one of the greatest scholars of his age. He has an outstanding output, culminating in his celebrated 'Ecclesiastical History of the English People', completed in 731. This history was not only written in good Latin, it was good history, showing strong powers of judgement and an ever-present anxiety to show his authorities and quote chapter and verse. He is still our best authority for the origins of the English, and although as a product of the Roman teaching he had a bias against the Celtic Church, he could still give praise where it was manifestly due, as in his noble picture of the Celtic saint, Aidan. It is in Bede that we find the famous and moving story of how Christianity was first received in Northumbria. An Ealdorman in Bede's history gave as his reason for accepting the new Christian faith the fact that the life of the pagan seemed to him like the swift flight of a lone sparrow through the banqueting-hall where men sit feasting in winter-time. Inside there is a comforting fire to warm the room; outside the winter storms of snow and rain are raging. While the sparrow is inside he is safe from the storms; but after a few moments of comfort he vanishes from sight, from winter into winter. Similarly man appears on earth for a little while. There-fore, the Ealdorman concludes, if this new teaching can reveal any more certain knowledge, it is right that man should follow it. Thus the downright, pragmatic, and weather-bound English-man speaks to us from the pages of Bede. He speaks to us directly as no Romano-Briton can do; his speech is our speech, and his thoughts are the thoughts common to Englishmen for over a thousand years, the thoughts of England and eternal life, his two homes. In Bede's work we recognize across the centuries a certain English way of looking at things; written with a certain noble simplicity and freshness not to be heard again until the advent of Chaucer.

Other small but peculiarly English characteristics can also be seen. The love of word-games, the quiz, the crossword puzzle, which makes quiz programmes so popular on radio and TV today, can be seen in the Anglo-Saxon passion for riddles, puns and nicknames. Whole books of riddles have survived, and many of their nicknames, which included 'Clean-hand', 'Bit-cat', 'Soft-bread', 'Foul-beard', 'Penny-purse', and 'Fresh-friend'. They loved old saws and proverbs such as 'Hapless is he who must needs live alone', or 'Weary shall he be who rows against the wind': and even St Boniface had a taste for secret ciphers. Alcuin, the first scholar of the School of York, and the great teacher of the Court of Charlemagne, invented nicknames for himself and his royal pupils, and a question-and-answer form of lesson, founded on riddles, for his adult-education classes.

Although Alfred's grandson, Athelstan, was recognized at his death as one of the leading princes of Europe, the Norse warlords were soon on the warpath again. There is no need to dwell on the harrowing years recorded in the Anglo-Saxon Chronicle, and the ignoble payment of the Danegeld. In the end, true unity was only achieved when the great Danish prince Cnut came to the throne in 1016. The Danelaw had conquered England, and England took her place for a time as part of a great Scandinavian empire. Jarls or earls ruled England now, instead of Alfred's ealdormen, and beneath Cnut's strong hand English and Danes were welded together to the lasting benefit of the island people. Cnut was nothing if not pious, and the authority of the Church increased mightily under his rule. Little wonder that the monks of Ely 'sang merrily as the King rowed thereby', as the Ely Chronicle recorded. His great thegns or earls, mostly of Danish stock, waxed mightily too. With their enormous wealth and their possessions scattered all over England they fatally unbalanced the Anglo-Saxon system of government and politics. The House of Godwin, Earls of Wessex, proved the downfall of the Anglo-Saxon polity. The Earl Godwin, with his acquisitiveness and his armies, proved bad enough, and alienated many of the old nobility; but the claims and quarrels of his sons were fatal. One son, Harold Godwinsson, became King of England in 1066 after political pressure had been brought to bear on the dying Edward the Confessor, who, childless himself though married to a Godwin, had openly favoured his nephew, the illegitimate William, Duke of Normandy. Whether Harold knowingly committed perjury, we shall never know; but the

Bayeux Tapestry remains an eloquent witness of the Norman
point of view, the central scene depicting the shipwrecked
Harold swearing allegiance to the Norman Duke over the sacred
relics of Bayeux.[1] Hence his manifold difficulties and death in
battle at Hastings; it was God's judgement on an upstart who,
moreover, had not the Papal blessing. The fact that Harold had
fought and won a first-class battle against his rebellious brother
Tostig and the invading King of Norway at Stamford Bridge,
had then hastily marched south on hearing of William's autumn
invasion of Sussex, and rushed into battle at Hastings with
comparatively few veteran house-carls and local fyrds; moreover,
that in this, which he must have regarded as a minor, *mêlée* (as
William's mercenary troops were negligible in number), he put
up a splendid fight and that the fatal arrow and the death of all
the Godwins was a shocking piece of misfortune that overthrew
the morale of his veterans, devoted as they were to their leader:
all this may be interpreted as God's will, for he seems to have
been on the Norman side; or as a logical consequence of the
growing weakness and disunity of the Anglo-Saxon people in
the eleventh century. Certainly there were many Normans
already in England during the reign of the Confessor (his mother
was a Norman, and anyway the Normans were only the French
Vikings or the French Danelaw), and in one way their invasion,
England's last, was but the logical end of the many Viking invasions of the last two centuries. The French Vikings completed
the work of the Danes and swallowed up the old Anglo-Saxon
kingdom, much as the Anglo-Saxons had finally and slowly
swallowed and digested the old Roman-British island. In both
cases the conquerors had been there a long time before the
conquest.

It is not surprising that our first big system of organized direct
taxation (since the Roman *annona*[2]) started with the payment of
the Danegeld. By the eleventh century the English willy-nilly

[1] See p. 58.
[2] The principal tax, paid in kind, occasionally in money, by the whole
Roman empire after Diocletian; it was based on land in terms of productive
value.

had got used to collecting all their silver pennies in barrow-loads from the Hundred Courts[1] through the agency of the leading thegns and royal officials. These silver coins were the first struck in England since Roman times and were destined to pay for taxation. The King was still supposed to live 'of his own': that is, as the greatest landowner, he had a system of 'food-farms' scattered everywhere, and was supposed to live on them and his rents. But the never-ceasing demands of the Danes, as the price of their withdrawal, had reduced the weaker descendants of Alfred to this paltry device, which only got rid of them temporarily; their constant reappearance led to constant direct taxation, and 'thus the whirligig of time brings in its revenges', and the ghost of the British Vortigern would have smiled at the predicament of the descendants of the rapacious Hengist and Horsa.

---

[1] The local courts for the rural areas known as Hundreds (still to be found on the maps of England).

3

The Anglo-Norman State

'What's that?' he said. His eyes had wandered further round the skyline, and where their road mounted he perceived a solitary, broad-spreading oak tree. From its great branches there descended three ropes, and at the ends of them, their feet pointing straight to the earth, their hands apparently clasped behind their backs, were the bodies of three men, their heads cocked at one side with a sort of jaunty defiance, whilst upon the crown of the highest sat a large raven. The nun looked at them with a friendly and cheerful smile.

'Trèsmeschiants gents, voleurs attrappés par le très noble Sire de Courcy avant son départ.'

'So Mr Courcy left them when he went away?' Mr Sorrell asked. 'Sort of visiting-card, I suppose? But how you can look at them like that so calmly just after you've been saying those pretty prayers, I can't think...'   FORD MADOX FORD, *Ladies whose Bright Eyes*

Some fine, great and beautiful things came out of the Norman Conquest, but at the time it was a cold-blooded, brutal, and highly successful take-over bid by the most energetic tycoons of the eleventh century. Their titled and enterprising chairman of directors was determined to take over a going concern, and to make it pay handsome profits. The best way to do this, once he had won the battle of Hastings, was to make out that nothing had happened except a change of landlords.

Neither Duke William himself, nor his followers, nor in a short time his victims, were prepared to permit any loose talk about a 'conquest'. Before long everyone was conspiring to establish his own version of what had happened, or had not happened, as 'the myth of the Norman Conquest'. To admit a conquest would have been fatal to 'the Whig interpretation of history'.[1] So, even before there were any Whigs, a conquest was not admitted. William was no conqueror, but 'a claimant to the

---

[1] The term serves as title of a famous book by Herbert Butterfield. It denotes that interpretation which reads history, and especially English history, as the history of liberty, proceeding ever onward and upward, and requiring conquests, revolutions, and such-like inconvenient 'breaks' to be papered over,

crown under ancient law who had vindicated his claim by trial of battle with Harold, a victory which brought him no title whatever to change the laws of England'.[1] If he had changed them, it would have been a lawless act, something to be wiped out by coronation charters, and by Magna Carta, in the course of time, restoring and confirming the ancient laws of Edward the Confessor. Precisely what those laws were nobody was quite clear about, but very soon the lawyers and chroniclers had set about inventing them in the shape of *leges Edwardi Confessoris, leges Willielmi, leges Henrici*... Thus the most notable break in the revolutionary history of England was promptly patched into the pattern of continuity, and the Normans—always adept at taking the protective colouring of the peoples they conquered —became the first Whigs, or the first conservatives, in the English tradition. 'We actually build bridges in our rear, we seek to join up again,' and not only after 1688.

The English were not a decadent people in 1066. They were the people of Bede and Alcuin, the race who sent St Boniface to christianize the Germans, and Alcuin of York to teach the court of Charlemagne; a race of fair-haired farmers, brave fighters, poets, and artists in precious metals; the basic stuff of the English nation as it emerged into modern history. Hitherto they had lacked the genius of government and administration, and they fell ready victims to the hard-headed managerial superiority of the Normans. Saxon genius and Norman talent together were to produce a miracle of cross-fertilization in the Anglo-Norman state of the twelfth and thirteenth centuries. In the England of the central Middle Ages, from the Great Charter (1215) to the reign of Edward I, the original genius of the English, the sub-jugated race, gleams through from beneath the surface of history. Strictly speaking, said Lord Macaulay (who so often used that phrase when he was writing loosely), during the century and a

or at any rate accounted for as having been all for the best in the long run. This kind of history was to be especially patronized by liberals (or latter-day Whigs) in the nineteenth century. The emergence of the Whigs as distinct from the Tories is touched upon in footnote 3 to p. 172, below.

[1] J. G. A. Pocock, *The Ancient Constitution and the Feudal Law* (Cambridge, 1957), p. 53.

half which followed the Norman Conquest there is no English history. It was with the loss of Normandy (1204) and King John's granting of the Charter in 1215 that the two peoples became reconciled. 'Here commences the history of the English nation.' The Conqueror had been *Rex Norm-Anglorum*, but King John was *Rex Angliae*. Domesday Book, compiled in 1086, records the condition of the two nations, the Norman aristocracy and the English natives. A century later we still hear of the Normans needing to be protected against the malice of the English who cut Norman throats in secret places, so that the King has to inflict collective punishments. By the end of the twelfth century, 'the presentment of Englishry' and 'the Murdrum fine' are becoming absurd and unjust because it is increasingly difficult to tell whether the corpse is that of a Norman or an Englishman. 'But now that the English and Normans have lived so long together and have intermarried, the nations have become so intermingled that we can scarce distinguish in these days betwixt Englishmen and Normans...'

The Law of Englishry, by which a corpse was assumed to be that of a Norman unless it could be proved to be that of an Englishman, resulting in a heavy fine on the nearest village in the one case, and nothing at all in the other, is a typical example of the kind of measures inflicted upon members of a resistance movement by an army of occupation in a backward country. King William had said, 'I will that all men whom I brought with me shall be in my peace and quiet...' But the English thought differently, and, as a speaker in the *Dialogue of the Exchequer* put it in 1177, 'passim ipsos in nemoribus et locis remotis, nacta opportunitate, clanculo jugulabant...'[1] Perhaps it is because the story of the Conquest has so often been told by learned gentlemen from Oxford and the southern counties who liked going to Normandy for their holidays that the type of Norman who came with Duke William tends to be thought of as a polite and dark-haired Frenchman, and the Conquest itself as a kind of pageant put on by fascinating visitors from Boulogne. Although

[1] 'Here and there they lay in wait in woods and secluded places [for the hated Normans] secretly to slay them as opportunity might offer...'

the gentlemen who came with the Duke were not, in Carlyle's absurd phrase, 'simply Saxons who had learnt to talk French', they were the 'frenchified' descendants of the terrible men of the black sails and the horned helmets who had wrung from English lips the supplication against 'the malice of the Danes' in the days of the West Saxon monarchy.[1] By the early eleventh century they were no longer a stranger race, for the higher levels of English society had already been extensively normanized in the days of Edward the Confessor. What took place after 1066 was a wholesale change of aristocratic personnel. Not only had the native aristocracy been decimated, dispossessed and driven into exile, but great numbers of the ordinary folk of England had been depressed into villeinage or serfdom, completing the process of depression which had been going on for many years beneath the weight of the Danegeld[2] and the manifold menace to life, limb and property in an age of invasion. The brutality of the Conquest itself is hardly to be judged from the formal campaign of Hastings, and the swift and effective strategy by which William took possession.

The Duke of Normandy received the submission of the great earls, the clergy, and the citizens of London at Berkhampstead after crossing the Thames at Wallingford, receiving oaths of allegiance and accepting the crown. He was crowned on Christmas Day, and in the following year he felt sufficiently confident of his position to absent himself for a visit to Normandy. On his return the real conquest began with the three great hammer-blows, south-west, north, and north-west, to shatter the recoil of the spring which he had hitherto merely depressed. Exeter, York, Durham, and Chester all felt his might. The infamous 'harrying of the north' serves as a blanket-term for a policy of devastation which was to be recorded by scores of entries of 'waste' in Domesday Book at the end of his reign. The 'going concern', the mere switch of landlords, was not the whole story, or anything like it. After the initial and highly efficient 'walk-

---

[1] Large numbers of Bretons came with William, too.
[2] Maitland considered that the Danegeld alone was sufficient to reduce a nation of freemen to serfdom.

over', it was a long and bloody business, replete with scorched-earth tactics to rival those of Sherman's march from Atlanta to the sea nearly 800 years later. 'There are no revolutionary cleavages in English history,' wrote the late Sir Maurice Powicke, 'and there have been few periods of widespread devastation.' He would allow two obvious exceptions: the Norman Conquest and the Reformation. Both struck northern England with peculiar force, the one in its farms and homesteads, the other in its great religious houses. 'The malice of the Normans' left not a habitable place between York and Durham. Many hundreds of square miles were reduced to a wilderness. The process of spreading death and destruction and calling it peace involved the annihilation of farm implements and food supplies, so that the wretched scarecrows who survived were left to starve and without means of recovery. Village after village was literally wiped off the map, men, women and children left only their eyes to weep with, and sometimes not even their eyes, for the Duke's men hanged and mutilated as freely as they slaughtered. These were not what might be called the inevitable barbarities of war, for William had already won. They were the terrorism of conquest, and on a scale that England has never known before or since. Only the lawyers were to maintain that there had not been a conquest.

William had done no more, and no less, in Maine and certain other territories that came beneath his sway. 'The harsh beginning of much, the harsh ending of much', as Carlyle said of the New Poor Law of 1834. The cauterizing of a wound? After all, William is accredited with having brought England into the mainstream of European civilization. She was to become, at least for a time, part of the pattern of medieval Europe with its contractual feudal relationships, its feudal law, its institutions for justice and defence based upon the feudal obligations of one man to another, up and down the social scale. Outwardly the country assumed the style and the manners of a civilization which lived by land, built in stone, and thought in terms of military might; a land panoplied in the clean-cut stone of castle and cathedral, keep and donjon, and flint-faced guildhall. It was the

45

England of *Ivanhoe*, the England that lay under the eyes of the American gentleman when he woke up in the reign of Henry III after a railway accident.[1] Mr Sorrell would have recognized the landscape with its hanged men, its perching ravens, its nuns riding mule-back, its Sire de Courcy stringing up a few robbers before setting out for the Holy Land *pour encourager les autres*. At the end of *Tess of the D'Urbervilles*, Hardy told us that 'the d'Urberville knights and dames slept on in their tombs unknowing', but their last long sleep was not yet. They were alive and full of blood and wide-awake, intensely busy changing the face of England: dames with long straight gowns and wooden faces, knights with tremendous walrus moustaches like that latter-day Norman, Gustave Flaubert, large fierce eyes staring from under iron caps and behind iron nose-shields, and long crustacean bodies shaped like hooped oxygen-cylinders. No doubt it was this, their fiercely comic aspect, that led T. E. Lawrence once to observe that 'the Normans were rather asses'.

They left upon the face of England the typical marks of a military aristocracy and a militant Church. Nothing tells us more of the shared military quality of Church and State in the Anglo-Norman realm than the squared white stone of the garrisons of God and the baronage. From Peveril's hold above Castleton to the military face of Battle Abbey by the Sussex shore, from the towers of Durham and Southwell to the pale ramparts of the King's keep in London, from the Welsh Marches to the Cinque Ports, from Helmsley to Hedingham and Pleshey, the emblems of lordship went up, terrible as an army with banners. Remote beside slow rivers and in the folds of woodlands, the parish church gave a hint of battlements even to the tamest little *ton* that had broken the soil since the Saxons came. It was long before the Normans replaced Saxon wood and rubble with the masonry of military feudalism in its monolithic might. Much of the castle-building of the first generation of the conquerors was improvised out of the debris of old destruction as they piled up mound and

[1] See *Ladies whose Bright Eyes*, by Ford Madox Ford. Some of the aspects of the medieval landscape surveyed by Mr Sorrell may be seen in the passage which serves as epigraph to the present chapter, p. 41 above.

motte to hold a strong-point in emergency. Towers fell and curtain-walls crumbled. The one thing certain was the unending supply of labour that could be lashed and driven to the tasks involved in making England safe for aristocracy. Even today, when one surveys the sheer bulk of Norman building up and down the land, after eight centuries of time's revenges, one is sometimes left wondering how the Normans had time to do much else than build. The answer, of course, must be that it was a choice between building and dying. Settlement and construction, having and holding, this was what life was about. Fortunately the builders were the busiest and most business-like race in Europe.

William parcelled out the English land as he took possession of it. The very nature of the physical conquest, along with the nature and the ambitions of his land-hungry followers, determined the character of the apportionment. His motley following of Normans, Bretons, Flemings had to be appeased as the land was taken over, from month to month, if not from day to day. Moreover, the Duke of Normandy had had sufficient experience as a vassal of the King of France to know what to seek and what to avoid in the establishment of a feudal monarchy. Not that it was a matter of introducing 'feudalism' at all. The *idea* of a so-called feudal *system* was not introduced into England until the middle of the eighteenth century, when, as Maitland told us long ago, certain lawyers put forward 'the notion of one grand idea and a few simple principles underlying the mass of medieval law, English and continental...' If we want to speak of 'the feudal system,' as Maitland also taught us, we have to understand that 'the feudalism of France differs radically from the feudalism of England, that the feudalism of the thirteenth is very different from that of the eleventh century'. Indeed, the phrase has become so large and vague that it would be possible to say that England was the first, or the last, country to be feudalized; or, 'that William the Conqueror introduced, or for that matter suppressed, the feudal system'.

Feudalism is a state of society in which the main social bond is a personal relationship between lord and man, based on land

47

SHORT HISTORY OF ENGLAND

tenure, and implying protection on the one hand and service
(including service in arms) on the other, the doing of justice on
the one hand and the doing of 'suit of court'[1] on the other. A
feudal society is one in which relationships are organized in this
way, with the king at its head, and a whole hierarchy of vassals
ranged in ranks beneath him. Towards such an organization
English society had been tending for centuries before the Norman
Conquest. 'We need not regard this change as a retrogression.'
Still less, Maitland remarked, should we indulge in the 'habit of
speaking of feudalism as though it were a disease of the body
politic'. It was indeed a natural and even a necessary stage in
British history, and, regarded from the angle of universal history,
'feudalism means civilization, the separation of employments,
the division of labour, the possibility of national defence, the
possibility of art, science, literature and learned leisure; the
cathedral, the scriptorium, the library, are as truly the work of
feudalism as is the baronial castle...' In speaking of feudalism
we shall not be speaking simply of subjection of the peasantry to
the justice of the lord or of the free village to the manor, 'not of
abnormal forces, not of retrogression, not of disease, but in the
main of normal and healthy growth'.

If one is inclined somewhat frequently to quote the name of
Maitland in discussing this question, that is because it was
Maitland who taught us not to look round corners for ingenious,
and generally minatory, explanations of what was after all a
perfectly natural order of society and social relationships at a
certain stage of social evolution. We have learnt to forget romantic abstractions like the wicked barons and knights in shining
armour, and to take it for granted that the feudal host consisted
of farmers and fighters and business-men with work to do, a
living to make, and a world to win between dawn and dusk.
Carlyle, with his superb imaginative insight, and despite all his
thunder-and-lightning style, did more than anyone before
Maitland to make us see this. He showed, in his *Past and Present*
(1843), that the feudal baron was more like the eighteenth-
century captain of industry Richard Arkwright than he was like

[1] That is, the obligation to attend the court of one's feudal lord at stated intervals.

48

Lord John Manners and the aristocrats of Disraeli's 'Young England' party. William I led many a man called *Taillefer*, which means *Ironcutter*, or Brooks of Sheffield,[1] busy cutting out jobs of real work, governing, fighting, and running a real society. Feudalism needed no more and no less 'explaining', or apology, than the Manchester cotton trade. The important thing for the historian to do about feudalism is to avoid turning it into a 'walking abstraction', something that appears to have been invented in order to be replaced ('in the logic of history') by another abstraction called 'capitalism', in turn to be replaced by another abstraction called 'Socialism', the whole series serving only to inflate the ego of professors of dialectic.

William saw to it that nobody had too much, or too much in one place, and he made a careful note of what everyone had. His Domesday Book, which was a gigantic inventory of his new realm and its contents, describes about 170 baronies held by laymen, of an annual value of well over £30,000.[2] Another £19,000 worth went to ecclesiastical landholders, and the King himself kept scarcely less than this in his own hands. Something like half the landed estate of England was in the hands of lay barons. Indeed, the barony, or 'honour', was the major unit of feudal society, the basis and the stronghold of the tenants-in-chief of the crown, the 'magnates', the men whose duty it was to do the king 'suit of court' at his *curia*, to attend his *magnum concilium*, to serve him personally in arms and with whatever quotas of armed knights he was pleased to levy upon them. How the tenant-in-chief maintained these knights for service in the feudal host was his own affair, though it was generally considered that a 'knight's fee', or the amount of land needed to maintain a heavily armed cavalry officer (which is what a knight was), and to keep him in the field for the forty days during which the king had a right to his services, was five hides, or 120 acres. All that concerned the king was that he got his knights according to the

[1] See above, p. 4.
[2] The money figures, as Sir Maurice Powicke said when he quoted them in his *Medieval England* (pp. 57–8), 'do not represent much in the nature of cash. They are only a rough-and-ready estimate of potential power...'

quota he had levied upon each of his tenants-in-chief. Whether the latter raised them by knight's fees of five hides, or by hiring the services of armed men when the occasion arose, was for him to determine.

That the quality of the knights thus produced for the king's service was not always satisfactory, and especially when the contributor was a churchman, can be seen from numerous signs, the most obvious being the early development of the practice of levying scutage, or shield tax, in lieu of service. Henry I accepted money payment when it pleased him, and by the reign of Henry II we find the king's motives and intentions clearly described by the chronicler in terms of his reluctance to trouble (*vexare*) his country knights (*agrarios milites*), taking into account the length and difficulty of the projected journey or expedition, and quite plainly interested in hiring mercenaries (*solidarios*) by means of the 'shield money' (actually, in this instance, described in terms of coats of mail, or *loricae*). It may very well be true that, as Oliver Cromwell's followers were to say, the lords of England were 'William the Conqueror's colonels', and the barons his majors, and the knights his captains; but within a short time of the Conquest we are hearing of agrarian knights, or rustic gentlemen, who would rather not be troubled with military service. 'Military feudalism' seems never to have bred much in the way of militarism in England. The Norman aristocracy soon took on the colour of the English. They preferred farming. Of course a century after Cromwell's major-generals had gone clanking into history, Tom Paine and the English Radicals were still harping on 'the crafty illegitimate of Normandy' as the progenitor of King George III, and on 'the robber barons' as the ancestors of the aristocratic monopolists of the unreformed House of Commons.

How did the Conqueror's followers find their way to the scattered manors with which the King had invested them? There was no 'seating-plan' available for this feast, and many of the new landholders must have been strangers to the rural landscape. On many a morrow after the battle of Hastings, England was lively with adventurers riding up hill and down dale looking for manors. One would vèry much like to know how Eustache de Vache from Flanders and Fulke de Bréauteville from Brittany solved the immediate and practical problem of finding their way to Hainoure or Cotenoure or Smitcote in the Erewash Valley. The question is not as trivial as it may seem, for it at once brings us face to face with one of the great realities of the situation, which is that the newcomers were from the beginning in some sense dependent upon the people who led along their horses and yielded up their carts or merely gathered at the roadside to point the way. That there was a good deal of *Schaden-freude* about it on the part of the natives one need not doubt. But fitting into a landscape is a problem in topography requiring for its solution the co-operation, willing or otherwise, of the figures already there. Priests, reeves, oldest inhabitants, tithing-men, no doubt all were recruited to the task. The old Saxon society of the tithing and the hundred was full of vigorous life, and the Normans brought with them the device of the *inquête*, the jury of sworn witnesses which was soon to be called upon to provide a great variety of the local fact-finding which in turn is the rudimentary basis of both justice and administration. The most famous example of the *inquête* is the panel of sworn witnesses which William was to employ, in all the shires and hundreds and vills of England, to collect the information he required for drawing up his great *descriptio* of his new realm in Domesday Book at the end of his reign.

The shire and hundred courts of Saxon times, which might be fairly regarded as the ancient popular institutions of the English, continued to meet under the new order, and in 1109–11 Henry I ensured the continuity of the old English institutions within the world of Norman innovation by issuing an order that the shire and hundred courts be held as *in tempora regis Edwardi et non aliter* ('in the time of King Edward [the Confessor] and not otherwise'). This was a significant measure in the cause of continuity, coming as it did from a king who was married to a princess directly descended from King Alfred, and who opened his reign with a Coronation Charter of Liberties, promising— for what it was worth—amendments in matters of justice *secundum lagam regis Edwardi* ('according to the laws of King Edward').

'Manors—manors everywhere', Maitland wrote of the new regime portrayed in Domesday Book. Manors were certainly ubiquitous, but to imagine that the manor now became universal at the expense of the old 'free villages' of the Saxon world would be to give a misleading and over-simplified portrait of medieval England at any time.[1] If by 'the manor' we simply mean *manerium* as 'manor-house' (and the term had no technical meaning at the time of Domesday Book), certainly England was full of them, and the Normans were particularly interested in seeing the country as a complex of manors because the manor was the administrative unit for the collection of the *geld*, the fiscal product of the realm, the principal thing that the King was interested in when he assembled his great survey in 1086. But as regards the working of the land, and the daily lives of the people who worked on it, the properly manorialized areas of England were the southern and western parts of the island. East Anglia and the northern Danelaw were far less uniform, East Anglia having many villages of freemen on small estates, while in the northern Danelaw (roughly from the Welland to the Tees), apart from areas where the Church held the land, men belonged to sokes and berewicks, hardly associated with the *manerium* at all. It was an immensely complex situation, hardly to be dignified with the name of 'system', let alone a 'manorial system'.

Structure depends upon function, and rural structure depends upon the qualities of the soil, and especially upon the proportion of pasture in relation to arable. Very extensive areas of England were, from an early date, devoted to sheep-farming, even the

---

[1] The typical manor consisted of a quantity of demesne land (land which the lord had in his own hands, equivalent to the 'home-farm' of a modern land-owner), and of lands held by freehold tenants and unfree 'tenants-in-villeinage' who owed the lord 'week-work' which they did on his demesne. All these lands usually lay together, and sometimes the manorial unit was coterminous with the vill or the township. Adjacent to the cultivated land under strip cultivation in two, or three, large open fields, lay the common or waste on which beasts were pastured. The 'typical manor' is a text-book abstraction for the lowest forms of schools. It disappears into a perplexing multiformity as soon as the actual situation in any one area comes under study.

ploughlands being used to fold sheep on fallow and stubble. The sheep were folded for their wool rather than for their meat, and until Robert Bakewell took over sheep-breeding in the eighteenth century they resembled, as regards flesh and bone, a species of gaunt and rangy hound. Their wool, however, was in great demand in the manufacturing areas of Italy and Flanders. England was exporting wool to the cloth manufacturers of Florence before the Norman Conquest, and by the thirteenth century the wool trade was reaching its Golden Age, when men said the hoof of the sheep turned sand into gold. The shepherd with his flock and his wattled hurdles was a key figure in the medieval rural scene, destined to immortality in poetry and song and pictorial art. Flocks might amount to three, four, and even five figures, especially on the lands of the great religious orders of the north country. Even a peasant hamlet like Merton in south Wiltshire with less than two hundred villagers is recorded as folding between three and four thousand. 'The pastoral world', as Eileen Power wrote, 'is a world with different settlements and different holdings from the world of arable agriculture. Its settlements are hamlets and homesteads.' It was, in a sense, a freer world, and as Miss Power went on to remark: 'Wordsworth was making a strictly economic observation when he said that the voice of freedom was the voice of the mountains'—or at least of the dales and fells where the sheep nibbled the shoulders of the hills. The self-sufficing medieval village, which is what we generally mean when we envisage 'the manor' with its open fields, its pasture and its waste, was undoubtedly a reality, but it was only a corner of the picture. Men were engaged, even in Norman times, with a great variety of cash-crops, 'industrial crops' like flax, woad, madder and saffron, not to mention the fact that many people lived by fishing and by the digging of coal. The picture of English life in the early Middle Ages is one of multifarious occupations, and 'life on the medieval manor' describes only a part of it.

The Normans, too, were great town-builders and began the transformation of the Saxon 'burgh' into the city. The towns have been described as 'islands in the sea of feudalism', though they were rural enough with their town fields and town bulls. However, a runaway villein[1] was acknowledged to be beyond recapture if he succeeded in domiciling himself in a corporate town for a year and a day. 'Town air', the saying went, 'is free air', though freedom was strictly monopolized by the burgesses who enjoyed, and very jealously guarded, the privileges accorded to them under their charters, especially the privileges embodied in the grant of their *gilda mercatoria*.[2] The privileges of the Gild Merchant concerning the monopoly and regulation of trade are typical of a 'scarcity economy'. If gildsmen kept close watch on fair dealing and the fair sharing of commercial opportunities, if they regarded traders from other towns as 'foreigners' to be taxed and tolled and carefully supervised while within the walls, this was because there was only a limited amount of trade to go round. No 'closed shop' of the modern industrial world can match the closeness of a medieval English town. The monopolists of the Gild Merchant were to injure urban trade development later on, but for a century and more after the Conquest their protectionism was beneficial, and the towns grew strong and prosperous under their regulative energies. By the reign of Henry II (1154–89), Lincoln, York, Norwich and Winchester, with their walls and battlements under the presiding might of castle and cathedral, with their fairs and markets, gild-halls and

[1] The notion that every villein was a potential escapist, like the American Negro slave on the Southern plantations, is a fantasy of the 'democratic' mind. To be 'tied to the soil' was the best thing to be in medieval society, whose abiding horror was the 'landless man'. The villein had at any rate a standing in terms of the commodity of universal value—the soil. He was protected at law against everyone but his own lord, and his lord was as little likely to injure or destroy him as he was likely to injure or destroy a draught beast of his demesne, a horse or an ox.

[2] Technically a 'burgess' was the holder of a 'burgage-tenure' in the land of the borough both within the walls and without. He enjoyed the privileges of the borough under its charter, such as membership of the Gild Merchant, which (where it existed) often coincided with the organ of general civic authority, 'portmoot', 'commune', or whatever. Gild Merchant and borough were generally 'two aspects of the same body', but men who were not burgesses might acquire membership of the Gild Merchant in order to enjoy amenities as traders, e.g. merchants of the county acquired membership of the gild at Lincoln. (See Charles Gross, *Gild Merchant*, vol. II, pp. 120, 146.)

gabled town-houses, were busy commercial centres to rival any of Europe north of the Alps, and London was as great as all the others in England put together. London was already the social centre of the realm, with its 'lordly habitations', its schools and law-courts, its charities, its water supply and drains, and even its restaurant on the north bank.[1]

The Church shared with the city as an agency of 'liberty'. When he composed his study *On the Constitution of Church and State, according to the idea of each,* in 1829, Samuel Taylor Coleridge chose to identify the mercantile and commercial classes with what he called the 'progression' of the country, its improvement and general freedom, while he sought to identify the landed order with the country's 'permanence'. During the period when the interest of 'progression' was only 'in the bud', or merely 'potential existence', the Church 'presented the only breathing hole of hope', relaxing the iron fate by which feudalism predestined every native of the realm to be lord or vassal. It was, Coleridge held, 'under the fostering wing of the Church' that a class of free citizens and burghers was reared. 'To the feudal system we owe the *forms,* to the Church the *substance,* of our liberty.' In the privileged vicinity of church and monastery the fugitive vassal and oppressed franklin[2] found a refuge, thus laying 'the first foundation of a class of freemen detached from the land'. It was the clergy who waged 'a holy war' against slavery and villeinage. The Church may be said to have provided the nearest thing to 'a career open to talent' for the sons of men of low degree, who might proceed via the cloister school to the highest offices in the realm. As early as 1164 the sixteenth and last of Henry II's *Constitutions of Clarendon,* which purported to enumerate the ancient customs governing the relations of Church and State, records an objection to the ordination of *filii*

---

[1] See *Medieval England,* ed. Austin Lane Poole, vol. I, ch. VII, *Towns and Trade,* by E. M. Carus-Wilson.

[2] 'Franklin' was the archaic term often employed by writers of the Romantic revival of the early nineteenth century for a landowner of free but not noble birth in the fourteenth and fifteenth centuries. The author of *Christabel* (published 1816), the quintessence of revived medievalism in poetry, readily adopts the Chaucerian term when writing his *Church and State* in 1829.

rusticorum without the consent of the lord of the manor. We have few recorded instances of the 'base-born' rising to eminence by ecclesiastical avenues, but the opportunity existed.

The Norman and Angevin kings were devout men after their fashion. They swore by various portions of God's body. The Conqueror swore generally by his teeth. Henry II had a preference for his eyes, or, as the Archbishop of Canterbury once ventured to correct him: 'per reverentiam oculorum quos jurasti, domine mi rex'.[1] All, with the possible exception of King John, were deeply, even if not devoutly, conscious of their dependence upon God's favour, and even John was on excellent terms with the see of Worcester, with whose excommunicated bishop he chose to spend Christmas on at least one occasion. It is true that they treated their God as something of a mascot, or lucky charm, but then so did the Roman emperors after Constantine, and so do fighting-men in all ages. Their historical reputations have often suffered unduly in consequence of the fact that churchmen were the principal chroniclers upon whom history had for long to depend. Similarly, they composed for long the sole source of supply for educated royal servants.

The Conqueror had had his banner blessed by the Pope on setting out upon the enterprise of England. When the enterprise came to a successful conclusion, however, he declined to do fealty to the Holy Father for his new realm. As for the payment of Peter's Pence, an obligation which he inherited as an annual tribute paid to the Pope by his predecessors as kings of England (an obligation, or a privilege, which they shared with the rulers of Poland and the Scandinavian lands), William was rather particular about the fact that he paid it as alms, not as tribute. Indeed, William I set the pattern of English kingship in its relations with Rome for centuries to come. It was the relationship of a loyal son to a respectful father. While he would have no nonsense, he welcomed a good working relation, as between gentlemen. One of the first things he effected when he took charge of England was the separation of spiritual and temporal jurisdictions. Somewhere between 1070 and 1076 he put forth

---

[1] 'By the blessed eyes, by which you swear, my lord king...'

an Ordinance of Separation, somewhat vague in its terms. It forbade the bringing of cases concerning the cure of souls, *regimen animarum*, before the lay courts, or *ad judicium secularium hominum*, thereby opening a rather large door to the encroachment of ecclesiastical upon temporal jurisdiction in later days. But it at least brought the English into line with the practice of continental Christendom. It seems to have been somewhat shocking to continental opinion that the Saxon bishops had sat along with the sheriff and ealdormen in the shire courts. Not that anyone imagined that the clergy should be kept out of civil courts. Most of the king's justices were perforce recruited from 'clerks' of his chapel anyway, for generations to come. But the 'rusticity' of the Saxon bishops in the days of the notorious pluralist Archbishop Stigand (likewise a disloyal subject and an adherent of the anti-pope) was now at an end. The bishops were to become urban, if not always urbane; tenants-in-chief of the Crown, scarcely distinguishable from lay barons, royal servants and valued administrative allies of the king in the affairs of state. William carried on the reformist tradition of St Dunstan. He worked in collaboration with the Norman Lanfranc, Archbishop of Canterbury (1070–89), and enjoyed the confidence of the reforming Pope, Hildebrand, Gregory VII. Under the new regime, canon law began to develop and flourish in England, as in the rest of Europe, though popes went on professing some surprise when the island produced good canonists.

The Church was the sole institutional check on the despotism of the Norman and Angevin kings, although the real limitations in older days were not institutional, and certainly should not be assessed in 'constitutional' terms. The sanctity of custom, and of customary ways of doing things, traditional modes of behaviour, counted for most of all in a society which had little else than custom, use and habit to refer to. William the Conqueror, *qua* conqueror, was the man in possession, and possession amounted to nine points of the law. William's attitude can be shown from the old story of his seizing a couple of handfuls of the soil when he took a toss from his horse on landing at Pevensey. He was, in feudal terms, 'taking seisin' of what, according to

Norman propaganda—and especially as we see it in the Bayeux Tapestry, the most famous example of the Norman genius for making everything, even needlework, serve the cause of public relations—had been promised by Edward the Confessor, if not by Harold when he visited William on the occasion of his celebrated shipwreck on the Norman shore in 1064.[1] His real claim to be Harold's successor as King, however, rested upon his acceptance by the great men of the realm at Berkhampstead and his coronation in London on Christmas Day 1066, the acknowledgement of accomplished fact. Succession, implemented by his victorious sword, gave him Harold's rights and duties as King of the English: the command of the fyrd, or national army, the right to impose the danegeld, or the national taxes, and the duty of making his 'peace' prevail over all the land. *Justitia est emolumentum* ('the administration of justice is highly profitable') was a favourite royal maxim. And what the King could not do as Harold's successor (which was very little) he could do as lord of 'omnes homines quos mecum adduxi aut post me venerunt' ('all the men I brought here or who followed me'). He had the right to feudal aids, in particular when he knighted his eldest son or married his daughter. He had the right to take a 'relief' (*relevium*, or fee) when an incoming heir entered upon his inheritance, and to enjoy the fruits of an estate while the future heir was under his wardship, a practice which was especially profitable when extended to a vacant see or abbacy. Kings would extend such vacancies as long as they could in conscience contrive, in order to enjoy such profit. William Rufus (the Conqueror's successor as William II) made a habit of such prolongation, although he filled the See of Canterbury in some haste when

---

[1] See above, ch. 2, p. 38. Two things should be remembered here. One is that Edward the Confessor had no right to give the crown away, or to promise it. The monarchy was elective, and at the very least no one could hope to assume it without the consent, or the consultation, of the Witan, or council of wise men of the land. In the second place, no one knows what kind of oath Harold swore before William, though it is obvious that it was sworn under duress, and therefore could legally be renounced. The story of the holy relics secreted beneath the altar on which Harold swore (suggested in the Bayeux Tapestry) does not appear until a later date as the basis for the charge that Harold was the victim of trickery.

he seemed likely to die of over-eating in 1093. Canterbury had then been vacant for four years.

Political exigency did much to bring these despotic rulers to acknowledge certain limitations and make certain concessions from time to time, especially where tactical advantages might be gained in the everlasting struggle to defeat rival claimants to the crown. Here again William II showed himself singularly adept. He came to the throne in 1087, and in 1088 we find him calling the English 'Anglos suos...Anglos probos et fortes viros...'[1] and promising them good laws, tax relief and travelling expenses if they rallied to him against the Norman conspirators ('bonasque leges et tributorum levamen, liberasque venationes...'). After him, his brother Henry I, in competition for the throne with his other brother Robert, made much play with his Charter of Liberties, a document which was to be produced in 1215 as the prototype of Magna Carta. It was said, and not altogether unjustly, that when he had gained his ends he forgot his promises, but at least he had, in addition to providing a model for future use, given hostages to the one great corporation which never died and never lost its memory: *Ecclesia Anglicana*. The first promise of his Charter of Liberties was 'Sanctam Dei ecclesiam imprimis liberam facio', and he went on to renounce all the unjust exactions of his predecessor, including the evil practice of keeping bishoprics and abbacies vacant. In 1107 he came to a compromise with Archbishop Anselm on the question of 'lay investiture' (the vesting of churchmen with spiritual symbols by the hands of laymen), the issue that kept pope and emperor at loggerheads in continental Europe for so long at this time, renouncing the practice of himself investing bishops and abbots with the symbols of spiritual authority, while Anselm undertook not to refuse consecration to prelates who had done homage to the king for their temporalities.[2] King Stephen, in the civil strife which occupied so much of his reign, made many more concessions to the Church in his *Carta...de libertatibus Ecclesiae Anglicanae* of 1136, particularly in regard to church property

---

[1] 'His Englishmen...Englishmen strong and true...'
[2] Lands and goods pertaining to a see or an abbey.

during vacancies and the extent of ecclesiastical jurisdiction, concessions which Henry II was later to try to whittle down in his contest with Becket.

Becket, indeed, was the first to stand up to the King over a matter of financial exaction, in the case of the 'Sheriff's Aid'. This was a kind of tip given to the sheriff by the county for his official services. It was purely customary, and no more (and no less) a form of taxation than is a Christmas-box. Henry ordered that it should in future be paid into the Exchequer. Sheriffs being what they were, it was well understood that the sheriff would somehow make himself out to be the loser and would recoup himself by compensatory exactions elsewhere. Becket resisted, the King swore by God's eyes, the Archbishop corrected him, swearing 'de jure ecclesiae' (the oath of a cleric) that the sum was not owed by the lands of Canterbury ('non dabantur de tota mea')—no, not one penny ('ne unius quidem denarius'). The demand had to be withdrawn. This kind of resistance, of course, was resistance on behalf of a particular area or community, and not on behalf of a general principle. Another upstanding churchman, St Hugh of Avalon, Bishop of Lincoln, in the reign of Richard I, was to champion the exemption (or privilege) of his see from military service to the King outside the realm of England. (He admitted Lincoln's obligation to provide knights' service, but in this country only: 'sed in hac terra solummodo'.) Had he given way, he appears to have said, it would have re- dounded to the detriment of his successors: he would have been —as men of this country are always so fond of saying in such situations—'creating a precedent'. Hugh of Lincoln anticipated that his successors would have said: 'The fathers have eaten sour grapes, and the children's teeth are set on edge.'

Resistance to royal exactions in the name of privilege could, and did, pave the way for resistance in the name of liberty. A privilege was, in medieval times, a 'liberty', and many liberties will amount in the long run to liberty. That is what came out of the many 'liberties', mainly baronial, championed in Magna Carta, a document which owed much to another archbishop, Stephen Langton.

4

Common Law and Charter

It is sometimes maintained that the story of medieval England is best told as the story of her kings. Certainly at that time the personality of the king played a more decisive part in shaping the story than in periods of more 'institutionalized' monarchy. Yet we are not so confident as we once were that kings in losing their personal authority lost very much of their influence on the course of events, or that personal monarchies were ever quite so powerful, for good or ill, as was once imagined. This is mainly because men no longer believe so confidently as they once did in the sovereignty of the human will, even the will of kings. The great personalities of history now play second fiddle to great impersonal forces and movements. Instead of saying, as our fathers did, how fortunate that King John was of a wilful and tyrannical disposition, so that Stephen Langton and the barons found it necessary to compel him to set his seal to Magna Carta at Runnymede in 1215, we are inclined to say that the charter would have come in another form, and another manner, at another time, if John had never been born, or had been a different kind of man, and anyway it was only an acknowledgement of baronial privileges wrung by selfish aristocrats from a debauchee, and that what really mattered was the King's sale of borough charters and the rise of the towns with their up-and-coming middle class, the gravediggers of feudalism. And yet the fact remains that King John was a wilful tyrant, and that things did happen in the way they are recorded to have happened, and that the actual course of history is far more important, and vastly more interesting, than anything that a historian can invent for the edification of his readers. The interplay of royal personalities and impersonal forces at work in the body of society,[1] together with a certain amount of sheer fluke, is what

[1] Which means in the minds of men.

distinguishes history from historicism, whether of the Communist Manifesto, the Old Testament, or *Old Moore's Almanack*.

The fact is that when Henry I died of his well-known 'surfeit of lampreys' on the day after St Andrew's Mass-day in 1135, leaving twenty-two children, two of whom were born in wedlock, there was—as the monk of Peterborough wrote—'treason soon in the land, for every man that could forthwith robbed another', which was not unusual, for 'the King's Peace' died with him.[1] When Sir John Seeley took the place of Charles Kingsley as Regius Professor of Modern History at Cambridge in 1870, a kindly don was heard to ask, on coming away from his inaugural lecture, 'Who would have thought we should regret dear Kingsley so soon?' Norman gentlemen had long lamented King Henry as a tyrant who played down to the English (so that some called him 'the last king of the English') but men now began to speak of him as 'the Lion of Justice', for, as the chronicler went on, 'there was great awe of him'. A man could go through the kingdom safely with his bosom full of gold and silver, and that was much to be thankful for. None could say as much of King Stephen's reign (1135–54), which went down to history as 'the nineteen long winters' when 'God and his angels slept'. Certainly Stephen's reign showed the vital importance of a strong and decisive personality on the throne in an age when feudalism could easily become another name for feuding. Stephen was a grandson of the Conqueror, and a nephew of Henry I; but Henry had left a legitimate daughter, Matilda, who was married to Geoffrey, Count of Anjou. The Norman baronage had little love for Matilda and her Angevin husband and children, and promptly gave their suffrage for the mild and easy-going Stephen of Blois, who gave away a good deal of Crown land and relaxed the tight rein of his predecessor in order to secure their support. Thus he began his reign on the wrong foot, and, as was usual in those days, he never got on to the right one.

---

[1] This went on until 1272 when, Prince Edward being absent on crusade, the new king's 'peace' was declared to have begun from the day when his father, Henry III, was 'alive and dead' instead of from the day of the new king's coronation. Thenceforth the throne has never been regarded as vacant by death. 'Le roi est mort. Vive le roi!'

Of course the Nineteen Long Winters, with God and his angels sleeping, was not the whole story, although it would be a mockery to make out, as historians are so fond of doing in such cases, that 'the anarchy has been much exaggerated'. The most that can be said has been said by Austin Lane Poole,[1] who points out that the appalling condition of England in these years was little different from the normal condition prevailing in twelfth-century Europe, 'where the feud and the private castle were not prohibited. It was just because England had been fortunate enough never to have known these instruments of oppression, these seeds of discord, that, when she at last experienced them, they appeared so particularly appalling. The English people had been "spoilt", as we might say, by more than half a century of peace and strong rule for a state of things which on the Continent was almost a commonplace.' It seems that we must, after all, allow for 'exaggeration' and 'impermissible generalization'. The monk of Peterborough who left us the most horrific account of the kind of thing that happened was living close to the area that suffered the worst ravages at the hands of the worst ruffian of the time, Geoffrey de Mandeville. 'How far this private war was general, and how far it dislocated the life of the country,' wrote Mr Lane Poole, 'it is difficult to determine; the evidence is insufficient and contradictory.' At any rate, it seems that we should amend 'nineteen' to 'nine' long winters, for by 1148 the worst was over. Geoffrey de Mandeville was laid low by an arrow at Burwell in 1144. The Lady Matilda left the country by 1147. She died in 1152 and in the following year a treaty was signed by which Stephen was assured of the throne for the rest of his life with Matilda's son, Henry of Anjou, as his heir. The most fortunate thing that happened, however, was the launching of the Second Crusade, in 1147, which took large numbers of the turbulent aristocracy away to the Holy Land. No more than during the Wars of the Roses, three centuries later, was the normal life of the country utterly at an end. There were even faint signs of improvements. It has been discovered that two of the great legal reforms generally accredited to Henry II, *novel disseisin* and

[1] *Domesday Book to Magna Carta* (*The Oxford History of England*, 1951), chapter 5.

the assize *utrum*, appeared sketchily in these years.[1] On the economic side, the great sheep-farmers of the future, the Cistercian monks, had begun to settle in the country even before Stephen came to the throne, and the Flemings had already been settled as weavers in Pembrokeshire for some quarter of a century.

It was not the baronage that caused all the trouble under King Stephen, nor did Henry II conduct a campaign against the baronage in order to put things right. The barons did not constitute an alien element in the body politic requiring to be excised or suppressed, and it is wholly to misconceive the character of medieval England, and of its history, to interpret it in terms of a chronic, or irrepressible, conflict between king and magnates. The medieval 'baronage' is a rather unsatisfactory collective noun for the men who decided how things went. To quote the late Sir Maurice Powicke: 'Whatever the system might be, they were part of it; indeed there is little exaggeration in saying that they *were* it.'[2] They held the land, and the land carried with it the duties of administration and police and the levying of armed men. The tenants-in-chief of the Crown were not only an element of the community but by far the most important people in public life. Nothing, for good or ill, could go on without them, and no medieval king would have thought for one moment of trying to suppress or eliminate them, any more than in the seventeenth century Cardinal Richelieu would have thought to eliminate the nobility of France. Richelieu cut off the heads of Montmorency-Bouteville and the Marquis de Cinq Mars, of le Comte de Chalais and le Maréchal de Marillac, in order to make it clear that noble traitors and conductors of private war must pay for treason and disorder with their heads. He would have had the head of Gaston d'Orléans, the King's brother, if the latter had not got out of his reach in Lorraine. This is what King Stephen in his generation failed to do. His bugbear was not the baronage but Geoffrey de Mandeville and the Earl of Chester, Robert Fitz-Hubert of Devizes and William of Dover. Barons became over-mighty subjects and took to 'self-help' because royal authority supplied, or threatened, no alternative.

[1] See below, pp. 71–2.   [2] *Medieval England, 1066–1485* (Oxford, 1931), pp. 51–6.

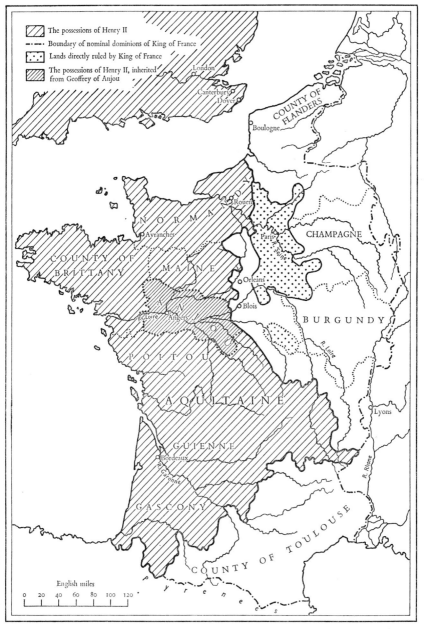

The possessions of Henry II
Boundary of nominal dominions of King of France
Lands directly ruled by King of France
The possessions of Henry II, inherited from Geoffrey of Anjou

London
Canterbury
Dover
COUNTY OF FLANDERS
Boulogne

Rouen
N O R M A N D Y
Avranches
Paris
Seine
CHAMPAGNE
COUNTY OF BRITTANY
M A I N E
Orleans
A N J O U
Loire
Angers
Blois
BURGUNDY
R. Loire
P O I T O U
A Q U I T A I N E
Lyons
G U I E N N E
Bordeaux
R. Garonne
R. Rhone
G A S C O N Y
C O U N T Y   O F   T O U L O U S E
P y r e n e e s

English miles
0 20 40 60 80 100 120

3   The dominions of Henry II

It would be absurd to imagine that the baronial holders of the land, for all their proclivity to violence, self-help, intrigue and corruption, wished to see their English estates reduced to a desert by internecine warfare. What they could do to moderate this kind of thing is illustrated by the arrangements made between the Earls of Chester and Leicester towards the end of the anarchy. They agreed not to make war on each other without fifteen days' notice, and to maintain a no-man's-land between their possessions, a demilitarized zone in which neither would build castles. They even had a couple of stake-holders in the Bishops of Chester and Lincoln. If their liege lord, the King, were to make war on either earl, the other might assist his brother earl to the extent of twenty knights, all plunder being returnable. This private treaty illustrates not only the complete lack of effective central government, but the desire and the ability of a pair of great feudatories to restore some measure of order in the midst of chaos. In the end it was by such local arrangements that a more settled state of things was brought about in the country at large.

The new king, Henry of Anjou, who came to the throne as Henricus Secundus in 1154, must not therefore be imagined as a simple 'baron-breaker'. He had more to do than police the turbulent lords of England, and all his life the first call on his superabundant energies was from the military, governmental and administrative problems of a continental empire in which England formed only an unsavoury corner. Not only had he Normandy from Matilda, his mother, but Anjou, Maine and Touraine from Geoffrey, Count of Anjou, his father. In 1152 Henry had married Eleanor of Aquitaine, former wife of Louis VII, King of France, and she had brought him also Poitou and Auvergne. But the English problem, though not the most extensive, was the most important in priority, for it was as King of England that he wore the crown which set him on a level with the kings of Europe, and especially with his feudal suzerain, or overlord for his French possessions, the King of France. He set about the English problem immediately after his coronation, his measures involving the expulsion of foreign levies, in especial the Flemings, the 'slighting' of 'adulterine', or illegally built, castles, and the recovery of the alienated Crown lands. Within five years of his accession in England we find him at war with his suzerain, the King of France, over Toulouse, which he claimed on behalf of his wife, and within the first ten years of his reign he conducted no less than three Welsh wars and one for the conquest of Ireland which established the ascendancy of the Pale, or the area around Dublin where the royal authority was strongest. He married his daughter Matilda to Henry the Lion, Duke of Saxony and Bavaria, and later in his life we find him acting as arbiter between the kings of Castile and Navarre. Although he bore no imperial title, his was a truly imperial sway, extending from Scotland to the Pyrenees. It was appropriate that Geoffrey of Monmouth had already produced his *Historia Regum Britanniae*, tracing the British monarchy back not merely to King Arthur but to Brutus the Trojan. This brilliant and imaginative work was to become a respected text-book throughout the Middle Ages. It was probably written at Oxford,[1] and its relation to historic truth is irrelevant. As the medieval historicists liked to say, with pleasing nonchalance: 'He that will trow (believe) it, trow it...' The whole purpose of a myth is to trow it, and not to ask questions. The British History of Geoffrey of Monmouth inaugurated the cult of an imperial destiny on the eve of England's recovery under a great king, an international figure on the European stage.

Henry II was a middling-sized man with close-cropped red hair, a violent temper, and an incapacity for sitting still. His intention to recover what was his own as King of England meant that he bent his energies to the problem of the recovery of stolen goods in general, so that the King's cause was the cause of all injured property-owners, and in serving his own interest he would be serving the realm. He set about establishing legal procedures, first for the defence of seisin, or land-possession, which was a matter of fact, and only secondly for the establishment, or re-establishment, of rightful ownership. Possession was to be defended by means of 'possessory assizes', of which there were four, concerned with Novel Disseisin (recent dispossession),

---

[1] *British Antiquity*, by T. D. Kendrick (Methuen, 1956), chapter 1.

Mort D'Ancestor (inheritance), Darrein Presentment (property in presentation to ecclesiastical livings), and Utrum (dispute *whether* land were held by ecclesiastical or lay tenure). Henry thus protected possession, rightful and wrongful alike, and only secondarily concerned himself to make provision for recovery by the unlawfully dispossessed. As Maitland put it, he protected the land-grabber against his victim so that land should not be grabbed in future. Thereby he discouraged self-help, the bane of the late reign, even on the part of the injured. The question of right came second to the safeguarding of peace, for Henry, like all successful rulers, was a *politique*, putting immediate peace before the ultimate triumph of truth and justice. Once the great standstill had been assured, the process of 'doing right' could be attended to, and not before. Both defending possession and eliciting rightful ownership involved the use of one or another of a whole assortment of royal writs or mandates, all opening with the words: 'Rex vice comiti salutem', and requiring the sheriff to put the appropriate procedures into operation, for the *vicecomes* or sheriff to whom the King thus sent his greeting was the royal officer in charge of the King's military and judicial affairs in every shire, the officer who collected his taxes, summoned meetings of the shire court, had custody of his 'pleas' or law-suits, not to mention his prisoners. Because he thus had a finger in every pie, and generally pulled out plums for himself as well as doing the King's business, he is the villain of the piece in medieval story-telling, notably in the tales of Robin Hood in the person of the Sheriff of Nottingham, and figuring still in the villain's role in Christmas pantomimes. Only by obtaining a Writ of Right commanding the sheriff to act could a dispute over a free tenure be brought into a baron's court in future. By a writ of Novel Disseisin the dispossessor was ordered to do right by the plaintiff or the King would do it for him. Writs were the King's monopoly, to be purchased from his Chancery, and the most rapid and effective in their operation were the most expensive. *Justitia magnum emolumentum est.*

Henry II was never to be known, like Henry I, as the Lion of Justice, nor, like Edward I, as the English Justinian. He was not a great and original law-giver, for many of his most important measures are now known to have been already in embryonic existence. Nor were many of his reforms brought about by formal enactment. The concept of statute as the source of innovation was beyond the medieval notion of legislation. Even 'Constitutions', like those made at Clarendon (1164) for instance, were regarded as simply the writing down of custom: 'consuetudines vero et dignitatum regni' (i.e. the King's ancient customs and dignities). Henry's work was done by instructions, sometimes verbal, to ministers and justices, conceived and put into operation in the ordinary tasks of doing the King's business as keeper of the peace and supreme judge. The King supplied the authority and the drive. The daily work that built up the tradition of common-law practice, and in the end the rule of law in England, was done by the King's men of business, justiciars like Hubert Walter and Ranulf Glanvil, and hard-riding itinerant justices who carried the King's justice far and wide. Not only was the King's justice itinerant, or circumferential. It was stable and centralized, too. For the King had opened the doors of his court at Westminster to litigation on the part of the mass of his subjects. Business there was brisk and profitable, for in no time or place were ordinary men and women more litigious than in the England of the medieval centuries. Maitland has made it possible for us to see and hear them at what was their favourite occupation and recreation, for litigation seems to have supplied the place of organized sport. 'A picture...of English life as it was in the thirteenth century,' he called his first book, *The Pleas of the Crown for the County of Gloucester*. Not a promising title for a contribution to social history, one would say. Yet it is there, before the King's justices on tour of the County of Gloucester, that we see them all. 'What is visible in the foreground is crime, and crime of a vulgar kind—murder and rape and robbery. This would be worth seeing were there no more to be seen, for crime is a fact of which history must take note, but the political life of England is in a near background.' Here is a fair field full of folk, men and women as full of blood as any vision of Piers Plowman: sheriffs and famous men, abbots and priors, reeves, smiths, millers and carpenters, and Edith Wackford bearing the disputed pig in her arms so that we hear its individual grunt.

There was little new or original in the means that Henry provided for the administration of his justice. The Jury of Presentment for presenting cases for trial, which was to become the grand jury, was probably in use in some form in the reign of Ethelred. The petty jury, as applied to the possessory assizes, and in the King's courts generally, was the successor of the sworn *inquête* of neighbours to supply facts and bear witness to facts which had been recruited for the compilation of Domesday Book: the King was offering it as an alternative and an improvement upon the crude old English appeal to the supernatural, or the ordeal by fire and water: as an alternative, also, to the hated Norman ordeal by battle. Even the itinerant justices went back at least to Henry I and the Norman kings. Henry II was a French prince, and his lawyers wrote and thought in French, and English law in the thirteenth century bears many resemblances to the *coutumes* of northern France. There is nothing particularly homespun about this French prince's ideas and practices. They not only owed a great deal to the prerogative procedures of the Frankish kings (the most likely root of trial by jury), but their coherence owed much to the influence of revived Roman jurisprudence being taught at this time in the law schools of Pavia and Bologna. A celebrated Roman jurist, Vacarius, was teaching Roman law in England by 1150. Nor must we underestimate what the King's lawyers learnt from the highly civilized and sophisticated canon law administered by their brethren of the ecclesiastical courts, so often their rivals but still more often their teachers.

English law and its modes of procedure, then, were not invented under, let alone by, Henry II. What happened was rather that English law became articulate. The result of articulation in the course of rather less than a hundred years was not a 'system' but a habit of legal practice, with its writs and its forms of action, its juries and its recognitions and its assizes. It was something sufficiently coherent and articulate to be described, something that was indeed to be described as early as

1188 in a formal treatise[1] by the Justiciar, Ranulf Glanvil (1180-9), or possibly by his nephew, Hubert Walter, who was both Justiciar and Archbishop of Canterbury. Best of all, though a little later, came the *Note Book of Henry of Bratton*, generally known as Bracton, who was one of Henry III's justices. This was the working note-book of a practitioner, concerned (as were they all) very little with the adumbration of principles but very much with the moving picture of the law in action, and especially (in the case of Bracton) with the precedents set by two recent and active justices, Martin Pateshull and William Raleigh. We can see that the law has already acquired three of the features which were to prove the despair of satirists and reformers as yet unborn: it was very complicated, it was very expensive, and it spoke the most dreadful jargon. Which meant, of course, that it was very slow in many of its courses. Despite all the briskness of Henry II and his servants, it was already something of 'a hass'. Yet, in the halcyon days that followed the anarchy, it was a vast improvement on any other law that was to be had anywhere in the Angevin empire. And it was certainly not unpopular, not even with the baronage whose feudal justice it undercut in so many respects. After all, the barons stood to gain more from Henry's establishment of order and stability than they were likely to lose by his intrusion into their field of jurisdiction. Nor, when they came to present his son John with the Great Charter, did they demand the abolition of the devices by which Henry II had made his justice effective. That there was no widespread dissatisfaction may be gathered from the fact that in Magna Carta the barons and their allies of the commonalty of England asked not for less use of the possessory assizes but for the 'recognitions' (assizes) to be held four times a year, which in fact proved too frequent. They did, however, require that *breve quod vocatur Praecipe*[2] should not henceforth be used to the detriment of their courts, for a writ like the one called *Praecipe* had the effect of drastically short-circuiting feudal justice by

---

[1] *De Legibus et Consuetudinibus Regni Angliae* (1188).
[2] 'The writ that is called *Praecipe*' (*Praecipe*=command), from the first word, as in Papal Encyclicals.

removing cases of free tenure straight to the king's court, without even requiring the baron to 'do right' first. Nor should it be imagined that clause 40 of the charter (*nulli vendemus, nulli negabimus, aut differemus, rectum aut judicium*: 'to no one will we sell, refuse, or delay right or justice') implied a criticism of the high price of writs. It was right and proper that these prerogative instruments should be expensive. They were unique and irresistible. If the king's justice ultimately drove out feudal jurisdictions it was because he put a better article on the market.

There was, however, another type of jurisdiction, that he was never to drive out, or even to limit: that of the Church and its Courts Christian. His quarrel with the Church came, as might be expected, during the vigorous reforming pontificate of the fiery Pope Gregory VII. Henry was unlucky enough to have in Thomas Becket an Archbishop of Canterbury who was prepared to out-pope the Bishop of Rome in the cause of what he conceived to be justice and righteousness, although one of the more moderate churchmen of the day observed that the dignitaries of the Church 'were more intent on defending the liberties and rights of the clergy than on correcting and restraining their vices'. Becket had previously been Henry's chancellor, his boon companion, his ally in the early and arduous years of the recovery of the realm after the anarchy. Hence much of the personal bitterness of the quarrel, for Becket revealed himself after he became Archbishop of Canterbury in 1162 as the extremist he was by nature in everything he undertook. Henry was concerned to recover at least some of the ground surrendered to the Church by Stephen, whose concessions he regarded as invalidated in any case by the fact that Stephen was a usurper.

The quarrel centred upon the trial of criminous clerks, priests who had committed civil crimes. In 1163, the year after Becket was raised to the primacy, one Philip of Broi, Canon of Bedford, had been allowed to clear himself of a charge of murder in the court of the Bishop of Lincoln. Henry called him to appear in a royal court and was met by a refusal to plead which amounted to a contempt of court. Becket at once took the part of the Canon and told the King that he must come to Canterbury for remedy in the ecclesiastical court. The King asserted his right to punish a clerk who had been tried and degraded in a Court Christian, which Becket insisted was punishing a man twice for the same offence, something that not even God does: 'Nec enim Deus judicat bis in idipsum.' Henry, at a conference at Westminster, desired to know whether the bishops were willing to observe the ancient customs of the realm. When the ancient customs were presented in the form of the Constitutions of Clarendon early in 1164, Becket gave his consent 'in good faith and without guile', but avoided setting his seal to the document. Little wonder, for although the Constitutions were a genuine statement of the usages of the past, they contained a number of clauses which ran contrary to the canons of the Church as reformed since the days of the Conqueror. 'We promised nothing at Clarendon', he was to declare later, 'except saving the honour of the Church...it is impossible to observe anything in good faith and according to law if it is contrary to the law of God and to the fealty due to the Church.' Throughout the quarrel, Becket often seems to have been intent on providing precedents in moral casuistry for the clergy of the Counter-Reformation.

Henry had made a mistake in putting ancient customs in writing. It became obvious to many, including the Pope, that Becket must now be supported. Several English bishops who had been inclined to compromise, or even to desert their leader, rallied now that they saw clearly what compromise meant. The third clause in the Constitutions, on the trial of criminous clerks, required that a clerk accused of anything constituting a breach of the king's peace or of temporal law should make answer or plead (*respondendum*) in the king's court and then proceed to the Court Christian for trial. If found guilty he should no longer be protected by the Church (*non debet de cetero eum ecclesia tueri*). Such a procedure found authority in a Decretal later employed by Pope Innocent III, and was no innovation of Henry II. However, it was condemned by the reigning pope, as were six more of the sixteen clauses, including William I's prohibition of the excommunication of his servants and his tenants-in-chief 'nisi prius dominus rex' (without first the king consenting), and (in effect) appeals to Rome 'absque assensu domini regis' (similarly without the lord king's consent). Other condemned clauses involved the Assize *utrum*,[1] the reservation to the king's courts of cases of debt, and the right of archbishops, bishops, 'et personis regni' (in effect, 'anyone') to leave the kingdom without royal licence.

Henry summoned the Archbishop before his Curia to answer the claims of one John the Marshal concerning a manor in Sussex, and in strict accordance with the feudal law ordered the forfeit of all his movables when he failed to appear. After this the King showed a good deal of vindictiveness, while for his part Becket was obviously trying on the martyr's crown. After some six years of self-imposed exile, during which he fulminated against the King from a variety of continental pulpits, the Archbishop returned to England, much to the embarrassment of the bishops, some of whom he suspended from their episcopal dignities. On Christmas Day 1170 he denounced and excommunicated his enemies from the pulpit at Canterbury. The season of peace and good-will was finally shattered a few days later by murder in the cathedral.

Henry did penance for Becket's murder and was absolved, undertaking to abolish all customs injurious to the Church. Becket had won the battle by his martyrdom, and very soon miracles were being worked at his tomb. The King's campaign for the rule of law was won by another Henry, the eighth of that name, nearly four centuries later, when he brought a writ of *quo warranto*[2] against 'Thomas, sometime Archbishop of Canterbury ...', for usurping the office of a saint. Henry VIII paid tribute to his great predecessor's tradition of legality, or legalism, by assigning Becket counsel at the public expense. Stubborn in death as in life, Becket failed to appear, and after proofs had been heard on both sides he was pronounced guilty of contumacy, treason, rebellion, etc. 'To fight and to judge is the office of a king.' To do justice was ever regarded as the highest and most god-like of the king's functions. To do this duty he is sworn at his crowning. He has his courts and his judges for the purpose. It is not merely his

[1] See above, p. 68.
[2] A royal command to show by what warrant...

right but his duty to establish whatever instruments of justice are requisite.[1] Henry II established writs to inaugurate the proper forms of action, methods of procedure, and modes of trial. He was concerned to make the system work, and with the practical consequences in terms of peace, order and fees. As ruler of an extensive, loosely knit empire, however, he spent much the greater part of his time in the pursuit of his twin-functions of fighting and, 'the counterfeit of war', hunting. In this he was like his sons, Richard and John, with whom he is often mistakenly contrasted. It is only in retrospect that he appears principally as the great king who established and maintained the complex of royal justice which has been inherited by many generations of English-speaking men and women who have populated the transpontine lands of his continental empire.

His sons were a caricature of both his virtues and his vices. Richard I (1189–99) was almost wholly devoted to the Angevin cult of war, and his contribution to English development was a series of expedients necessitated by his prolonged absences from the realm. John (1199–1216) had more than his father's ability as a soldier and his taste for presiding personally over the administration of justice. Both princes had their father's taste for letters. Richard was famed as a patron of troubadour poets and poetry. John had the nucleus of a personal library which contained both Pliny and the *De Civitate Dei* of St Augustine. He was probably the first medieval king to buy a dressing-gown ('supertunicam ...ad surgendum de nocte xxs') and he took frequent baths. The shortcomings of both brothers as kings of England had their fortunate side. John, by his loss of Normandy to the French king Philip Augustus, compelled his barons who held land in both England and Normandy to make up their minds whether they would be Englishmen or Frenchmen. Whichever way they chose, of course, they were deeply aggrieved with King John. 'Shut up

[1] 'So howsoever many courts of ordinary resort shall be established by him, yet if either they have not authority to apply remedy for all wrongs and diseases, or that power and authority which they have may not enjoy her free course and passage, then must the King either exercise his pre-eminent and royal jurisdiction, or else must the injuriously afflicted be deprived...' (Lambarde's *Archeion*, c. 1591).

by the sea with the people whom they had hitherto oppressed and despised,' the barons found in the Great Charter 'the first pledge of their reconciliation' with the body of the English people. So Lord Macaulay chose to put it. 'Here,' he announced, not without justification, 'here commences the history of the English nation.'

The nineteenth-century historian Bishop Stubbs called the reign of Richard I an age of 'self-agency', when, in the absence of the King, the people were used to govern themselves, although he refrained from the supposition that there was any conscious policy to educate the people in the art of self-government. By 'self-agency' he meant that every man came to see that his well-being depended on peace and good behaviour. In so far as those who managed affairs—justiciars and chancellors like Hubert Walter and William Longchamp—called 'the people into participation in the work of government and administration', it was to employ them as they had for long been used to employment, as members of 'inquests', fact-finders and gossips. When Walter of Coutances, Archbishop of Rouen, became justiciar in 1191, his main task was to raise money for the King's ransom (150,000 marks, an unprecedented sum) out of the hands of the King of France. Every possible way of raising money, old and new, was resorted to, including the levy of a quarter of the revenue and movables of everyone. This was the first time that revenue and movables had been directly taxed by central government, and the Saladin Tithe[1] was a precedent for the taxation of personal property, turning into the tenths, thirteenths, fifteenths and so on which were to be the basis for subsidies in the following century. All this involved no national consultation on ways and means, 'the people' coming into the operation only as local juries of information or assessment.

With Hubert Walter, who became Justiciar in 1193, affairs came into the hands of an ex-itinerant justice fully cognizant of the principles governing the reforms of Henry II. In 1194 he promulgated the Great Iter, an elaborate series of instructions to the justices on finance and administration. Fiscally, it was based on the precedent of the Inquest of Sheriffs of 1170, and produced

[1] A levy of a tenth of rents and movables, in 1188, to finance the attempt to recover Jerusalem from the infidel.

much evidence that, while the increasing fertility of the land had raised the sheriff's receipts, the Exchequer remained impoverished. Despite Henry II's attempt to replace baronial sheriffs with 'novi homines, de pulvere' (new men, raised from the dust), the King was still unable to rely on these vitally important servants for honesty and fair dealing. Not for nothing does the saga of Robin Hood and the Sheriff of Nottingham centre upon the age of Richard and John. The judicial side of the Great Iter is important for its instructions on the method of choosing the grand jury (jury of presentment) in every county, and for selecting guardians or keepers of the king's pleas. The process is somewhat clumsy, but the word 'election' is used, and not only 'milites' (knights) are required to take part, but 'legales et liberos homines' (free and equal men). When in doubt about the prevalence of the principle of election in the twelfth and thirteenth centuries it is best to assume that nomination by the sheriff was more likely in practice than any 'democratic' process. Other people than barons and knights, however, are appearing on the blurred edges of the picture. Perhaps the most notable example of what Stubbs meant by 'self-agency' is to be found in the *Edictum Regium* of 1195, which requires everyone over the age of fifteen to take an oath to keep the peace and to assist in the capture of malefactors (resembling the Hue and Cry of pre-Conquest times). The work of taking these oaths is assigned to 'Milites vero', and these gentlemen are generally thought to be the prototypes of the justices of the peace of so many later centuries of English history.

If, as is said, art has often been *le gaspillage des princes*, it is no less certain that the beginnings of a widely based participation in the work of government and administration owe much to princely necessity and the need to restrain royal wilfulness. It is when the crisis of King John's reign was approaching its climax that we find the hard-pressed King sending out orders for the summons of his council at Oxford, and requiring the Sheriff of Oxford to include 'quatuor discretos milites de comitatu tuo illuc venire facias ad nos ad eundem terminum ad loquendum nobiscum de negotiis regni nostri', four discreet knights to appear as representatives of the county to consult with the King about

77

the affairs of his realm. We know nothing of what took place at this meeting, but the summoning of 'discretos milites' is an early sign of much that was to come. These men, had they gone to council, would have been 'knights of the shire', little different from those soon to attend the House of Commons. Similarly, when the barons at Runnymede set up the law above the King, and named a committee of themselves to see that he kept his promises, we may detect a faint and distant foreshadowing, in feudal terms, of the Petition of Right of 1628. At any rate, the seventeenth-century lawyers of the Long Parliament saw it like that, and they knew nothing about 'feudal terms'. To them, it was the fundamental law coming down from Edward the Confessor and their liberty-loving Saxon forefathers. At last, they rejoiced to proclaim, the English genius had conquered the Conqueror, the 'crafty illegitimate', and all his tyrannical race. At the moment, however, that midsummer moment of June 1215, in the meadow by the Thames, it was 'a feudal donation of franchises',[1] and a treaty of peace between King John and his rebellious vassals.

It was fashionable in the early years of the present century, when the seventh centenary of the Charter was due for celebration, to make little of it, even to speak of 'the myth of Magna Carta'. Bishop Stubbs had said in 1870 that 'the whole of the constitutional history of England is a commentary on this Charter', rather as Alfred North Whitehead said that the whole history of political thought is a series of footnotes to Plato's *Republic*. Such oracular pronouncements are not always the enemies of the truth, but the fervid language of such as Bishop Stubbs rang somewhat hollow in 1915, when the triumphs of peace and liberty seemed so darkly threatened by the enemies of the liberal world and all its works. In the years that followed the First World War liberal optimism was even more stricken by the pale cynicism of Lytton Strachey and the fashionable depreciation of the Victorians and their seemingly naive notions of ancestral wisdom.

No doubt it was healthful to be recalled to the habit of looking at Magna Carta as a feudal document in a feudal world, the

---

[1] The concession, or in this instance acknowledgement, of feudal rights and privileges.

achievement of a baronial party intent on making England safe for the baronage. The fact remains, however, that the Charter contained clauses affecting the well-being of merchants and even villeins as well as of the magnates. It is true, of course, that any alleviations of the lot of the tillers of the soil were framed with primary regard for their lot as part and parcel of the incomes of their masters. For instance, clauses 21, 22 and 23, which concern 'amercements' (that is, fines), provide for the assessment, of such levies by fairer methods, but it is clear that the benefit to the villein is really intended to prevent the king from ruining the villein, not as a member of the commonwealth, but rather as an asset in the wealth of his lord. Freeholders, likewise, are afforded a certain protection by clauses 15 and 43, which have regard to subtenants and their defence against exactions by both the king and their overlords. But it is pointless to insist upon direct benefits to anyone but the mighty. The indirect benefits of such famous clauses as 12 and 39 were only to become manifest in the course of centuries when the principles of 'no taxation without consent' and trial by jury had been exiguously squeezed out of them. Most valuable of all was the total impression to be gained from the mere fact that a king had been compelled to acknowledge principles, even feudal principles, as law which he must observe, and a certain rudimentary (and baronial) machinery which should bring him to book if he ignored them in future. Precisely what *laws* the king was subordinate to in future is less important than the fact that he was now proclaimed to be under *law*. John had offended all classes, and all classes were present at the day of reckoning at Runnymede, even if the creature later called 'the common man' was present only in the form of 'noises off'. To talk of 'the myth of Magna Carta' is not an effective mode of disparaging it. Myths are what men live by, and in future ages this particular myth was to be a tamer, and even a killer, of tyrants. It is, as the Lord Chief Justice, Edward Coke, was to declare several centuries later, 'such a fellow as will have no equal'. It is true enough that Shakespeare could write his *King John* without mentioning it, but its power to create a valuable superstition was to show itself within a very few years of John's death.

5

The High Middle Ages

When King John died at his castle of Newark on 18 October 1215, half England was in the hands of the King of France and his allies of the English baronage. John's elder son was a child of nine, and for the first time since the Conquest England was to come under a regency. Yet the minority of Henry III was not to prove a return to the anarchy of King Stephen's reign. Barons and prelates at once sounded the keynote of the new reign by assuming responsibility for the 'state' of the Crown until the King came of age, which meant primarily the maintenance of his estates, the material basis of his regality. On a number of occasions during a reign of more than fifty years, Henry's vassals were to declare their responsibility for maintaining the state of the Crown, even against the will of the King. It was a responsibility that the House of Commons was to assume, 400 years later, when it sought to take over command of the armed forces from Charles I by the Militia Ordinance of 1642, declaring it to be their duty to take such measures as were requisite to the security of the realm 'although His Majesty, seduced by evil counsel, do in his own person oppose or interrupt the same'. In the early thirteenth century, the immediate assumption of such responsibility by the baronage marked an epoch in the history of English institutions and in the English outlook on political life.

In 1216, and for long after, it was regarded as axiomatic that the King should 'live of his own', seeking augmentation of his resources only on special occasions and for extraordinary purposes. For him to live 'of his own' depended upon his having 'his own' to live of, or off, without ordinarily coming down on his vassals for assistance. It was his duty to maintain, and augment, his substance. Much that may seem to later ages to have been claimed by the King as a right was in fact simply the fulfilment of a duty. Prudence alone dictated that a prince should consult with his chief vassals in weighty matters affecting Crown and realm. 'Such prudence was not regarded as incompatible with but rather as a condition of power. In the thought of the thirteenth century, absolutism, in the sense of irresponsibility, was a proof of weakness or a bad education in kingcraft.' The reign of Henry III, a reign full of baronial quarrelling, baronial efforts to reform the royal government by restraining or controlling it, is only to be understood rightly in the light of such concepts. From the baronial assumption of responsibility for the child king's 'state' in 1216, to the Provisions of Oxford[1] in 1258, and onwards to the ordinances of 1311[2] imposed on his grandson, Edward II, we are watching a single process, sporadic, sometimes factious, ultimately unsuccessful: an attempt not at baronial usurpation but at baronial regnancy.

The story is confusing in its detail and may seem disappointing in its outcome. Perhaps we might have expected to find in the committee of twenty-five barons who engaged themselves, according to the 61st clause of Magna Carta, to make the King keep his promises, the take-off for an effective institutional check on royal despotism and misrule, the first treads on a flight of stairs leading upwards and onwards to the latter-day landings of constitutional government. Instead we quickly find ourselves in the swampy ground of baronial politics, bemused only by the signposts pointing to THE LORDS ORDAINERS, THE PROVISIONS OF OXFORD, REVOCATION OF THE ORDINANCES, and THE PARLIAMENT OF YORK. The error is to imagine that Magna Carta was 'a mile-stone on the road to parliamentary government', and the barons the medieval prototypes of Pym and Hampden, with Henry III playing the part of a thirteenth-century Charles I, or 'bad king'. Parliamentary government, indeed Parliament itself, sprang not so much from baronial opposition as from the royal

[1] A set of provisions issued by the Mad Parliament of 1268, arranging for the government to be run by committees selected by king and barons respectively.
[2] Ordinances under 41 heads set out by the Lords Ordainers in 1311 to regulate the government after Edward II had shown himself extravagant, wanting in judgement, and devoted to favourites. Principally, the ordinances dealt with the royal favourites, the appointment of ministers, and the meeting of parliaments.

prerogative and the king's necessities. The medieval king ruled through his Council, which was entirely his creature and creation. When in the long run he summoned non-baronial elements—knights of the shire, burgesses of the towns—to his Council ('reinforcing his Council with non-feudal elements', as the historians have called it), that was at no one's behest but his own. When such elements, in the course of time, transformed his Council into Parliament, that was not because he had any ambition to be remembered as 'the Father of Parliament', but, like most other things that happen in 'constitutional history', because the king wanted it that way, and for the everyday necessities of everyday government.

The first institutional necessity of any monarchy is a Council. Counsel, advice, consultation is as important to a king as money and arms, indeed it may be the surest way of getting money and arms. Counsel taken need not be acted upon. Everyone with difficult tasks to perform, difficult decisions to make, will ask for it, if only to strengthen a mind already made up. In government, 'counsel' means a 'council', though for long enough a medieval king's Council possessed few of the attributes of a recognizably modern institution: fixed membership, regular sessions and procedures. The king's Council was a body of men whom the king summoned because he thought their advice would be useful, or whose opinions and interests it would be unwise, even dangerous, to neglect. It had no competence which did not arise from his own free will, or prerogative. It could do nothing that he did not wish it to do, and it had no existence apart from him. It existed not to decide what the king ought to do, but to enable him to do what he ought.[1] It might be a *magnum concilium*, a great council, specially and solemnly summoned by the king which had special and solemn business to do. It might be a good deal less than *magnum*. Sometimes the king found it best to work with an inner circle of advisers, in private, a *concilium privatum*, though the word *privatum* was for long the description of an occasion, not the title of an institution, the Privy Council.

The first English king to reinforce his Council with non-feudal

[1] See Kenneth Pickthorn, *Early Tudor Government: Henry VIII* (Cambridge, 1934), chapter 2.

elements—knights and burgesses—was Edward I (1272-1307). He had everything it takes to furnish forth a memorable ruler, imposing physical stature, an agreeable presence, abounding energy, courage, intelligence, a crusading zeal combined with a thoroughly practical sense of possibilities: the most eminent 'actor of majesty' before the appearance of Henry VIII in 1509. Edward was on crusade when he came to the throne in 1272. He was on campaign on the Solway when he died in his seventieth year in 1307. Indeed it is as a warrior that we should think of him, and that is no doubt as he would have wished it. The Edward I who is called 'the English Justinian' is an altogether lesser and more equivocal figure than the Edward I who conquered the Welsh, banished the Jews, and hanged William Wallace at Smithfield. As 'the Father of parliamentary representation', Edward never existed at all. If he is to be associated in historic memory with the celebrated institution which later had its seat at Westminster, it is because he had the political sense, and reigned long enough, to establish the identity of the 'state' of the king with the well-being of the community He proved that the king would increase, not suffer, in weight and influence, in peace and majesty, by co-operation with not only the nobles, but the *Commune concilium regni*.

It was at one time imagined that Edward I was well aware of what he was doing in this matter of Parliament, even that he was conducting what might be called a 'controlled experiment', building up stage by stage a comprehensively representative assembly. The so-called 'Model' Parliament of 1295 wherein were present lay and spiritual lords, representatives of the higher and lower clergy, two knights from each shire, and two burgesses from each town, was held to be the culmination of a deliberate process of experiment and planning. The single fact that Edward must have gone back on his public-spirited intentions during the last twelve years of his reign, when no such comprehensive assembly is to be heard of, threw doubts on this intellectual fallacy, which is now dead. It might be added, at this point, as Sir Llewellyn Woodward has remarked, that the English probably acquired the habit of self-government not because they had a talent for self-government, but rather because they had a Parliament. That they had a Parliament was at any rate as much the achievement of Edward I as the triumph of the Common Law was the achievement of Henry II; but both were the offspring of the royal prerogative. A writ may be described as a prerogative instrument, whether it is a writ of Grand Assize or a writ for the election of a member of Parliament. Both are sent to the sheriff. Both bring local men, mostly knights, *coram rege*, to the king's court. Parliament is 'the Grand Assize', or the 'Grand Inquest' of the nation.

Edward I, although he spent a good deal of his time and energy campaigning in Snowdonia and the Scottish lowlands, properly belonged to southern Europe. He was a southerner by blood; son, grandson and great-grandson of the women of Provence and Aquitaine. By his great-grandmother, Eleanor, wife of Henry II, he was Duke of Aquitaine. Gascony was his to rule as a vassal of the King of France. By his marriage to Eleanor of Castile he came to the possession of Ponthieu and was brought into the politics of the Pyrenean world of Aragon and Navarre. South from Flanders, from the estuary of the Somme, through Aquitaine and Gascony, to the Pyrenees and the Mediterranean, Edward had his hands upon a great complex of fiefs and kingdoms which composed the 'state' of western Christendom, a Christendom that he longed to see at peace within itself so that it might bend its forces to the great task of realizing the fading vision of the thirteenth century: the relief of Jerusalem. If we wish to ascribe a visionary aim to Edward I, it must be this, the resumption of the holy task from which he had been recalled at his accession. We can, if we wish, see his local labours in Wales and Scotland, and even his work in codifying English law, as episodes incident to, or preparatory to, the great enterprise that he was never to undertake. Like so many of the diversionary activities of the great characters of history, these (to him) lesser tasks were to be the tasks for which history remembers him. In his notions of the crusade, as in his notions about feudalism, he was more than a little old-fashioned. The crusading ideal was somewhat faded by the later thirteenth century.

As for feudal relationships, which he sought to define and regulate by many of his most memorable statutes, the traditional relations of lord and vassal were already fading into those of sovereign and subject after the style of the modern world. The statute *Quia Emptores* (1290), which was intended to check subinfeudation or subletting of fiefs in the interest of feudal lords, great and small, actually had the undeliberated effect of dissolving the nexus of tenure which constituted the manor. The relationship of lord and man was gradually being deprived of its tenurial basis. That part of the great statute of 1285 (Westminster II) which is remembered as *De Donis Conditionalibus* was intended to put a brake on the alienation of estates. It did in effect saddle English land-law with the system of *entails*, by which the law maintains inalienable possession of land in family succession. The great *Quo Warranto* inquiry which was set on foot by the Statute of Gloucester (1278) was an investigation into private jurisdictions, or local liberties, which interfered with public justice. Such local or private jurisdictions were not necessarily recovered by the Crown; but, despite much baronial indignation, Edward established the principle that they subsisted, if not by royal grant, at least by royal tolerance. The sovereignty, and the ultimate supremacy, of public over private law and authority was asserted in no uncertain fashion.

The mode of promulgating these wide-ranging legislative commands (for they were not, properly speaking, 'statutes' within the modern meaning of the term) was even more important than their content, which was often ambiguous, susceptible of 'glossing' by the men entrusted with their execution. 'Don't gloss the statute,' Chief Justice Hengham told a pleader in 1305. 'We know it better than you do because we made it.' But 'glossing' of statutes went on all the same, and frequently resulted in consequences unintended and unforeseen by their framers.

For all his stature as a school-book hero—perhaps even because of it—Edward I fails somehow to come through as a completely convincing figure. It may be, as Sir Maurice Powicke suggested, that Edward was a conventional man in an age of change. His lot was cast in a wonderful time, surely the height of 'the High

Middle Ages', the age of Giotto, Dante and Roger Bacon, of St Louis and Thomas Aquinas, of the pointed arch and the birth of the perpendicular style, of the great glories of medieval Europe in glass and stone. How far the King of England was aware of all this we do not know, for we have little record of either intellectual or artistic interests on his part. After all, like a true king he was busy with his 'state', laying the foundations of an empire which was to be known one day as Great Britain—not least in consequence of his mighty energies in Wales and Scotland and (more remotely) Ireland. Likewise in his pursuit of what were, for England, to prove culs-de-sac in Aquitaine and Gascony, he was dominated always and everywhere by the exigencies of war and law and politics. Only here, in his concern with the problems of politics, can we actually see him at work and dimly trace the interplay of old and new ideas. The busy characters of history are rarely moved to record what they took for granted, and least of all to appease the curiosity of historians.

The reign of his successor Edward II (1307–27) contains much that is important in administrative history, notably the development of the offices of the royal household—Wardrobe and Chamber in particular[1]—wherein the routine work of government was increasingly carried on. Edward II's preference for household administration was, of course, in large part determined by his desire to elude control by the baronial party among his enemies who had control of the great offices of state. The evasive policy of a weak king may bear more fruit in terms of administrative development than the bold inventiveness of a strong one. Edward's reign also contains the great come-back of the Scots under Robert Bruce at Bannockburn in 1314.

When Edward III (1327–77) succeeded to the throne as a boy of fourteen early in 1327, peace with the Scots was already on the way, and in the most humiliating terms. The Treaty of Northampton which ratified the settlement was known as the *turpis pax* in very much the same way as Lord Bute's Peace of Paris of 1763

---

[1] Offices which, by their very intimate nature, were easy for the king to retain under personal control when his enemies had seized control of others, e.g. the Exchequer.

was to be known, after John Wilkes's gibe, as 'the peace that passeth all understanding', and for somewhat the same reason, namely that it was made by a man (Roger Mortimer) who was not merely suspected of being the paramour of the young king's mother, but was known to have been living in adultery with her for several years. Edward III did not dispose of Mortimer until 1330, but it is certain that he never intended to take the *turpis pax* as anything more than a shameful and provisional measure. The third Edward was a warrior by taste and intention from his earliest years, nursed and reared in the dangerous games of chivalry soon to be celebrated by Froissart. He was, indeed, something of an exhibitionist, but an exhibitionist on the throne was very much what was needed after Edward II.

Edward III intended from the first to pursue what later generations were to call 'a forward foreign policy'. The Hundred Years War with France, which began in 1336, was in one respect at least a resumption of the campaign of Edward I for the conquest of Scotland. When David Bruce or David II, King of Scotland, was deposed by Edward Balliol with English assistance after the Battle of Halidon Hill in 1333 (a partial tit-for-tat for Bannockburn), he fled to the Court of Philip VI of France. It was Philip's invasion of Gascony, together with his attempt to put a spoke in the Anglo-Flemish wool trade, which gave the signal for the opening of the Hundred Years War. The defeat of Philip at Crécy in 1346 had its counterpart in the defeat of David II at Nevile's Cross near Durham in the same year. David fell into Edward's hands and remained his prisoner for ten years. Thus Edward III wiped out the stain of his father's defeat at Bannockburn, much as his invasion of Normandy, with the victory of Crécy and the capture of Calais, seemed to have wiped out the stain of the loss of Normandy by King John. The years of victory, from Crécy to Poitiers, atoned for much in the memories of Englishmen of the fourteenth century, and the memory lasted. Only when the French chronicler Froissart gave way to Dryasdust,[1] or when the war threatened to last a hundred years, with its

---

[1] Thomas Carlyle's pseudonym for the academic historian who, it seemed to him, was always taking the colour out of history.

attendant cost and the release of disorderly men-at-arms and final defeat, did historians begin to talk of the futility of trying to put back the clock of history.

Freshly crowned with the laurels of Crécy, Edward founded the Order of the Garter on St George's Day in 1348. Froissart gives the date as 1344, but the later date seems more likely to have been the year of inauguration. And for once modern research seems to have served rather to lend credence to than to discredit a romantic story: that of a lady's fallen garter and the king's binding it beneath his knee with the immemorial motto, *honi soit qui mal y pense.*

The year of the Garter was also the year of the Black Death, which, along with other less serious outbreaks in 1361 and 1369, probably reduced the population of England by half by the end of the century. Both pneumonic and bubonic in form, it spread from the West Country to London, and thence across East Anglia and into the North. It caused neither panic nor flight, though by familiarizing men with the spectacle of sudden death even more spectacularly than did normal life in the medieval centuries, it no doubt contributed something to the morbid and macabre character of late medieval literature and art. Its effect on economic life was to intensify tendencies already at work. The wool trade suffered only a brief set-back, but the shortage of labour was to be an important element in the background of the Peasants' Revolt in the following reign. Fortunately the plague, even in its second wave known as *mortalité des enfants,* failed to undo the greatest event of the reign, the birth of Geoffrey Chaucer in or about the year 1340. Chaucer was to see the century out despite all vicissitudes of war and plague and courtly life. Edward III ransomed him as a prisoner of the French shortly before the Peace of Brétigny which ended the first phase of the Hundred Years War in 1360. When Edward died in 1377 England was entering the world of the Canterbury Pilgrims, the Paston Letters, and the background of Shakespeare's historical plays.

The great Duke of Marlborough once said that he learnt his history from the plays of Shakespeare,[1] and even now a man

[1] 'Shakespeare, the only History of England I ever read.'

might do worse. Such a course would do something to restore the loss of perspective which afflicts the historian when he looks back upon the two centuries between the death of Edward I and the accession of Henry VIII. Instead of heading our chapters Bastard Feudalism, Rise of the Nation State, Waning of the Middle Ages, we might discover why (apart from the publication of the second edition of Raphael Holinshed's *Chronicle* in 1586), Shakespeare and sixteenth-century Englishmen in general looked back to the England of John of Gaunt and Wyclif, Warwick and Talbot and Harry the King as an age not of sunset and decline but of banners bright with the morning; why 'The Troublesome Reign of King John' contains no reference to Magna Carta but a good deal about Philip of France and Cardinal Pandulph and a Pope called Innocent; and even why the Lord High Chancellor of England rests, as the piers of Old London Bridge rested, upon sacking stuffed with wool. 'The fate of these two centuries in our national consciousness', said Sir Maurice Powicke, 'has been very curious...'

It has indeed. They have been relegated to the world of myth and romance in favour of either the two centuries of 'origins' further back or the two centuries of Tudor and Stuart achievement which followed. The Elizabethans knew better. To them, looking back from the other side of the gulf which is the Reformation, the later years of the English Middle Ages were years of glory, of the glitter of chivalry, of triumph over the national enemy across the Narrow Seas. The echoes of so much that belonged to those years still rang clearly in men's minds, the shadows of so many great figures who had lived then still lay across the scenes of their past splendours. The great wool-churches stood white in their new-cut masonry, and the finance capitalists of the great age of the wool trade who had helped to build them had become legendary, if cautionary, figures of the *haute bourgeoisie*. It seemed only yesterday that William de la Pole, 'second to no merchant in England', and first wool merchant to found a noble family, had gone down to ruin after lending Edward III £18,000 for the financing of the Hundred Years War. Agincourt rested on English tongues as a newly adopted English place-name, as English as Juliet, the new-minted name of an English girl.

If there were any ends or beginnings in the story we call history, the murder of Richard II at Pontefract castle in 1400 would be an appropriate date to mark the end of the English Middle Ages. Richard had been foolish enough to talk of the laws being locked up in his own bosom. Still worse, he had laid hands on the inheritance of his most powerful vassal. Henry Boling-broke, Duke of Lancaster, soon to be the founder of a line of kings, went into exile and bided his time. Richard, a temperamental and cultivated man, made the tactical error of turning his back on his enemies. He was in Ireland, and delayed by contrary winds, at the crucial hour of armed action by his enemies at home. What happened to him when he returned was swift, sudden and disgraceful, but it must be confessed that he had for long been asking for the kind of trouble he got in the winter of 1399. Henry of Lancaster, on assuming the crown as Henry IV (1399–1413), never ceased to be a haunted man. He was haunted not only by the sin of regicide but by the high cost that he had to pay in the shape of concessions to those who brought him to the throne. It would be too much to say that his hands were tied from the first, but he meant a good deal more than most monarchs mean when he originated the sentiment: Uneasy lies the head that wears a crown. No doubt, too, he experienced the pangs of retributive justice if indeed he caught his son Prince Hal trying on the crown before the breath was out of his father's body.

For another 200 years, the rulers of England preferred to look back to his grandson, Henry VI (1422–61), a 'simple' man and a saint, as their favourite ancestor. Shakespeare, the greatest propagandist that the Tudors, indeed any dynasty, ever had, made the story of what happened to Richard II into an awful warning against the sort of thing that must never be allowed to happen again, least of all to a Tudor. King-killing was out for another 250 years. With the murder of that poor, unhappy gentleman, the first tremor had been registered in the ultimately seismic vibration which was to shatter the spell of medieval monarchy. Within little more than half a century of Richard's death, the lion and the unicorn were fighting for the crown at St Albans and Wakefield, at Towton and Tewkesbury, fleshing their swords over a piece of real property which nowadays, as Maitland put it, 'does nothing but lie in the tower of London to be gazed at by sight-seers'. At Bosworth Field in 1485, which ended the last round of the Wars of the Roses, Richard III rode into battle with it on his head, and when the fight was over it was picked out of a thornbush and set on the head of Henry Richmond. Of course, no one could know that Bosworth ended the last round, or that Henry Richmond was as Henry VII the first of a dynasty that would last for more than a hundred years. Presently Parliament was to pass a statute known as *De Facto* which promised (somewhat absurdly) exemption from the penalties for treason for those who faithfully served 'the king for the time being'. The Myth of Monarchy had suffered a taint of tarnish. As Trevelyan was to say of another, and later, occasion, 'it was never to be glad confident morning again'.

No doubt Bishop Stubbs was tiring of his mighty task when, towards the end of his three-volume masterpiece, he summed up the fifteenth century as 'futile, bloody and immoral'. Even now it is difficult for the common reader to see that century in its own right and not simply as the deliquescence of the Middle Ages or a rehearsal for the great performance of the Tudors. There was a time when historians held the reign of Henry IV, the first of the Lancastrians, in some esteem as a period of 'premature constitutional government', or of 'the Lancastrian Experiment', a trial run for the limited monarchy of later times. In fact there was no experiment about it, and if there was any constitutional government it was only because of the equivocal position of Henry IV, who had had to make the best terms he could with his more powerful vassals, after they brought him to the throne, and perhaps to show some respect for the 'commonalty', who had given their assent to the *fait accompli* brought about by their betters. The balance of forces, however, emerged in a pattern gratifying to constitutional lawyers of a later age looking for precedents. The monarchy had always been regarded as limited by law in some sort, at any rate since the Great Charter of 1215, and by the middle of the fifteenth century there was nothing much more than a certain chauvinism about Sir John Fortescue's proud boast that England was a kingdom of *jus politicum et regale*, where the king 'may not rule his people by other laws than such as they assent unto', while France was a realm of mere *jus regale* where the king might rule his people 'by such laws as he maketh himself'. Professor Chrimes best sums it up when he concludes: 'Government was still the king's business, and it was not for the Commons to meddle with matters of State and high policy. But within certain limits and for certain purposes the monarchy had become a parliamentary monarchy.'

The chauvinism of Sir John Fortescue was as nothing compared with that of Tudor Englishmen when they looked back to Henry V. Henry IV had been able to disarm his enemies, but he had never been able to lay the ghost of the central character of *Le Trahison et Mort du Roy Richard*, and he is said to have died with the remark, 'God alone knows by what title I hold the crown'. His son suffered from no such inhibitions. Henry V (1413–22) was above all else a man of certainties. He was no less certain of his title to the throne of France than to that of England. We may be sure that had he ever spoken the brave speeches that Shakespeare put into his mouth no one would have thought them odd or out of character. Nor need we talk of anachronism when he cried at Harfleur, 'On, on, you noblest English!', for this was the dawning if not of the national state, at least of the spirit of nationalism. The thing only becomes absurd when made into a history lesson by Bernard Shaw. When in *Saint Joan* Shaw puts 'nationalism' into the mouth of Monseigneur Cauchon, Bishop of Beauvais, in 1429, as a politico-sociological term (along with 'Protestantism' in the mouth of the Earl of Warwick), we flinch. So did John de Stogumber. 'I do not understand what your lordships mean by Protestant and Nationalist,' said the chaplain. 'You are too learned and subtle for a poor clerk like myself.' Which is hardly surprising.

Henry V's army for the invasion of France was an English army raised not by feudal levy but by indentured captains, with 6,000 archers paid at sixpence a day. The good yeomen whose limbs were made in England really were the men who had been practising at the butts beside the churchyard wall, and the king who talked with Michael Williams and John Bates and Alexander Court beneath the orchard trees on the night before Agincourt was no giddy youth lately reformed after frolics with Falstaff at the *Boar's Head* but a seasoned campaigner with the good company commander's understanding of morale and eye for terrain. His campaign of 1415 was no commando raid but a large-scale attempt to put into reverse the swing of the pendulum of Anglo-French power relationships since the reign of King John. When in 1419 he overran the Ile de France itself and by the Treaty of Troyes secured his succession to the crown of France, Henry V was at the head of a realm extending from the Tweed to the Pyrenees, an empire exceeding that of Henry II. Little more than a century later, another Henry, the eighth to wear the English crown, was to announce the independence of his imperial crown from the authority of the see of Rome. Henry V, an athletic young man of thirty-three, had affrighted his enemies and startled Christendom at the head of that terrible phenomenon of modern history, the nation-state. He had also conjured up for one moment at the point of his sword the vision of that Anglo-French dominion proposed by Winston Churchill in 1940.

It was not to be. Henry's *voie de fait* was the offspring of predatory nationalism, and the French, too, were at the threshhold of national self-affirmation. The English cry 'Haro! Haro!' had frozen the blood of Frenchmen in their veins, but soon they were to shout for 'God and the Maid!' and by 1453 only Calais remained in the hands of the Goddams. Henry's Treaty of Troyes, the laurelled wreath on his brow when he entered London with his Queen, Katherine of Valois, in February 1421, carried a poisoned thorn, for Katherine was the daughter of the mad King of France, Charles VI. In the following year she bore Henry an heir, the future Henry VI, and the fitful sanity of this monarch was to be a crucial factor in the troubled history of England of the next half-century. Henry VI was 'simple' rather than insane, and only really mad for the three years 1453–6. The 'Royal Saint' who founded the twin colleges of Eton and King's College, Cambridge, was no doubt the product of an unlucky conjunction of genes, for when his widowed mother took to herself a Welsh

gentleman of the name of Owen Tudor, she became the grandmother of Henry VII, and whatever may have afflicted the Tudors
it was certainly nothing to do with their wits.

The infant Henry VI suffered from an excess of uncles, mostly
Beauforts; not on the whole wicked uncles, but men with a lively
concern about the succession. The Beauforts, descendants of
Edward III through the third marriage of his third son, John of
Gaunt, with Katherine Swynford, had been legitimized by Act of
Parliament. They were legally incapable of inheriting the crown
themselves, but since they owed all their wealth and influence to
John of Gaunt, Duke of Lancaster, they could be depended on to
stand or fall with the Lancastrians. Perhaps it was fortunate that
the death rate among noblemen at this time was high, especially
among those who stood near the throne. Battle, plague and
poison worked hugely for mortality. Henry VI's lovable character, too, as he grew to man's estate, was capable of working
miracles in inclining men to periodic amity. The procession he
organized to St Paul's in 1458, himself walking in front, wearing
his crown; the Duke of Somerset (Henry Beaufort II) following
after, hand in hand with the Yorkist Earl of Salisbury; the Duke
of Exeter (another Beaufort) hand in hand with Richard Neville,
Earl of Warwick (Yorkist and 'Kingmaker'); with Queen
Margaret following on, hand in hand with none other than the
Duke of York himself: this wondrous spectacle of public amity
must have been a sight for sore eyes after many months of
manœuvre between the Duke of York and the Lancastrian lords
for the Protectorate.

First blood had already been drawn in the family feud to be
known as 'The Wars of the Roses' at St Albans in May 1455.
The year 1459 was to see both sides in battle array at Blore Heath,
and 1460 was to see the Duke of York committed to a *coup d'état*.
After the second battle of St Albans in February 1461, the Duke's
son Edward of York entered London beside the Kingmaker for
his coronation as Edward IV. There were still to follow ten years
of sporadic fight and flight, insurrection and invasion before, in
the year 1471, Henry VI died in the Tower of London. The wonder of it all is not the frequency of battle, but the slowness, even

the reluctance, of recourse to extremes. It required the passage of some forty years after the premature death of Henry V to show that the House of Lancaster could not govern, and to put the eldest son of the Duke of York on the throne as a viable king at the age of nineteen. Between Edward IV and the coming of the House of Tudor there was to intervene the Duke of Gloucester, remembered as Richard III, whose brief reign was established on the disappearance in the Tower of London of his nephews, the children of Edward IV, who are still remembered as 'the princes in the Tower', victims of one of the unsolved crimes of history.

'The Wars of the Roses' were invented by Sir Walter Scott in 1829.[1] No one who took part in them ever thought or spoke of them under such a title. The plucking of the white rose and the red rose in the garden of the Temple, which Shakespeare brought into his *Henry VI*, might have been invented for the benefit of future writers of school text-books.

I have read that some gentlemen were walking together in the Temple garden after dinner, and disputing about the King and the Duke of York; one of them took the king's part, and said that, though he was silly, his little son Edward, who was just born, might be wise, and he was determined to defend King Henry and his family, and desired all who agreed with him to do as he did, and pluck a red rose, and wear it in their caps, as a sign that they would defend the family of Lancaster.

The gentlemen who thought it would be best to have the Duke of York for their king turned to a white-rose bush, and each took a white rose, and put it in his cap, as a sign he loved the Duke of York; and for more than thirty years afterwards the civil wars in England were called the Wars of the Roses.

Thus Lady Callcott writing the thirty-second chapter of *Little Arthur's History of England*. In fact only the white rose of York was worn as a badge during the fighting. The red rose was but one of the many emblems of the House of Lancaster, and when the first Tudor came to the throne and married Elizabeth of York, a daughter of Edward IV and sister of the 'princes in the Tower', he superimposed the white rose on the red, possibly to symbolize

---

[1] See *Anne of Geierstein*, chapter VII.

the union, although this was rather the concern of Tudor chroniclers and propagandists than of Henry VII. As Sir Winston
Churchill once said of the tale of 'Fair Rosamond' in the reign of
Henry II: 'Tiresome investigators have undermined this excellent
tale, but it certainly should find a place in any history worthy of
the name.' Wars of the Roses they were, and Wars of the Roses
they may well remain, for there is little else that is attractive about
the dreary chronicle save their name.[1]

The contest was not a dynastic quarrel in the sense of a quarrel
between rival families. The contestants were all descendants of the
children of Edward III, and especially those of John of Gaunt,
Duke of Lancaster (1340–99), who begot offspring upon no less
than three several consorts. The Lancastrians came down from
the first of the three, Blanche of Lancaster. The Yorkists descended from Gaunt's brother Lionel, Duke of Clarence, after the
extinction of the line of the eldest brother, the Black Prince, in
the person of his son Richard II. The Tudors, who came victorious out of this prolonged knock-out competition, were descended from neither, but from Henry V's widow, the Valois
Princess Katherine. They too had some Beaufort blood, from the
marriage of Katherine's son, Edmund Tudor, with a great-grand-
daughter of John of Gaunt's third and last consort, Katherine
Swynford. Like most family quarrels, the contest was prolonged
and bitter, though, as we have seen, while the amiable Henry
VI lived and was in possession of some of his wits, it was susceptible of periods of moderation. The wars were really a series of
battles interspersed with periods of armed hostility.

The country as a whole suffered strikingly little except in the
immediate neighbourhood of a stand-up fight. The worst ravage
of the countryside was that suffered by the retreat of the Lancastrian forces northward before the Battle of Towton in the
spring of 1461. For the most part, however, peasants and middle
class stood aside (so far as they were able) and left the barons, a
small class, to carry on what some historians have mistakenly

[1] It would indeed be graceless to imply that Professor Chrimes belongs to the
race of tiresome investigators. His discussion of the name 'Wars of the Roses'
forms a most useful preface to his *Lancastrians, Yorkists, and Henry VII* (1964).

called 'the fights of kites and crows'. The barons were trying, un-availingly and no doubt clumsily, to settle the most important question for the politics of that and most other ages: who should wear the crown, or who should wield political power? While this question was in the course of settlement by the sword, daily life went on in its accustomed manner for the generality of men, and foreign visitors seem to have been mostly astonished, and delighted, at the infrequency of signs of a war-torn country. True, the foreign traveller saw chiefly the southern counties, but all accounts paid tribute to the richness and the fertility of the land and its people. Misery, of course, there was, but an Englishman who had lived through those troublous times would have been astonished to learn from an Elizabethan (and Elizabethans were fond of harping on the miseries of their ancestors in pre-Tudor days) that he had suffered a generation of frightfulness.

The effect of the wars upon English trade is to be seen most notably in the fluctuations which took place in the country's greatest form of commerce, the export of raw wool. The lowest ebb was reached in the years 1459–62, when the Yorkist cause was in the balance at Bloreheath and Northampton, Wakefield and Mortimer's Cross, and at the second Battle of St Albans. In these years the average number of sacks of wool exported was down to 5,000, and in the ten months before August 1460—the critical time of the Duke of York's open bid for the throne, and of his death at the battle of Wakefield—there was an almost complete suspension of export. As the Yorkists came into control under the new Duke of York (the future Edward IV), in the years 1462–5, the figure went up to an annual average of 7,000; and between 1465 and 1469, when the authority of Edward IV was attaining more stability, there was a notable recovery. There was another interval of depression between 1469 and 1471 when Queen Margaret and the Kingmaker invaded England on behalf of Henry VI's son, Edward, a bid which they finally lost at Barnet and Tewkesbury (where Prince Edward died) in the final year. The average export for the years of Yorkist success (1465–9) reached more than 9,000 sacks, a tribute to Yorkist attention to the safety of the Narrow Seas and the security of Calais.

The cloth trade underwent similar cyclical movement. Perhaps it was the more sensitive to fluctuations in the domestic situation because it was more dependent on industrial activity than on the land itself. Conditions abroad had even more effect here. The loss to the English crown of Guienne and Gascony (1451), and the dislocation of the continental markets for English cloth in the Baltic lands and Low Countries helped to cause depression in the years 1448–76. The English were at a disadvantage in rivalry with the powerful merchants of the Hanse towns in the mid-fifteenth century, at least in part because of domestic disturbance, though partly as a result of the political and military situation abroad. Edward IV was constrained to grant valuable concessions to the Hanse merchants in return for financial support for his return to England in 1472. In 1475 the Hanse merchants were established here with privileges that the Crown could scarcely hope to curtail until well into Tudor times. The Company of the Merchants of the Staple, at the centre of the wool trade in Calais, however, were the main contractors for government loans, and could generally bring a good deal of pressure to bear upon the Crown in conducting a policy favourable to the interests of their trade. And throughout these troubled years the merchants of Bristol went on building up their wealth in a peace and prosperity which, as Miss Carus-Wilson has said, 'stands out in striking contrast to the disorder and misery occasioned by partisan strife elsewhere'. Here, at any rate, whatever the case where barons exhausted themselves and their fortunes in bloody strife, English merchants went on quietly amassing wealth and worldly wisdom. On the whole, however, economic advance in relation to the merchants and manufacturers of other countries was at any rate frustrated and delayed by political conditions at home. Such vicissitudes put England at a disadvantage in competition until late in the century.

English demesne farming[1] itself in these years was undergoing a period of stagnation. War and pestilence, together with all the insecurity that goes with defective governance, brought down agricultural prices, and as the profits of agriculture declined and population diminished, there was little or no development of new

[1] Farming of land in the immediate ownership of the lord of the manor.

areas of husbandry: the internal colonization that had been a pre-requisite of the slowly expanding economy of earlier generations. Arable and sheep farming suffered alike. Lords were increasingly letting out their demesnes and living on their rents, while husbandry was passing more and more into the hands of tenants, whether bondsmen, free peasants, or 'new men' from the towns. Now was the time when it was said, for once with truth, that 'Hodge rules the field', whether ploughland or pasture, building up farms that lay between the big estate and the old manor-strip in size. These were the men whom later generations were to look back upon as 'the yeomen of England', middling farmers, good bowmen, 'adding field to field' wherever they had the chance: the original enclosers, long before the great men took to the practice on a big scale in the next two centuries and more. We have prototypes of these men at the roots of many families of the country-gentleman class of later generations. The Paston family, who were to produce justices and knights of the shire, were said to be descended from men who had been recently *adscripti glebae* (bound to the soil), transmitting lands held by servile tenure, Clement Paston being no more than a 'thrifty husbandman', and marrying a bondwoman. Yet Clement borrowed money to educate his son William in the law, and William Paston became a Judge of Common Pleas in 1429, and married an heiress.

And as Hodge came to 'rule the field', as farming became more and more the business of a multitude of men of middling substance, so the marketing of agricultural produce, and more especially of wool, produced the middlemen, the men whom later generations called 'broggers', which was the Early English for 'brokers'. Instead of wholesale contracts between big producers and exporters which gave rise to the *haute bourgeoisie*—the class of merchant capitalists which included men like William de la Pole, the fourteenth-century progenitor of the Dukes of Suffolk —we have the 'woolmen', the lesser middlemen who built their houses and the 'wool churches' of the Cotswolds and East Anglia, men commemorated in brass and glass at Northleach and Chipping Campden, Fairford and Lechlade and Cirencester. In a society of prosperous peasant farmers the woolmen were the essential link, if the unpopular link, between a multitude of small farmers and the market. The society where men like these were ruling field and market was full of strains, like all thriving societies, but it was the nearest thing England ever had to that 'Merrie England' to which men looked back in a haze of regret after the setting in of the enclosure movement of Tudor times, the debasement of the coinage, and the onset of much misery at the lower levels of society. The social changes that were going on in the society of England during the 'Wars of the Roses' supply a withering commentary on the facile notion that economic history ever proceeds by steady advances or unbroken lines of progress. The economic history of England in the later Middle Ages is replete with recessions, cyclical fluctuations, and relapses from concentration to diffusion of wealth.

The century of York and Lancaster is more recognizable to the men and women of the mid-twentieth century than any other of the Middle Ages. It was an age of violence, extravagance and superstition. Noblemen slit each other's weasands, or chopped off each other's heads, as a suitable epilogue to a pitched battle. The young men wore their hair on their shoulders and stuck their feet into fantastically pointed shoes. They went one further by fastening their shoe-points to their garters. Every young man of family seems to have been intent on being mistaken for a 'knave' with his ragged hair-do, his tight hose, his snake-skin jerkin. They wore huge and hideous rings on fingers and thumbs, and they ate highly spiced food. Their manners and fashions were those of chivalry *in extremis*. Our last vision of that violent, dirty, over-dressed society may well be of John Paston sitting over his Chaucer in his wind-riddled house by the sea down in Norfolk. It is nearly as melancholy as the portrait of Dickens's Sir Leicester Dedlock down at Chesney Wold in Lincolnshire four centuries later. There he sits, the smoke stinging his eyes, the wind battering the chimneys, and his father's tombstone twelve years unmade over at Bromholm Priory. 'Over it all broods a sense of discomfort and nakedness; of unwashed limbs thrust into splendid clothing; of tapestry blowing on the draughty walls; of the bedroom with its privy; of winds sweeping straight over land unmitigated by hedge or town; of Caister Castle covering with solid stone six acres of ground, and of the plain-faced Pastons indefatigably accumulating wealth, treading out the roads of Norfolk, and persisting with an obstinate courage which does them infinite credit in furnishing the bareness of England.'[1] Nothing has power to hold John Paston long. He will put off anything, writing, mending his house, making his father's tombstone. He is 'one of those ambiguous characters who haunt the boundary line where one age merges into another and not able to inhabit either'. It is easy to see from the Paston Letters, as Virginia Woolf once said, why Chaucer wrote not *Lear* or *Romeo and Juliet*, but *The Canterbury Tales*, for Chaucer never flinched from the life that was being lived at the moment before his eyes, and was little given to abstract contemplation. John Paston, whose father had bought his manor of Gresham from the poet's son, could find in Chaucer the world he knew, and so can we. Here in a few pages the whole story in which he had his part was laid before him. So he could sit in his chair, with the wind lifting the rushes on the floor and the tapestry on the walls, to learn the end of it. Geoffrey Chaucer was to his age what the modern novelist is to ours.

[1] Virginia Woolf, *The Common Reader* ('The Pastons and Chaucer').

6

The Nation-State

There is no obvious reason why the dates marking a century should coincide with the beginning or the end of a distinctive epoch in a nation's life. D'Alembert, writing at the middle of the eighteenth century, thought that mid-century marks were more appropriate for punctuating the history of modern Europe. The capture of Constantinople by the Turk (1453); the climax of the Reformation with the Peace of Augsburg (1555); the Peace of Westphalia (1648); the publication of the first volume of the Encyclopaedia of Diderot and D'Alembert (1751); all these events might seem to bear him out. In the history of England, 1455 marked the beginning of the Wars of the Roses. Precisely 100 years later, Mary Tudor set about burning Protestants at Smithfield, thereby ensuring that England should be an anti-Catholic country and the enemy of Spain. It is here rather than in 1485, let alone 1500, that the next chapter in our history opens. By taking her place irrevocably in Protestant Europe, and in her alienation from the Spanish orbit, England became Great Britain and a world power. 'What was shaping itself in the northern seas', Maitland wrote, 'already looked ominously like a Protestant Great Britain. Two small Catholic powers traditionally at war with each other, the one (England) a satellite of the Hapsburg luminary, the other (Scotland) a satellite of France, seemed to be fusing themselves in one Power that might be very great... A new nation, a British Nation, was in the making.' If any date is to be affixed to this mighty event, it must be 1560.

The laying of the foundations of the new nation took more than a century, and was initiated by the abundant energies of Edward IV and Henry VII in restoring what men at that time called 'good governance'. The foundation of the celebrated 'New Monarchy' which re-established the authority of the king and allayed, if it did not cure, the worst maladies which had afflicted the body politic since the beginning of the fifteenth century, was laid not by Henry VII but by Edward IV, the Yorkist victor of Hedgeley Moor and Hexham in 1464. What those maladies meant in general terms may be seen from a reading of Sir John Fortescue's treatise on *The Governance of England*. What they meant in concrete and particular instances in the lives of ordinary English people at the time may be glimpsed in *The Paston Letters*. The Chief Justice writes of the poverty of the king; the need to make the king's livelihood exceed that of any of his subjects; the need to reconstitute the king's Council so that its members shall be sworn to the king's exclusive service; but more especially of the resumption of the Crown lands alienated to the Church. Here, in the 'getting of plenty', lay the key to the restitution of the royal authority and all the blessings of peace and justice that flow therefrom. A well-endowed Crown would enable the king to 'do daily more alms than shall be done by all the foundations that ever were made in England', and every man in the realm 'shall for this foundation every day be the merrier, the surer, fare the better in his body and all his goods'. Sir John spoke like a lawyer, a lord chief justice, a pillar of the House of Lancaster whose cause he had seen go down in ruin at Tewkesbury in 1471. He also spoke as a man who, as one correspondent told another in 1451, had been expecting every night for a week to be assaulted in his own house, though nothing had come of it, 'more's the pity'. What the Pastons experienced at the hands of this 'lack of governance' is indicated vividly by John Paston's wife when she advises her husband, in London on a law-suit: 'I pray you heartily have a good fellowship with you when you shall walk out'; and again: 'For God's sake be ware what medicines you take of any physicians of London.' The best advice to a man with a grievance was 'spend somewhat of your good now, and get you lordship', for, as Jack Cade's manifesto declared, 'the law serveth of naught else but for to do wrong, for nothing is sped almost but for meed, dread and favour...'.[1]

---

[1] Jack Cade's rebellion, 1450, was a rising of the Kentishmen in protest against the incompetence and financial oppression of the government led by the Duke of Suffolk. Cade's manifesto sums up most of the features of 'lack of governance' at this time.

Local magnates employed their abundant energies in bribing sheriffs and justices, in intimidating and bribing juries (which was the more expensive because juries were reputed to be ambidextrous, and to take bribes from both sides), and, when all else failed, in attacking each other with private armies of retainers in their houses.

There is no need to suppose that Edward IV read up his appropriate policies in Sir John Fortescue's book, but he certainly pursued policies which Sir John would have applauded during the ten short years after the Battle of Tewkesbury in 1471. Nor was his effective successor, and the last of the Yorkist line, Richard III, far behind him in this, although he suffered much as a successful ruler by reason of his evil repute in consequence upon his supposed (but as yet unproved) disposal of the little princes, his brother Edward's children, who stood between him and the crown. Edward IV pursued the endowment of the Crown with vigour and success, bringing to it the extensive possessions of the Duchy of York, the confiscated Duchy of Lancaster, and a number of forfeited estates of attainted rebels, not all of them Lancastrians. To handle these assets he revived the Chamber of the Household as the effective finance office of both receipt and expenditure. He even made a profit out of the recoinage of 1464–5, and engaged in profitable investment in overseas trade. In fact, he went a long way towards realizing the medieval notion that the king should live 'of his own', and put the royal finances on a more sound and secure basis than any king for a century. The key to his success lies in his personal energy and resolution. No doubt, as the school-books never fail to insist, he was licentious, but he was certainly not idle.

Domestic disorder was at least in part a legacy of the Hundred Years War. With the recovery of France and the loss of England's French possessions, unemployed gentlemen and disbanded soldiery were ready for mischief at home. Statute after statute had been framed against the keeping of retainers—at least six since 1399—before Henry VII brought in his *Retentionibus Illicitis* in 1504. The Court of Star Chamber,[1] whose effect it was, as Sir

---

[1] Although the statute 3 Henry VII neither inaugurated nor defined the Star Chamber Court, it indicates what the Court was presumed to do, and who were

Thomas Smith declared in *The Commonwealth of England* (first published in 1581), 'to bridle such stout noblemen or gentlemen which would offer wrong by force to any manner men...', was not in itself the cure for such ills. Courts, statutes, the common law itself, depended for their efficacy on the authority of the man who wore the crown. Only the lapse of time, and the continuance of a wise and strong man on the throne for a reasonable term of years, could stamp out the evil habits engendered by a couple of generations of foreign war and domestic disorder, and engender others in their place. The Yorkist kings, Edward IV and Richard III, set the pace, but their time was too short. Henry VII's later success owed much to their spade-work and their example, but it owed most of all to the fact that he reigned for twenty-four years, and was succeeded by a magnificent bull of a monarch who lasted for thirty-eight.

The England of Henry VII was already a satellite of Spain, 'a small rough spot on the rim of sixteenth-century Europe', veritably 'little England', a green island off the coast of a continent, much as Ireland was for long to be 'the other island' of John Bull. Little indeed she was, for Scotland was still a separate kingdom, as alien as France, to whose orbit she belonged. There were less than 3,000,000 people living within the rough wedge of land which pointed away to the Celtic fringes of the Duchy of Cornwall and the Principality of Wales. Even within these narrow confines there were extensive regions where the king's writ ran but lamely, franchises like the Counties Palatine of Durham and Chester where the word of a bishop was better heeded than the word of the king's justices, not to mention the great hinterland north of the Trent which men still called 'the northern parts' and where there was 'no king but a Percy'. The regions of this small

imagined to be its principal judges. The types of case mentioned include giving unlawful liveries, maintenance of retainers, bribery of sheriffs, riots, unlawful assemblies, bribery of juries; the judges were the Chancellor, Treasurer, Lord Privy Seal, a bishop, a temporal lord of the King's Council, the two chief justices of King's Bench and Common Pleas. It proceeded on bill of information, and dispensed with a jury. It punished by fines principally, and did not inflict capital punishment. Obviously, as the court was in effect the King's Council in its criminal capacity, it was unlikely to be intimidated by anyone.

but diversified island were the more difficult and disparate because communications were (and were to remain for two centuries yet) a good deal less serviceable than the Romans had left them. Until the age of the railways rebellion almost anywhere had at least twenty-four hours' start of central government. Extensive areas were still clad in forest, and many thousands of acres submerged in marsh and fen. As for England overseas, apart from Calais and the Pale around Dublin, there was none until the settlement of Virginia inaugurated a new world after the death of the last Tudor sovereign. England was no sun but a satellite, as yet.

The rulers of France and Spain made passes at England. It is hardly an exaggeration to say that they thought of the island as the Romans had once thought of it: as an off-shore base to be taken into custody sooner or later, as strategy or trade requirements might determine. The sixteenth-century dynasts, however, could and did take account of the island in terms of matrimonial affiliations. In 1501 the King of Spain married his daughter Catherine of Aragon to Arthur, Prince of Wales, and when he died next year his brother Henry took his place. In 1554 the daughter of the marriage of Henry and Catherine, Mary Tudor, married the King of Spain, Philip II. When Mary died four years later, Philip proposed that her sister, Elizabeth, should take her place. Elizabeth declined, and next year the King of France put in his claim to England on the strength of his having married Mary Stuart, the Queen of Scots, grand-daughter of Henry VII's daughter, Margaret. Queen Elizabeth I settled the matter in 1587 by cutting off Mary Stuart's head. She had for some time past made it clear (though never too clear, as was her way) that there was to be no future for French princes angling for the crown of England. The Virgin Queen did her best service to England by putting up the shutters on the marriage-market. Even before Mary Stuart's head fell at Fotheringay, Sir Walter Raleigh had made his first abortive venture in Virginia. The settlement succeeded twenty years later, and in 1620 the Pilgrim Fathers were in New England. The satellite was on the way to becoming a sun.

THE NATION-STATE

Few in 1485 can have dreamt of the material or the spiritual riches of the future. We can see now that England was potentially rich and powerful, with her coastal waters reaching out east and west to the markets of the Low Countries, the Baltic and the great transatlantic unknown; her merchants waxing rich despite civil discord; her seamen already well skilled in navigation; her men-at-arms already accustomed to be feared by greater kingdoms on the mainland of Europe; her mineral deposits as yet poorly exploited when compared with the enterprise of her ancient wool-masters. The realm awaited the aggressive energies and intelligence of a masterful monarchy. This is what the House of Tudor brought to her. There was little new in what they did. To call their monarchy 'the New Monarchy' would be to say both too much and too little. Too much because it would ignore their Yorkist inheritance, too little because it misses the point of the revived dynamism, the sheer political ability, they brought to the tasks of governance. Within a century, this remarkable family had set the English on the road to their modern destiny.

The genius of the Tudors was above all else political. They had other gifts in plenty. Henry VII could have made even a nationalized industry pay its way. Henry VIII was athlete, poet, theologian and musician; not perhaps the *uomo universale* of the Italian Renaissance, but an early example of that English phenomenon, the gifted amateur. Elizabeth I was a scholar, a linguist, a high-stepping dancer, above all a consummate actress. Edward VI was a cold-hearted little scholarship-boy who would have 'got in' at any university, past or present. Even Mary Tudor possessed the Tudor stomach for a fight and the Tudor gift for political manœuvre. Every member of this astounding family of kings and queens had a genius for politics, for compassing what they wanted, and for wanting generally what their people wanted, thereby harnessing the best powers of their servants to popular causes. They had, too, a wonderful capacity for self-preservation. Heretics (except Mary) in an overwhelmingly Catholic world, they all died in their beds, except Elizabeth, who preferred to die on the floor, propped up on cushions. It was an age and a world perilous to heretic potentates. William the Silent of the

107

Netherlands and Admiral Coligny of France fell to the assassin in Elizabeth's lifetime as the agents of Catholic orthodoxy carved gaps in the Protestant front. A handful of beefeaters at the Tower of London and a few trained bands comprised almost the whole of the armed forces of the Crown.

Plainly, this dynasty can have been no despotism maintained by force of arms upon a reluctant people. When at the end of her life Elizabeth told her people that she counted it the chief glory of her reign that she had ruled with their loves, she spoke for all the Tudors in more or less degree, for all that really mattered was that they shared a generally enthusiastic 'identity of interest' with the politically important people for long enough to break the back of their appointed task. When the dynasty came to an end in 1603, that identity of interest was wearing thin. The Stuarts un-failingly destroyed it. The key to Tudor success, and the explana-tion of their survival for so long despite all the sharp turns and tergiversations of religion, is only to be discovered in their hold on the key figures in a 'lordship society'. Most men kept their eyes on what, in the army, are called the 'markers': the men upon whom the rest dress their ranks. The one failure of the Tudor family was in the matter of begetting healthy male heirs. Not one of them succeeded in this elementary task after Henry VII, whereas the House of Stuart bred men children regularly, to their own and every one else's misfortune. It was as if, having produced the miracle of the Tudor genius, nature broke the mould. It was, perhaps, too rare for mass production.

Yet it scarcely looked like that in the beginning. Henry Duke of Richmond, the victor of Bosworth Field in 1485, can hardly have known, nor can his subjects, that he was to be the founder of a great line. He must have seemed, as the De Facto Act (Statute of Treasons, II Henry VII, c. 1) called him, 'the King and Sover-eign Lord of this land for the time being', the latest victor in the long knock-out competition for the crown, the sovereign lord to whom the law now made it (perhaps problematically) safe to give allegiance. When Richmond became Henry VII of England his first (and almost his last) task was to make this long-dubious safeguard a reality. He achieved it by amassing wealth, monopo-

lizing artillery, and overruling every medieval franchise or
'liberty' he could lay his hands on—save that of the Church, the
crowning acquisition which he left to the abundant energies of
his successor. But first, of course, he had to make sure that he was
king, or, what mattered more, that he was accepted as such, for
he who played the king in medieval (and for long in modern)
times had vast powers at his disposal for the achievement of all
else. Henry's simple device was to say he was king and act
accordingly. He repudiated (without the necessity of legalistic
argument) the notion that he owed his position to any other
authority than the God of Battle who gave him victory at
Bosworth. That, after all, is the meaning of the royal motto
Dieu et mon Droit, a more pleasant heraldic version of 'Might is
Right'. By dating his reign from the day before Bosworth, and
eschewing any formal grant of the succession by Parliament,
Council or Church, other than the 'recognition' of his sovereignty
when a parliament met some three months later (and a parliament
which was only a lawful assembly because he had summoned it),
and by marrying the Yorkist heiress, Elizabeth of York, in the
new year, as if by an afterthought: by these measures he did all
that was needed in a situation where most people wanted only to
submit to a strong monarchical yoke for salvation. Everything
was on his side: depleted baronage, subservient clergy, war-
weary people. Of course, there were still rivalries and con-
spiracies to come: Yorkists lamenting Richard III, dangerous
claimants in both Scotland and Ireland, not to mention Lancashire
and Cornwall. There was still the puppetry of Lambert Simnel
and Perkin Warbeck, pretenders whom interested persons were
glad to mistake for children of Edward IV or Richard III or anyone else who suited them, pitiful catspaws who retain a certain
serio-comic remembrance in history, perhaps because of their
charming names. It is easy now to underrate the peril of these
manœuvres by Henry VII's enemies. Not until the end of the
century were they brought to an end by sporadic warfare and
judicial murder. It was like Henry to take less blood than treasure
from the destruction of these surviving kites and crows of the
Wars of the Roses. Nothing could round off an old tale more

suitably than the later career of Lambert Simnel among the king's cooks and falconers.

Henry VII was somewhat less than thirty years of age when he came to the throne. Like Charles II and some other shrewd and successful kings, he had been educated by exile in the salutary experience of penury and insecurity. Moreover, in the Lady Margaret Beaufort he had a mother who fulfilled in his life something of the role of Letizia Bonaparte in the life of Napoleon. It is much less than just, and hardly historical, to imagine the King as the 'dark, long-nosed man in a fur cap' of Kipling's story, who knighted a shipwright for saving him £30 on the gilding of the *Sovereign*. It is perfectly true that Henry audited his accounts with his own hand, but so did Napoleon, searching after the last *sou*. To depict Henry as ending his days in a frenzy of rapacity, a sort of sixteenth-century version of a miser in a Victorian melodrama (say Henry Irving in *The Bells*), ignores his constancy of purpose as a king who, like his predecessors in the medieval tradition of personal monarchy, had no choice but to 'live of his own' or not to live at all. His treasury was a household office, the king's chamber, and at the end of his reign it was handling an annual turnover of some £100,000. He introduced no new administrative system but simply made the most, and the best, of the very extensive resources of royal income: Crown lands (many resumed after long alienation), royal duchies, which constituted the solid basis of his wealth, averaging some £35,000 per annum at the end of Henry's administration, as compared with about £10,000 at the beginning; profits of justice, along with large windfalls from confiscations and fines from noble traitors and law-breakers; feudal incidents, customs duties and investment in trading enterprises; forced loans and benevolences, not wholly devised by extortioners like his infamous collectors of revenue, Empson and Dudley. Potentially, the Crown was very rich, and by making the judicial and fiscal system work effectively, the king could derive a very large income from his perfectly just and regular exactions.

Like a shrewd financier in an age of uncertain credit facilities, Henry invested largely in plate and jewelry. 'Hard cash' was essential in the form of a war-chest in those days, and for a long time to come. Henry also took care of foreign trade, more especially the trade in cloth, and carefully attended to his best asset in the money-market—his credit and his good name. If he looked after 'the middle class', that was because the men of business were his most profitable subjects. If he employed professional fund-raisers, he is scarcely to be blamed by academic historians of the twentieth century who are not unknown to do the same on behalf of college building funds. Henry VII's college was his country, 'a college in which shall sing and pray for evermore all the men of England', as the somewhat flatulent Sir John Fortescue had been wont to say, if only the King took his advice. Henry VII needed not his advice. It was common sense. All that he did was in the best of causes, the national stability and prosperity, perhaps even survival. In order to form a just notion of the man who did all this, and did it so well, one need only spend a few moments before the bust made by Pietro Torrigiano, now in the Victoria and Albert Museum. It is the likeness of a grave, pensive, sad (in the antique sense of 'serious') man, by no means merciless, and with the shadow of an ironic humour about the fine-drawn eyes and lips.

Henry worked through his council,[1] and especially through the council in its judicial aspects when it bore such names as the Star Chamber. He was not expected to summon his Parliament for the day-to-day work of government and financial support. He had six meetings with his Parliament in his twenty-three years as king. He chose his servants for their usefulness rather than their social rank. Like all kings who cherish their solvency, and something more (and what king does not?), he attended carefully to the trading community. This does not mean that he chose his servants from 'the middle class' any more than from any other section of society, or that he subjected his policies to predominantly middle-class interests. There is nothing essentially 'middle-class' about being a good man of business. He left a fortune of between one and two million pounds to his surviving younger son, who managed to run through it with the speed of many

---

[1] See above, pp. 104-5.

another spoilt child of the founder of a family's fortunes, ungrate-
fully and cruelly throwing his father's unpopular fund-raisers
(notably the unfortunate Empson and Dudley) to the wolves of
public ill-feeling. Henry VIII (1509-47) inherited from his father
the traditional organs of government, revitalized and in good
working order. He inherited not a tithe of his father's business
sense, clemency, or sober modesty of purpose. His father had
rescued the Crown from the gaming-table of aristocratic politics,
and set it on an eminence, withdrawn, aloof, invested with a
somewhat tawdry splendour. His brother Arthur and his sister
Margaret had been married to the daughter and son not of
native noblemen but of foreign princes of Spain and Scotland.
Within less than half a century Henry VIII was to carry through a
revolution in sovereignty, but the basis of his achievement lay in
the long, careful, courageous labour of the first Tudor king.

The Tudor revolution in government which founded in
England the sovereign state of modern history was carried
through ostensibly by Henry VIII but actually by the son of a
blacksmith who kept a public house at Putney, one Thomas
Cromwell. This man might well be called the first modern administrative genius, although he was a great deal more and other
than that. His royal master inherited him from Thomas Wolsey,
who has sometimes been called in his turn the last ecclesiastical
statesman of the English Middle Ages. These 'firsts' and 'lasts',
belong to the adjectival heritage of outworn text-books, but they
are not always unprofitable. In Wolsey's case there is something
to be gained from an old tag, for the man bore many of the marks
of the world that was passing away. For one thing, he carved out
a career through the Church, that medieval career *ouverte aux
talents*. From a butcher and grazier's house in Ipswich he had gone
to Oxford to become a fellow and bursar of his college, and
thence, through a chaplaincy to the Archbishop of Canterbury,
into the service of the king. When Henry VII died in 1509, the
new king took Thomas Wolsey into his Council, employing him
in the organization of the French War of 1512-14, that darling
project of a young king eager to open his reign with a feat of
arms after the style of Henry V. Wolsey conducted the business

side of the campaign with the same zeal and efficiency he showed in the feathering of his own nest with deaneries and bishoprics, and in 1514 landed for himself the archbishopric of York. In the following year, he accepted a Cardinal's hat from Pope Leo X, and in that year too he became Chancellor. At little more than forty, the butcher's son was the King's right-hand man (and, one might suggest, his left, too), one of the wealthiest and certainly the most powerful of the King's subjects.

The young king lacked his father's appetite for hard work. He preferred his pleasures, hunting and archery, making music and making love. While remaining final arbiter in all affairs of state, he was for long content to leave the greater part of the government of his realm to his chancellor. For a number of years Wolsey had borne a regality as great as that of any prince in all but name. It is said that when he referred to 'the King and I' he often omitted the first words, or left men to make what they would of the royal 'We'. George Cavendish, his gentleman usher, writing the life of his master, has left us a famous picture of the Cardinal Chancellor going in his state to Westminster Hall, apparelled all in red, in fine scarlet or crimson satin, wearing a round pillion on his head, a tippet of fine sables about his neck, and holding to his nose an orange stuffed with a sponge steeped in vinegar and other confections against the pestilential airs which rose from the press of his suitors. Before him were borne the Great Seal of England and his Cardinal's hat, crosses and pillars of silver, and a great mace of silver gilt. 'On, my lord and masters, on before!' cried his gentlemen ushers, 'make way for my Lord's Grace!'

Thus passed he down from his chamber through the hall; and when he came to the hall door, there was attendant for him his mule, trapped all together in crimson velvet, and gilt stirrups. Then he was mounted, with his cross bearers, and pillar bearers, also upon great horses trapped with fine scarlet. Then marched he forward, with his train and furniture in manner as I have declared, having about him four footmen, with gilt pollaxes in their hands; and thus went he until he came to Westminster Hall door...And from thence he would divers times go into the star chamber; where he spared neither high nor low, but judged every estate according to their merits and deserts.

He certainly served the realm well in his Chancery, at the Star Chamber, and in his court of poor men's causes, or requests, in the White Hall. He even tried to abate the course of enclosure, that crying complaint of poor men in the Tudor century,[1] thereby incidentally adding to his unpopularity as an upstart minister among the landed gentry. In his pride, his pomp and his greed, in his worldly greatness and his overbearing style, he combined in himself a showy conjunction of Church and State, a reproach to piety, a magnificent model of the overmighty subject. When he fell from power in 1530, he was on his way north to visit his see of York for the first time in sixteen years. He presented to the English mind a symbol of all that was wrong, and of little that was right, with medieval ecclesiasticism on the eve of its dissolution. He probably did more than any other single figure to create the English anti-clerical neurosis which was to remain for so long a powerful and constant feature of the national character.

It was in the shadow of this enormous and somewhat sinister career that Thomas Cromwell came to eminence in the early 1530s. While the Cardinal was conducting the somewhat meretricious balance-of-power diplomacy which enabled the young Henry VIII to preen himself between France and Spain on the international see-saw on such occasions as the Field of the Cloth of Gold (1520), the younger Thomas was knocking about Europe, trailing a pike in the Italian wars, making money in Flanders, and acquiring a generally low opinion of mankind in the sort of world which had shaped the calculating and cynical mind of Niccolò Machiavelli. It used to be said that Thomas Cromwell made *The Prince* his text-book and recommended its study to his royal master. The story has gone the way of Henry VII's supposititious debt to Fortescue's *Governance of England* and George III's debt to Bolingbroke's *Idea of a Patriot King*. Certainly neither Thomas Cromwell nor Henry VIII needed a text-book for his course in the politics of power. The King had caught sight of Anne Boleyn and was determined to put away his brother's widow, who had failed to give him a male heir. Henry prided himself on his theological expertise, which in fact was, like

[1] See below, pp. 130–2.

his music and his poetry, but not his athleticism, a commonplace among princes of the Renaissance age. But when he seized upon Leviticus xx. 21,[1] men might well ask who was so trustworthy a spokesman of biblical exegesis as the prince whom the Pope had honoured with the title of Defender of the Faith for his book against Luther in the year of the Diet of Worms (1521). Wolsey had failed to secure from the Pope the annulment of Henry's marriage with Catherine (who was, after all, the aunt of the Emperor Charles V, who had the Pope in his pocket after sacking Rome in 1527), and Henry was not only mad about Anne Boleyn but about the prospect of the male heir that she might bear him —the heir which, in the event, turned out to be Queen Elizabeth. His sexual inclinations and reasons of State were beautifully matched, and such a conjunction sealed the doom of the unhappy Queen Catherine. It was unthinkable that England should suffer again the dynastic filibustering of the fifteenth century, with all its dire consequences for the rule of law, the national unity, and the advancement of a society but lately restored to material well-being. Thomas Cromwell, after his return to England about 1512, had become Wolsey's man of business, and after his master's fall and some ten years of apprenticeship in the King's Council and administration, was prepared to take on Wolsey's final and fatally unsuccessful endeavour, with all his old master's abilities and with infinitely superior advantages for the particular task in hand.

For one thing, Cromwell was no priest. He was completely secular-minded, and he had little or no respect for clergymen. Indeed, he was like the generality of Englishmen of his generation, imbued with a wholesome contempt for a religious establishment long afflicted with hardening of the arteries and yet still jealous of its unearned increment of power and property. Most important of all, he had the clearest, coolest, and in many respects most power-ful mind of any servant of the Crown before the age of Pitt and Peel and the administrator statesmen of the nineteenth century. With Thomas Cromwell one feels that one is within an ambience

[1] 'And if a man shall take his brother's wife, it is an unclean thing...they shall be childless.'

that would make Wolsey appear not only medieval but antique, and most later politicians at least old-fashioned. Oliver Cromwell, who was the son of Thomas's sister's great-grandson, shared nothing with Thomas but his name, and shared that only by adoption, along with a certain amount of family wealth which descended to him from *malleus monasticorum*. Oliver once said that no man goes farther than the man who knows not where he is going. Thomas always knew. Having made up his mind, nothing short of the axe could deflect him, and when that happened in July 1540 it was a sad day for England's fortunes in her transit to the undivided sovereignty of the modern State. He was, and he remains, what his best historian has called him: the most remarkable revolutionary in English history. Not a lovable man perhaps; but a revolutionary who aims to remake a State by law, and not to undo it by force of arms, can seldom hope to be that. He is bound to make many enemies, and since Thomas Cromwell's enemies, like those of King John, were mainly churchmen, the men who for centuries were to furnish nine-tenths of the materials for the writing of English history, his enemies had for centuries not only the first but last word. It is important regularly to recall Voltaire's attempt to redress the balance: 'It is not for a priest to write history; one must be unbiased about everything and a priest is unbiased about nothing.'

The revolution we associate with the name of Thomas Cromwell was not the Reformation but the Breach with Rome, not the reform of English religion but the rejection of papal authority. It was quite literally a revolution in government. The nation state, as J. R. Tanner expressed it, was contracting itself upon its insularity. 'Where by divers sundry old authentic histories and chronicles it is manifestly declared and expressed that this realm of England is an empire,' ran the preamble of the Act in Restraint of Appeals, 1533. Nor was this a matter of political philosophy, although the preamble, having the usual propaganda purpose of most preambles in those days, went into the question with the kind of phraseology we associate with the language of Thomas Hobbes more than a century later. Hobbes said in properly pungent style that 'temporal and spiritual government are but two words brought into the world, to make men see double, and mistake their lawful sovereign'. The Act in Restraint of Appeals declares England to be governed by 'one Supreme Head and King...unto whom a body politic, compact of all sorts and degrees of people divided in terms and names of Spiritualty and Temporalty, be bounden and owe to bear next to God a natural and humble obedience...' That past of the said body politic called the spiritualty, now being usually called the English Church, is declared to be 'sufficient and meet of itself without the intermeddling of any exterior person or persons' to take care of its own affairs. The purpose of such statements, and the attachment of statutory penalties to the breach of such single authority, was in the first place perfectly practical: to restrict 'the King's Great Matter', or divorce proceedings, within the realm, that is, to the court of the Archbishop of Canterbury, Thomas Cranmer, Henry's nominee, a reformer, and a convinced believer in the royal supremacy.

For centuries the Bishop of Rome (to whom the Tudors were increasingly to refer as 'falsely called the Pope') had exercised enormous authority over English domestic concerns through appeals to his Curia. By a whole succession of measures (the most important of which was the summarizing Statute of Praemunire of 1393), the Kings of England had striven to protect their regality against such interference. Most notably, William the Conqueror and Henry II had regulated appeals beyond the realm by royal edict. Now such royal regulation was to be replaced by statutory prohibition fraught with penalties imposed by Parliament and enforceable by the common-law courts. The process involved a whole course of legislation, not only cutting off appeals to Rome but putting a halt, and finally a stop, to papal revenue from England, the erstwhile 'milch-cow of the Papacy'. The First Act of Annates (1532) had already transferred to the King the first-fruits (or first-year's income) of the bishoprics, and in 1534 an Act abolished Peter's Pence.[1] In the same year, the Second Act of Annates not only ratified and enlarged the first one, but gave the King what he had long enjoyed in practice—the control of

[1] See above, p. 56.

episcopal appointments by the system of *Congé d'élire*, which amounted to nomination.[1] At that time, too, the First Act of Supremacy formally abolished the Pope's authority in England and invested the King with the title of 'Supreme Head on earth of the Church in England'—no longer qualified by the clause which had been added when the royal headship was imposed on the clergy in 1531, 'as far as the law of Christ will allow'. In 1535 Cromwell was appointed Vicar General[2] and opened an investigation into the condition of the monasteries. The smaller houses were dissolved in the following year, and the greater ones in 1539. In seven momentous legislative years the Church and its property may be said to have been 'nationalized'. With Thomas Cromwell beside him, the King had instituted a form of Caesaro-Papism, or the triumph of the laity over the clergy, the *regnum* over the *sacerdotium*.

The revolution was carried through with superb *ordonnance*. The Pope was cajoled and threatened and squeezed with mounting intensity in a tactical course which often seems to anticipate the little-by-little reduction of the royal prerogative by the Long Parliament in the reign of Charles I. The success of these tactics appears, after the event, like a foregone conclusion, testifying to the unpopularity of the ecclesiastical establishment, and more especially to the defective morale of its leaders. Henry made it clear throughout by such promulgations as the Ten Articles of 1536 and more especially the Six Articles of 1539 that he intended to maintain the main articles of the Catholic faith. As the years passed, he showed himself scarcely less inimical to Protestants

---

[1] It had long been the custom in the case of a vacant abbey for the chapter to apply to the founder, or his heir, for 'leave to elect' a new abbot. The founder would sometimes send with the *Congé d'élire* (leave to elect) a 'letter missive' indicating a certain candidate for election. The kings of England claiming to be the founders of the bishoprics, the same procedure was followed here. Though the election by the cathedral chapter in theory remained free, the king's recommendation in effect really settled the issue. The Act of 1534 only made the royal interference habitual, and made it penal to ignore the royal choice.

[2] It need hardly be said that the title implied no priestly function, but simply Cromwell's title to supervise the visitation of religious houses as the King's *vicarius*, or deputy.

than to Papalists. The Church in England was not yet the Church of England, but by the end of his life it was well on the way to becoming that. Most people scarcely noticed the difference, except that the King now stood in the Pope's place at the head of the ancient Catholic religion of England. Martyrs there were, great personages like John Fisher and Thomas More, but they suffered as traitors rather than as heretics. The bones of Thomas More, a traitor, still lie beneath the floor of the Chapel of St Peter ad Vincula in the Tower of London, and an Anglican parish church was refused a Faculty from the Bishop to commemorate him within its walls as a martyr. But there are traitors and traitors, it would seem. A Labour majority of the city fathers of Norwich has been able to secure the commemoration of the traitor Robert Kett on the walls of the castle where he was hanged in 1537. Only the Roman Catholic Mary Tudor succeeded in making martyrdom a popular cause. But she burnt only Protestants.

Henry VIII's headship was essentially personal, but by admitting Parliament into the proceedings—even if only as a sleeping partner, in order to secure its enforcement by essential penalties— he had inaugurated an enormous shift in the balance of power, albeit the size of it was not to be properly apparent for more than a hundred years. It would be not only facile but untrue to say that the revolution of the seventeenth century was the offspring of the reformation of the sixteenth, except in the sense that everything that happens in history must in some sort be a 'cause' of everything that happens after it. But connection is not the same thing as causation. To mention the Reformation Parliament in the same breath as the Long Parliament is very nearly as absurd as to accuse Henry VIII of the execution of Charles I. There is, indeed, a perverted interpretation of history whose take-off has always been the dissolution of the monasteries. It got going with Cobbett and Disraeli, and it came to its apogee in the *monstrum horrendum* known as the Chesterbelloc. As late as 1927, in an essay on Oliver Cromwell, Hilaire Belloc, the tail end of the monster, trotted out the 'class of new millionaires' (including the Cromwells, the Hampdens and the Russells) who, glutted on the loot of the Church, and fearful for their ill-gotten gains if the Stuarts ever took England back to Rome, killed one king in 1649 and drove out another in 1688. Gilbert Keith Chesterton, the front end of the monster, in an otherwise attractive poem called 'The Secret People', wept for the king trapped by these gentry:

> The new grave lords closed round him, that had eaten the
>   abbeys' fruits,
> And the men of the new religion, with their bibles in their
>   boots...

These frolics of the monster have served only to convince mankind that decency lies with the Whigs.

7

The First Elizabethan Age

It is a mistake to describe the Reformation in England as an act of state. The Breach with Rome was the act of state—a political, indeed, a revolutionary act, which had to come first if the reformation was to be undertaken with some degree of order and effectiveness. For the next hundred years, reformation was to be the leitmotiv of the English experience, and England was to be vastly more religious after the breach with Rome than it had been before it. Reformation was indeed the child of the modern state, not its parent. So was 'the personal principle', the notion of the individuated man. The Middle Ages were the ages of mass man. The nation-state provided the essential conditions for the growth of respect for individual personality.

Of course, there had been numerous signs and tokens of reformation in the religious life and practices of the English since the salt of the Catholic faith lost its savour in the days of the Avignon Papacy, the time when the friars turned priests into tramps and scroungers in the everyday experience of everyday men. John Wyclif (c. 1330–84), often known as 'the Morning Star of the Reformation', had left behind him the movement known as Lollardy, which challenged Church authority and order by appealing to Scripture. Lollardy had never died, and early in the reign of Henry VIII a number of incidents gave prominence to such abuses of clerical privilege as 'benefit of clergy', and revealed an anti-clericalism which went deep among all classes. The most notorious case was that in 1515 of Richard Hunne, a Londoner of anti-clerical sentiment and Lollard affiliations, who was found hanging in his cell in the Bishop of London's prison, raising strong suspicion that he had been privately murdered. To the Lollard criticism of the Church in the later fifteenth century was added a tinge of Lutheranism from Germany, notably in the universities, more especially at Cambridge, in the sixteenth. Doctrinal change, however, was tardy. Henry VIII, 'the majestic lord who broke the bonds of Rome', was mainly concerned to set himself up in the place of the Pope as the head of a Catholic Church in England. Changes in faith and doctrine had to wait upon the energies of a generation of men who had known exile in the haunts of continental Protestantism during the retrogression to Papalism under Queen Mary and her Spanish consort. Nor did the first Elizabeth bear any love for the sons or stepsons of Jean Calvin. Like her father, Elizabeth had a taste for candles to her worship, not to mention other 'dregs of bye-gone idolatry'. She had, too, a rather more than Trollopeian distaste for bishops' wives.

What happened after the death of Henry VIII has been described as 'left incline and right-about turn', and then, with Queen Elizabeth I, the re-formation of the ranks. Re-formation rather than reformation; and so it seemed to the Protestants who had gone into exile under Queen Mary, men who looked for 'plainness' everywhere, the prototypes of the Puritans to come. Under Edward VI, 'left incline' had meant a movement towards a more positive Protestantism than anything that would have been tolerated by the Anglo-Catholic Henry VIII. The Protectors, Somerset and Northumberland, instituted for the minority of the child king Edward VI, presided over this movement with more or less alacrity. In worship, it meant the New Prayer Book, two versions of which were promulgated in 1549 and 1552 and each accompanied by an Act of Uniformity to enforce its use. From this time dates the impact of the Anglican liturgy upon the English consciousness. Those stately if equivocal rhythms, more especially after the remodelling under Elizabeth, which we associate with 'The Book of Common Prayer' were to enter into the blood-stream of the English people in their parish churches for more than three centuries, perhaps the most subtle and beautiful example of indoctrination on record. Enthusiasm for the change, whose inception was here, remained sluggish until after Mary Tudor had ensured it with the blood and fire of Smithfield. Thereafter, Elizabeth achieved its effectiveness by making it costly to be absent from Sunday worship in the parish church, where generation after generation of children were brought up within sight and sound of the Prayer Book ritual, even while their parents, bowing in the House of Rimmon, professed to close their eyes and ears.

At first, the new forms of worship met with mockery and even with open resistance; not, to be sure, out of theological conviction, but out of the innate conservatism of a people who did not care to have their diurnal practices, or habits, commanded by people like the Duke of Northumberland, the rascally successor of 'the good Duke', Protector Somerset. Moreover religious changes were accompanied, as usual, by the looting of various forms of Church property in which the common people felt they enjoyed an inheritance. Once it had been the monasteries. Now, in 1547, it was the turn of the chantries, those little shrines devoted by the living to the health of the dead, often by gilds and fraternities. Nor was it likely that in some parts of the country, notably in the Welsh- and Cornish-speaking west, that the people would appreciate an *English* Prayer Book. If it was a matter of understanding what was going on in church, Cornishmen thought they understood something of what was meant by the ancient and familiar-sounding Latin, whereas English was 'foreign', strange, thoroughly suspect. It took all the 'devildoms of Spain' on the high seas, and the Spanish monopoly of the western trades, to wed west-countrymen to Protestantism. A Cambridge Professor of Modern History once wrote of the day when 'Gospel-light first dawned from Bullen's eyes'.[1] For Cornishmen it dawned from the western approaches beyond the land's end in the days of the Elizabethan sea-dogs.

Mary Tudor's bigotry, her Spanish husband, her error in burning poor men and women instead of the rich and powerful, not to mention the attachment of the latter to their monastic spoils in face of a monarch who threatened to restore, not only the forms but the property of religion to Romish use, all served to make sure that when 'Bullen's daughter' came to the throne in 1558 as Queen Elizabeth England would return to the middle course her father had steered before the divagations, left and right,

---

[1] 'Bullen' was the contemporary pronunciation of 'Boleyn'. The Professor was Thomas Gray, better remembered for his 'Elegy'.

under Edward VI and Mary. Complete *renversements* of this kind, however, are never possible in history. The return of the Marian exiles, proto-Puritans for the most part, made it equally certain that Elizabeth would be under pressure leftward, if such a term is permissible, from the start. With the tactical fence-sitting of a *politique* who, like all her breed, preferred peace on earth to salvation elsewhere, and the psychological heritage of a young woman whose head had wobbled on her shoulders in the time of her sister's rule, Elizabeth was constrained to accept a settlement of religion that was very far from being the *via media* so often associated with her name.[1] The two great Statutes of 1559, of Supremacy and of Uniformity, restored to her, as 'Supreme Governor', all the authority and jurisdiction enjoyed by her father, and enjoined (with elaborate statutory penalties for dis-obedience) the exclusive use of the Second Book of Common Prayer of King Edward VI, with certain amendments in the Litany and the service of Holy Communion. By the eighth clause of the Act of Supremacy the Queen was empowered to delegate to such persons as she should think meet all or any part of her juris-diction in matters ecclesiastical—the statutory basis of the Court of High Commission for 'the increase of virtue and the conserva-tion of the peace and unity of this realm'. Only in 1581, ten years after the Bull *Regnans in Excelsis* had excommunicated the heretic queen and thereby made her fair game for any assassin inspired by the Counter-Reformation, did Parliament pass a statute imposing heavy fines for absence from 'church, chapel or usual place of common prayer'. Elizabeth once declared that she was unwilling 'to make windows into men's souls', but outward conformity in those dangerous days was an elementary political necessity. To argue that those who suffered persecution under Elizabeth I were persecuted for their politics rather than their religion would have been a meaningless refinement in a world where popes offered heavenly prizes for the murder of heretic

[1] The idea that Elizabeth enforced a middle way in religion is not wholly incorrect: she may have been immediately constrained to accept more Protes-tant courses by the Protestant reaction when she succeeded to 'Bloody Mary', but she strove for moderation in enforcing the settlement.

rulers and where modern distinctions between politics and religion were not to be imagined. At any rate, Elizabeth's victims were comparatively few, and she did not make out that she punished them for the good of their own souls but rather for her own safety and peace, and that of her realm. She was never one to do wrong for the wrong reasons, though her Puritan subjects thought she sometimes did it to the wrong persons, more especially when her Court of High Commission[1] took to chivvying Puritans as well as Roman Catholics.

Philip II of Spain was a pioneer of marriage to deceased wife's sister, but Elizabeth declined the match. Her supposititious virginity was to remain one of her chief assets in the game of power politics for as long as she remained a marriageable woman, and longer, so that her people came to accept the notion that she was married to them. When she told them that she counted it the chief glory of her reign that she had reigned with their loves, she was only adding the master-stroke to a flirtation that had gone on through all the years of her life. In 1585, three years before the Armada, Parliament put the sentiments of the nation into a statute 'for the surety of the Queen's Majesty's most royal person and the continuance of the realm in peace', the formal expression of the Bond and Association by which a Council consisting of certain Lords of the Privy Council and of Parliament, together with the Judges, was bound, in case of the Queen's demise 'by any violent or unnatural means (which God defend)', to prosecute unto death all who should be found to have aided and abetted the offence, while all her Majesty's good and faithful subjects were required to assist the said Council to the uttermost of their power. For everyone knew that one not very beautiful body stood between them and perdition, though they (and more especially the poets) habitually described it as the body of a goddess of peerless strength and beauty. Even when the beautiful Queen of Scots sought refuge in England, she could not compete with the aging

---

[1] The Act of Supremacy of 1559 expressly authorized the Crown to exercise the supremacy by commission, and from about 1580 a tribunal of that name, consisting of ecclesiastics, was sitting in London and exercising wide and not very precisely defined jurisdiction in spiritual causes.

red-headed lady who called her 'cousin' and passed her on from castle to castle, manor-house to manor-house, while the faithful Commons petitioned for Mary's just and speedy execution in order to the continuance of the true religion and the preservation of the realm. Elizabeth said she commiserated Mary's former dignity and former fortunes, and was most anxious 'to forbear the taking of her blood'. When the faithful Commons pressed her further, she answered like a true daughter of Shakespeare's England:

If I should say unto you that I mean not to grant your petition, by my faith I should say unto you more than perhaps I mean. And if I should say unto you I mean to grant your petition, I should then tell you more than is fit for you to know. And thus I must deliver you an answer answerless.

In the following year, however, she took the Queen of Scots' blood, or rather she let it be taken while she was looking the other way. After all, for a queen to shed the blood of a queen, even a queen like Mary Stuart, was not a good thing for monarchy, quite apart from the heart and conscience of Elizabeth Tudor, who had herself come so near to the axe's edge on her way to the throne.

Mary fell a victim to the Reformation in Scotland. Her death was the climax of that brief period in the mid-sixteenth century when for an hour Scotland occupied a central position on the stage of European history. 'Suddenly all far-sighted eyes had turned to a backward country.' They saw, and we may still see through Maitland's magic mirror,[1] 'that wonderful scene, the Scotland of Mary Stuart and John Knox: not merely because it is such glorious tragedy, but also because it is such modern history'. What was being decided there was the fate of the Protestant Reformation, and the making of a new nation, the British nation of the future, and indeed of the English-speaking peoples throughout the world in generations yet unborn. Scotland was still a medieval kingdom, the fringe of northern savagery. Its nobles

[1] See the masterly chapter XVI which he wrote for the second volume of the *Cambridge Modern History* in 1903.

were chieftains with a patina of French manners, for 'the auld
alliance' was Scotland's pipeline to whatever 'politeness' Europe
had to offer. Its parliaments, although they contained representatives of the three estates, nobility, burghers and clergy, were
largely factious feudal assemblies. The Scottish kings were the
thralls of the noble families and their retainers; like medieval
kings in general, they were expected to live of their own substance, and were chronically impoverished for lack of a regular
system of taxation. The population of all Scotland would have
found room and to spare in modern Glasgow. The Church was
rich and corrupt; bishops and abbots of the fighting kind had
plenty while the parish clergy were painfully exemplary in their
poverty. Nowhere in Europe were there more evident grounds
for reformation. The printing-press had come thirty years after
Caxton set up at Westminster. Lollardy survived in odd corners,
and Lutheranism had already its martyrs. There had even been a
flash of humanism with George Buchanan and the poet Sir David
Lindsay. 'In short, there was combustible material lying about in
large quantities, and sparks were flying.'

Into this scene there came in 1561 Mary, the lovely young
widow of King Francis II of France, a princess descended from
the English King Henry VII by the marriage of his daughter
Margaret to James IV of Scotland. Mary Stuart could, and did,
claim the throne of England, too, and in the eyes of Catholic
Europe her claim was infinitely superior to that of the daughter of
Anne Boleyn. In Scotland, however, John Knox had already
returned from Geneva to preach the Reformation, and the
Protestant cause quickly entered into alliance with the cause of
national independence, the cause of Robert the Bruce and Bannockburn in 1314, the cause that had gone down thereafter in
defeat at Flodden Field (1513), and at Solway Moss (1542) and
Pinkie (1547). John Knox and the spread of Calvinism brought
Scotland ultimately into equivocal alliance with Elizabeth of
England (another target for Knox's blast of the trumpet against
the monstrous regiment of women, 'regiment' meaning regimen,
or regime, or government). It was this combination, reluctant
but politic on both sides, that in a very few years sent the Catholic

Queen of Scots to seek refuge south of the border, *en route* for her death at Fotheringay less than ten years later. Mary Stuart had been the pawn of the Catholic Counter-Reformation and its thorn in the flesh of England's heretic Queen. Her son by her marriage to Henry Darnley, son of Matthew Stuart, Earl of Lennox, was to come to the throne of England at the death of Elizabeth, as James the Sixth of Scotland and First of England. The realm of Scotland, which was not to be united with England for another century, sent the Scots of the Covenant to fight for the Parliament in the Civil War that brought James's son to the block in 1649, just sixty-two years after the execution of his grandmother at Fotheringay.

It would be an error to imagine that Elizabeth ever 'went in with' Knox and the Scots rebels against their Queen. She never 'went in with' anyone wholeheartedly, least of all with rebels. In every situation she watched the odds closely and made use of the contending forces wherever there was inexpensive profit to be had. When, at the beginning of her reign, she assisted Mary to the throne of Scotland, it was less for love of Mary than for the sake of achieving sufficient control of the situation to get the French out of that country. It was the same in the question of the Dutch revolt against Spain which flared up into general rebellion in 1572. King Philip was the enemy, but it was not for another thirteen years that Elizabeth signed the treaty under which Leicester took English troops to the Netherlands. The massacre of the Huguenots on St Bartholomew's Eve was in 1572, the Jesuit attack led by Campion and Parsons was launched against England in 1580, the Throgmorton Plot for assassinating the Queen under Jesuit influence and at aristocratic hands was uncovered three years later, twelve months after William of Orange had fallen to the pistol of Balthasar Gerard. Elizabeth had the best of reasons to know that the world had never been less than a dangerous place for heretic rulers, and by the year 1585—the year of the Bond and Association—it was getting very hot indeed. Yet she did little more than privately encourage her seamen to singe the King of Spain's beard and make away with his treasure-ships like licensed pirates while she went through the motions of negotiating a French alliance by flirting with the Duke of Anjou. Procrastination, an air of innocence, many fair words and not a few politic lies, an occasional apology, a constant and careful shifting of her weight on the scales of the European balance of power in accordance with the interests and safety of her country —anything and everything to fend off enemies with whom she did not wish, and could not afford, to come to open war. Without declaring war on Spain, she—and God's winds—shattered one Spanish armada in 1588 and two more in 1596 and 1597. By the last decade and a half of her reign, Elizabeth had achieved her inexpensive glory, and her people were beginning to show that they could breathe more freely. 'Look, we have come through ...,' they might have boasted in those latter years. They were even questioning the great Queen's Majesty in parliamentary criticism, though in consideration of her great age and the tenderness of her long vigil and care for them they were prepared to 'play it cool'. When, in 1571, the Queen in Council had ordered a certain Mr Strickland not to appear again in the House of Commons, and the House had protested, it was said that 'in this happy time of lenity, among so good and honourable personages, under so gracious a prince, nothing of extremity or injury was to be feared; yet the times might be altered...' As indeed they were. When in 1603 the Patriot Queen gave place to James I, a highbrow pacifist from Scotland, the mood and the political temperature were to undergo rapid revolutionary change.

Revolutionary changes prepare themselves secretly, and silently, for generations before they show themselves at the surface of history. All through the century which culminated in the glories of Elizabeth, important economic and social changes had been taking place in the body of society. The first great period of expansion of the coal industry begins in the middle of the six- teenth century. Output had remained steady at around 200,000 tons per annum during the later Middle Ages, but now there were signs that the old prejudice against coal fuel for domestic use was declining, and the turning over of much monastic land to secular owners had assisted the exploitation of mineral wealth in some areas which were soon to become leading British coalfields. By the end of the seventeenth century annual output had reached nearly 3,000,000 tons annually, and coal fuel was being used increasingly in industrial processes, for example salt-panning, and coal even began to appear in literature with the Elizabethan poets and playwrights. Of course, coal production on a really modern scale depended upon the evolution of effective pumping machinery in order to mine at suitable depths, and this again was dependent upon the readiness of investors to risk the large amounts of capital necessary for so expensive an enterprise. Historians have discarded the notion that the century 1550–1650 saw 'a minor industrial revolution'. But it is interesting to note that the most important Elizabethan house in Nottinghamshire, and one of the most important in all England, was built by a coal magnate, Sir Francis Willoughby, at Wollaton, one of the best mining sites in the country. Wollaton Hall is highly ornate, not to say spectacular, and at least as pretentious as any Victorian business-man's mock-Tudor chateau.

Large-scale enterprise was also increasingly active in agriculture, for this was the first great age of enclosure, often for sheep-farming. Consolidation of holdings by small men exchanging their individual strips had gone on without undue protest for centuries, and sheep-farming had for long been the basis of England's staple overseas trade. In Tudor times, whenever conversion of arable to pasture involved the turning away of ploughmen and reliance upon a few shepherds, sheep-farming took on the evil aspect of a rich man's crime. The notion grew that sheep were devouring men, and anyway—it was rather glibly said— shepherds make but poor archers, so that the health and strength of the realm was diminished. The silly faces of the woolly race began to loom up in the popular imagination like the visages of man-eating tigers. The Kett rebels, encamped on Mousehold Heath above Norwich in 1549, took a peculiar pleasure in killing and roasting sheep, feasting merrily on the flesh of their enemies, as they supposed. Actually enclosure affected probably not more than 4 per cent of the total arable area of Tudor England, and about half the country was not cultivated at all even in the middle of the seventeenth century. The areas worst hit by enclosure were the Midlands, and some parts of the east and south-east. Of course, it is easy for the modern historian to remind us of these lessening facts, but where the social effects of agricultural changes were at all acute they were very acute indeed, while the concentration of enclosure into certain comparatively restricted regions meant that the extent of the distress was easily magnified. Nor was enclosure the sole cause or reason for rural complaint. We hear much too of the decline of 'house-keeping', or the keeping up of dependent households of clients or followers which may be represented by the way in which many gentlemen, deserting the patriarchal and neighbourly manners of an older time, were isolating themselves in their houses in the midst of parks and at the end of pretentious approach-avenues of trees. The medieval rural scene, with the life of the farm going on under the windows, was giving place to the scene that was to reach its apogee of style and beauty in the eighteenth century, with hedged fields, or 'closes', and the urban-style house set down in a country setting. Farming was being run on increasingly 'business' lines, although it would be an illusion to suppose that land had ever been run on principles different from those of trade, let alone that the buying and selling of land as a commodity was an invention of commercially minded Tudor business-men.

'Griefs' or 'pleynts', as men in those times called their grievances, found expression more easily than they ever had before, with the printing-press and the vocalism of preachers and writers like Hugh Latimer and More, the author of *Utopia*. Revolt, or aggravated riot, was becoming a commonplace. There were several widespread and dangerous movements during the Tudor century, and many instances of turbulence fomented by some peculiar local situation. Sometimes, a local feud would assume wider proportions like a snowball. The quarrel of the brothers Kett at Wymondham in 1549 with the rascally lawyer Sergeant Flowerdew, a local encloser, mainly over the despoliation of the abbey church—a quarrel over the spoils of the dissolution, to which the Ketts rightly thought themselves justly entitled as local donors and worshippers—came in a short time to assume the proportions of a regional revolution. Like the Pilgrimage of

Grace of 1536, which arose out of the peculiar grievances of northerners after the dissolution of the great Yorkshire abbeys, these rebellions were only suppressed by the exercise of a good deal of chicanery and bluff on the part of the King and his servants, for central government had neither a police force nor an army adequate for a large-scale emergency. Fortunately, as sometimes happens in peasant countries, rebels often made out that their main intent was to rescue the King from 'wicked counsellors', though English rebels never went so far as their peasant brethren in Muscovy with their claim to be striking a blow for the true Tsar against some 'false Dmitri' who had, so they liked to imagine, got control of the state. Robert Kett on Mousehold Heath called himself 'The King's Lieutenant' and his camp 'The King's Camp', which is perhaps not surprising when we recall that the King was the boy Edward VI, and that his realm was once more falling into the hands of overmighty subjects, the Protectors Somerset and Northumberland. Elizabeth I had more plots than rebellions to cope with, mostly engineered by agents of the Counter-Reformation. The Rising of the Northern Earls in 1569 on behalf not only of Rome but of Mary Stuart, and the rising of the Earl of Essex in 1601, were both blows on the part of somewhat belated overmighty subjects, phenomena sometimes incorrectly imagined to have been finally dealt with by Henry VII but in fact apparent in gentlemen wearing the dress of Whig oligarchs like the Duke of Newcastle and the Marquess of Rockingham 200 years later.

The Tudors had to evolve a rudimentary 'welfare policy' to cope with the worst problems of poverty and unemployment. Perhaps a 'police policy' would be a more accurate description. The preamble of such a statute as the Act for the Maintenance of Husbandry and Tillage, of 1598, reveals almost all the motives for government intervention at this time. Husbandry and tillage are declared to be the occasion of the increase and multiplying of people for service of the realm in war and peace, the best guarantee that the realm shall 'stand upon itself', that property shall be kept dispersed and distributed in many hands, and the people kept from 'idleness, drunkenness, unlawful games and all other lewd practices...' Health, wealth, industriousness, national self-sufficiency, and above all the public peace: these are the principal considerations. A similar concern for stability is to be seen in industrial legislation like the Statute of Labourers and Apprentices of 1563. Here there is a careful distinction between the higher and the lower crafts, the skilled and the unskilled worker. High qualification, in the shape of parental income, is to be required for apprenticeship in certain trades, such as those in wool and cloth, dyeing, tailoring, shoemaking, and the metal trades. The unapprenticed are liable to be drafted into husbandry by the year, and servants are forbidden to depart from their employers without notice or until the end of their lawful term of engagement. Persons leaving work on the land are not to wander about looking for work, nor to depart from the city or parish where they last served, without carrying a testimonial. For Tudor England lived in terror of the tramp, and it is to this time that we can trace back the nursery rhyme:

> Hark, hark, the dogs do bark,
> The beggars are coming to town!

Justices of the peace were required, by the Statute of Apprentices of 1563, to rate and appoint wages annually, a provision that was only fitfully observed, though it was the occasion of the Berkshire magistrates lighting upon the notorious non-contributory dole system in 1795, remembered as 'Speenhamland'.[1] The statute of 1563 was trying to regulate at the behest of 'the state', and through the energies of the unpaid magistracy, much of what the medieval gilds had once regulated. Neither the machinery used nor the principles it was attempted to apply were adequate or appropriate to the task. The stratification of crafts, the attempt to check the mobility of labour, the command that masters shall keep one journeyman (skilled labourer, paid by the day) for every three apprentices, all this and much else was attempting to regulate industrial life far beyond what was either practicable or even desirable at this time. The Statute of Labourers and Apprentices provides some striking evidence of the persistence of medieval

[1] See below, p. 238.

133

attitudes, more in what it reveals of the intentions of its framers than in what it achieved. The hope was expressed in the preamble that 'the law being duly executed should banish idleness, advance husbandry and yield unto the hired person both in the time of scarcity and in the time of plenty a convenient proportion of wages...' Status, stability, a comprehensive incomes and prices policy—all are to be hoped for. Needless to say, hardly any of them were forthcoming.

Since poverty and unemployment eluded all efforts at prevention, Elizabethan government steadily evolved a Poor Law, a code which reached completion in the great Statute of 1601, the basis of the English poor law until 1834. Over a long course of years, the Tudors came to make proper distinction between the sturdy rogue and vagabond, on the one hand, and the genuinely poor and needy on the other. They also attempted to tackle the problem nearer to its roots by making provision for the parish apprenticeship of the children of the poor. The imposition of a poor rate, and the appointment of overseers of the poor, marking the transition from voluntary contribution to compulsion by law, saw the initiation of 'Bumbledom', and the familiar background of *Oliver Twist*. But the voluntary principle remained, a tradition of private generosity and personal service which was to run like a golden thread through English government, more especially local government, for more than three centuries, of which the English are justifiably proud. Professor Jordan's work on the charitable bequests of Tudor England[1] has thrown a good deal of doubt on the greed and selfishness which are supposed to have dominated wealthy people in that age of monastic robbery and enclosing landlords.

How much did the English of the sixteenth century understand about the root causes of the social distress they experienced? To judge from a document like the *Discourse of the Common Weal of this Realm of England* (probably written by John Hales about 1565), there were thoughtful observers who knew a good deal. The author was one of the commissioners set up by Protector Somerset in 1548 to look into the question of enclosures. He puts

---

[1] W. K. Jordan, *Philanthropy in England, 1480–1660* (London, 1959).

his dialogues (there are three of them) into the mouths of what might be called 'representative men', namely a knight, a doctor, a merchant, a craftsman and a husbandman, and their conclusion is that the root trouble is to be found in 'the alteration of the coyne'—the debasement of the coinage. This was the evil consequence of the policy of Henry VIII, 'by whose commaundment the same was altered', and of the price rise, or inflation, which, as usual, afflicted chiefly those who lived on fixed incomes (to use a later terminology), notably the landed men who had to buy at enhanced prices while receiving rents at rates determined by old leases. The general effect, of course, was to compel such victims of inflation to raise rents whenever they could and to go in for enclosure, or sheep-farming, and more efficient estate management, in order to adjust their incomes to the higher cost of living. The French political theorist Jean Bodin was, it seems, the first to ascribe the price rise of the sixteenth century to the influx of precious metals from the new world, in his *Discours sur les causes de l'extrême cherté* in 1574, and in an edition of his *Discourse* of 1581 Hales made masterly use in English of Bodin's argument, although it is at least possible that he may have arrived at it independently by that time. Hales also gave expression to the principle which is generally known as 'Gresham's Law', that bad money drives out good, for, as his Doctor is made to say, when a man finds he has 'as much for the worse grote as for the better, will not he lay up the better grote always, and turn it to some other use, and put forth the worse?' Elizabeth's recoinage of 1570, calling in debased money, was undertaken with Gresham's assistance and probably did something to improve matters, but neither the Queen (who, it might be remembered, was always ready to lay hands on Spanish treasure) nor anyone else could do much about the torrent of American silver that was upsetting European prices. Only some inconceivable device like the locking up of gold in Fort Knox in our own century could have made much impression. Tudor England, and for a long time Stuart England, too, was in the grip of inflation that makes our own experience look comparatively mild.

'The Price Revolution' is not too strong a term to describe

what happened between the middle of the sixteenth century and the early decades of the seventeenth. Prices rose threefold, wreaking much havoc upon classes of men with fixed incomes or saddled with 'inflexible consumption'. The upshot, of course, was a great shift in the balance of property, and in consequence a change in the fortunes of the aristocracy great and small. Between 1540 and 1640 there occurred what can only be described as 'the crisis of the aristocracy', even though we may not yet be in a position to determine its precise and detailed character. At any rate, the crisis had a profound bearing upon the outbreak of the Civil War in 1642, and the English revolution of the seventeenth century as a whole. Historians no longer find adequate explanation of these events in terms of the personalities and policies of men engaged in the government of Church and State, of Archbishop Laud and the Earl of Strafford, of Charles and James, or of the growth of 'isms' like Puritanism and constitutionalism. Nor are they disposed to frame the problem in terms of anything so simple as an economic conflict between feudal and capitalist phases of production, between a decaying landed aristocracy and a rising mercantile and industrial *bourgeoisie*. Instead, they concentrate their attention upon the changing fortunes of those segments of society which threw up the men who possessed political and social initiative. Obviously these men were, and always had been, and would be for a long time yet, the landed aristocracy, whether nobility or gentry, those indispensable 'brave halfe paces between a throne and a people' as Fulke Greville once called them. As a result, the political and constitutional history of England in the seventeenth century is now seen in terms of a gigantic adaptation, or failure of adaptation, on the part of this aristocracy to a rapidly changing environment—indeed to the transition from medieval to modern England. In this account, the England of the first Elizabeth may come to be seen not so much as a unique and splendid flower but more as the seed-bed of changes scarcely less momentous than those generated in the reign of the second.

Nevertheless, the splendour of the flower remains incomparable. We may think we know how wealthy and worshipful an

136

aristocracy must be in order to afford Sir Francis Willoughby's gaudy Netherlandish house at Wollaton; or Bess of Hardwick's handsome glass and stone rampart, Hardwick Hall, on the hill above the Notts and Derby border; or Knole, the great house like a town where Virginia Woolf's Orlando sliced at the Moor's head swinging in the breeze that never ceased to blow through the attic rooms; or Hampton Court, or Greenwich Palace, or the vanished splendours of Nonsuch; or the Strand houses of Elizabethan noblemen leading down to the Thames. We can pace out and estimate something of the cash and care that went to the making of the boxed beauty of the herb-garden and the topiary, the pleasaunce and the park. The age and the realm, we may say, were at last sufficiently safe to turn the fortified manor-house into a toy, retaining battlements that were never meant for battle, letting the moat run dry, widening the arrow-slits to wide casements. The age was, we understand, already sophisticated enough to hanker after the wild wood and the Forest of Arden and the greenwood tree. Yet, do we know, or dare we even ask, how rich a people must be to afford a Shakespeare? Before the age ended, Richard Hooker had set the Anglican Church to music in the sonorities of his *Laws of Ecclesiastical Polity*, and within less than ten years of the departure of the great Queen the matchless prose of King James's Authorized Version of the Bible had enshrined the blossom-time of the Elizabethan mind and tongue. With the poetry of Shakespeare, this amazing achievement is likely to outlive both marble and the gilded monuments of princes.

Thomas Cromwell, in his Injunctions of 1538, had required an official translation of the Bible, based on Miles Coverdale's version (in turn based on Tyndale) to be bought for the parish churches. As might have been expected there was no headlong rush to read it, or to hear it read, although the bishops habitually enjoined preaching and teaching upon their clergy. Of course, conservatives did not fail to say that many a man had read the Bible to his own damnation, and even before the death of Henry VIII Parliament was concerned to regulate both the possession and the reading of the Scriptures by a statute 'for the advancement of true religion and for the abolishment of the contrary'. It was a singularly silly statute, ordering fines and even imprisonment upon persons below a certain social status (below the class of yeoman, noblewoman, or gentlewoman, for example) who should possess or read even the authorized translation. Not that the statute can have had much effect. But after the seven years' hard labour of King James's ecclesiastical committee the Authorized Version, with its rhythms, its grandiloquence and its vocabulary, was to become part and parcel of the English sensibility. There are those who hold that the influence of King James's Bible on English prose, like that of John Milton on English poetry, has not been an unmixed blessing. The Bible, they point out, is an oriental book, of alien imagery, hyperbole, and luscious metaphor, in many ways foreign to the English genius. 'I cannot but think', Mr Somerset Maugham once wrote, 'that not the least of the misfortunes that the Secession from Rome brought upon the spiritual life of our country is that this work for so long a period became the daily, and with many the only, reading of our people.' Henceforth, English prose had to struggle against a tendency to luxuriance, and plain, honest English speech was overwhelmed. This may be true. And we may go further than the matter of language. The very thought-forms of ordinary English people were to be moulded for generations by the simple fact that the Bible was to become one of the cheapest and most accessible books from which the young could be taught to read.[1] The Authorized Version made the English 'the People of a Book' as surely as the Koran made Islam. The Puritan tradition, whose shaping influence on modern England has been second to none, was to be for a century and more the twin tradition of 'The Bible and the Sword'. And when at length the sword slept, the tradition was to survive, for good or ill, in the evangelical edge of the Nonconformist Conscience, bloodless perhaps, but no less sharp.

[1] Notably after the foundation of the British and Foreign Bible Society in 1804 with its mass production of cheap Bibles. It was said at the time: 'The Devil trembles when he sees/Bibles sold as cheap as these.'

8

The Civil War

During the first half of the seventeenth century something very odd happened in England...a body of gentlemen and townsmen supported by a handful of dissident peers had the amazing effrontery to challenge the King, the bishops, most of the peerage, and their gentry supporters; it even defeated them...Thus the middle of the seventeenth century saw the eclipse of the monarchy...of the peerage...and of the Anglican Church...Why did all this happen?

LAWRENCE STONE, *The Crisis of the Aristocracy*

Men were to look back to the reign of Queen Elizabeth as an epoch of unexampled unanimity, a unanimity grounded on moral feeling, if not inspired by heaven itself. The very stars in their courses had seemed to fight for them, Providence having provided a common focus in the war with Spain. Few things afforded patriots more legitimate pride than the loyalty of the English Catholics to the heretic heroine in the crisis year 1588, the year of the Armada, and every schoolboy once cherished the tale of Master Stubbs who, with one hand cut off for libelling the Queen's government, raised his hat with the other and cried 'God save the Queen!' Beneath the surface of this 'happy time of lenity', of course, there were deep and dangerous currents of tension, and men knew that 'the times might be altered'. They were. In the year of the Armada the first generation of the aging Queen's most valued servants started to pass away. Leicester died in that year; Walsingham in 1591; Burghley, the ablest of them all, in 1598, a departure which the Queen took 'very grievously, shedding...tears, and separating herself from all company'. The tale of great names goes on, for it was hardly to be imagined that such a reign should ever lack stars of the brightest luminosity: Robert Cecil, sly and prim; Walter Raleigh, darkly brilliant; the darling Robert Devereux, Earl of Essex, in whom the Queen herself discovered a favourite to fear ('By God's son, I am no Queen; this man is above me,' she is reputed to have said before she took off his handsome head).

139

The sullen London crowds who watched the Earl of Essex riding in arms against the Queen on a dark February day in 1601 were witnessing the last mad flourish of an overmighty subject, a gesture without principle, senseless, vain, ignoble. Scarcely more than forty years later, on a summer day in 1642, the two Houses of Parliament resolved to live and die with the latest Earl of Essex, whom they had appointed their General to command an army 'for the safety of the King's person, defence of both Houses of Parliament...and preserving of the true religion, the laws, liberty and peace of the kingdom'. Indeed and indeed, the case was altered, within somewhat less than half a century.

The Great Civil War is the central historical experience of the English people, and when they look back on it they still ask why it happened. It is the kind of thing that James Boswell was thinking of when he remarked to Dr Johnson on the incredibility of English history. It may fairly be said that no one wanted it. When it started, in 1642, men found themselves suddenly and unexpectedly faced with terrible decisions, and during the tragic years that followed, hopes and endeavours for a negotiated peace never wholly died.

The coming of the war is not susceptible of the analytical methods of historical causation. No one can say in terms of cause and effect why it happened. It is possible only to reach a degree of understanding of the conditions that made it possible. Historians are still trying to do this, with special reference to the fortunes of the politically effective classes of society. It would hardly be too much to say that the whole Tudor Age constituted an educative process for the production of the revolution of the Stuart century. It produced not only the notorious 'unsolved problems of the Tudors'—price rise and the rise of Puritanism the chief of them—but the very minds and habits of the men who were constrained to solve them. Other societies in western Europe were producing their versions of a rising or a falling gentry, but it was only in England that this order of men was to prove capable of bringing about the eclipse of monarchy, peerage and Church, at least for a time, and thereby to give a whole nation the salutary experience of the ultimately preservative effect of revolution on the political and social institutions of a historic people. To a Frenchwoman who wished to know why democratic institutions seemed to work so much more smoothly in England than in France, the most somnolent of the dukes of Devonshire once replied: 'Madame, the reason is quite obvious. We cut off our king's head a hundred and forty-four years before you did yours.'

Foremost among the habits of the English of the early seventeenth century was the habit of self-government. Century by century, back to their germinal origins in the twelfth century, the 'Shallows and Silences of real life', as Maitland called them,[1] had been making England most truly the country, if not of self-government, at any rate of government by country gentlemen. Exercising 'self-government at the King's command', these men, with their worm's-eye view of the tasks of government in terms of the ordinary affairs of ordinary men and women, ruled England where England lived—in the countryside. They were neither rustic boors nor exiled courtiers, but men of business educated by the market-place, the petty-assize bench, and some increasing number of them at the universities and the Inns of Court.[2] The number of university men who came to the Elizabethan House of Commons increased from 67 in 1563 to 161 by 1593. No less than twelve new colleges were endowed by benefactors during the sixteenth century, and the colleges of Oxford and Cambridge were being increasingly adapted to the interests of young men who were not necessarily there to take degrees but as a prelude to studies at the Inns, or foreign travel, or management of family estates. The universities were far from being ivory towers devoted to divinity and metaphysics. As ever, they reflected the changing social scene: the Protestant and propertied world as it evolved in the Tudor century, the world of the private household, the entailed estate, the individual conscience.

It is against this background that we must view the origins and

[1] Collected Papers, vol. I, pp. 467–79.
[2] The Inns of Court were and still are the hostels where barristers lodge in London, and in the nature of colleges of legal education as well as lodgings.

the conduct of the men who composed the opposition to Stuart misrule. The House of Commons which presented the Petition of Right[1] and passed the Grand Remonstrance[2] is not to be explained simply as suffering from an infection caught from a few ill-affected men who sowed dissension between King and Commons (as Charles I avowed when he sent them home after the Petition of Right), nor by the ambition or desperation of a rising or declining gentry, but as the offspring of a long course of government by country gentlemen in the counties and a comparatively recent change of climate in the schools and universities and Inns of Court. These men had begun to breathe more freely after the removal of the threat of the Spanish Armada and to feel less constrained to choke down criticism of the way their country's affairs were being run. There had taken place among these men a decline in respect for, and habitual obedience to, the monarchy, partly owing to the personal ineptitude of the first Stuart kings, and partly owing to their dislike of the Stuart use of the royal patronage on unpopular men. These stresses and strains had created an ever-widening breach between Court and Country, a gulf involving deep currents of moral feeling, profoundly conflicting ways of life.

The breach had shown itself in the time of Queen Elizabeth. It had widened with the disreputability of the court of James I. These were the years of Shakespeare's nausea with the human race, the years of *Measure for Measure* (1603), *Troilus and Cressida* (1608), and all the 'sad stuff' that George III later complained about, as well as the monsters of Ben Jonson and the chamber of horrors which presented Sir Giles Overreach, the Duchess of Malfi and the White Devil. The hideous wickedness of the Overbury Murder—a case of slow poisoning by a pair of aristocratic adulterers—seemed to show that real life could be no less nauseating than contemporary drama and fiction. Above loomed the gorgeous painted ceilings of Peter Paul Rubens. The background

[1] See below, p. 146.
[2] A vote of censure on the King's government and policies, passed somewhat narrowly in 1641. Its 204 clauses contained not only a condemnation of the past but a parliamentary manifesto for the future.

was adorned by the over-dressed masques of Inigo Jones and the ponderous vulgarity of Jacobean wood-carving. Nothing that Charles I could do afterwards had the power to restrain the avalanche of disgust that was set rolling in the first decades of the century. The Caroline divines, such men as Andrewes and Sheldon and Cudworth, shine in the lowering sky of these years like fixed stars, but ordinary Englishmen saw less of the Beauty of Holiness than of the irritable features of Laud with his nagging insistence on 'things indifferent',[1] and sometimes things that had the outward appearance of Popery. What the English craved at this time was not so much the things of the altar but the things of the pulpit. The one bad mistake Elizabeth ever made, it has been said, was in not providing the Church with preachers. Neither the great Queen nor her Stuart successors ever grasped the passion of their people for sermons, preferably long ones. 'The fatal error into which the peculiar character of the English Reformation threw our Church', Coleridge was to say, two centuries later, 'has borne bitter fruit ever since—I mean that of its clinging to Court and State, instead of cultivating the people ...As it is, I fear the Church has let the hearts of the common people be stolen from it.' These hungry hearts were turning ever more to the Puritan preacher, the prayer-meeting, the conventicle, the 'little Bethels' of Protestant nonconformity which proliferated over England throughout the next three centuries.

As for the supposed 'antagonism of the merchant oligarchies' to aristocratic dominance—oligarchies which had come to thrive, notably in London, with the chartered companies of Stuart England, and whose interests are imagined to have felt thwarted by 'the fetters of a decaying feudal aristocracy'—every term in this favourite equation of the Marxist is suspect. Such oligarchies as existed among the mercantile and industrial capitalists were intent rather on joining the aristocratic 'establishment' than on destroying it, while peers and gentry, as usually in England, shared the business outlook and habit of mind of a society permeated from top to bottom by a mercantile ethos. Any 'challenge'

[1] That is, things that are not essential to salvation: for example, whether we talk of priests, presbyters or ministers.

to the social and political authority of the peerage came not from a capitalist *bourgeoisie* but from other and slightly lower ranks of the landed aristocracy itself. Any attempt to discover the origins of the Great Civil War in terms of a class war must proceed on very treacherous ground indeed. Explanations in terms of either a 'rising' or a 'declining' gentry are likely to prove optical illusions. There were as many declining gentry as there were rising gentry in these years, a time of unprecedented economic mobility throughout the whole of the middling land-owning part of society. The 'crisis' in the affairs of the gentry, as Professor Lawrence Stone has lately shown us,[1] was a many-sided crisis. It did not of itself bring about the Civil War, but it helped to produce the conditions which made the Civil War possible.

In the Parliament which stood up to Charles I, his oppressive financial exactions and perilous religious perversities, the House of Commons was far more important than the House of Lords. For one thing, the Commons could have bought the House of Lords twice over. This dominant House of Commons of the early years of the Stuart revolution consisted of no 'mere' or 'impoverished' gentry but of the landed men who had done very well out of the land-boom which had been going on for half a century and more. They were the politically vital characters of the realm: deputy lieutenants, sheriffs, justices of the peace, and royal commissioners in the counties, men of 'port and worship' in their neighbourhoods. These rich country gentlemen of the Lower House were to occupy the central stage of Stuart constitutional history. Some 60 per cent of the members of the Long Parliament in 1640–1 had annual incomes of more than £1,000 a year, and it seems probable that only 10 per cent had incomes below £500. Nearly all of them were attached, generally territorially, to the regions they represented in Parliament. They were the kind of men who had for generations been engaged in what may be called 'self-government at the King's command'. No generation of men in the parliamentary history of England can match them for all-round political ability and (what was especially needed at that hour) political courage. They did not aim to

[1] Lawrence Stone, *The Crisis of the Aristocracy* (Oxford, 1965).

supersede the king or to rule the realm. Not for another hundred years and more did the inveterate oppositional habits which the House of Commons acquired in these years give way to a properly constructive attitude to political power and its responsibilities.

Charles I, 'the fair and fatal king' whose statue was to ride at Charing Cross for so long, 'hard by his own Whitehall', was in fact a short, bandy-legged man with a stammer who felt too often the need to prove his mastery in the eyes of his French Queen, and generally took care to have himself portrayed for posterity on a very high horse. Devout, chaste, and of scholarly tastes, he was the pattern of a fine gentleman, and along with his fair Queen he brought a wholesome change in manners and morals after the sordid joviality of his father. Charles came to an inheritance which he was well fitted to adorn by his taste in painting but only to undo in the art of politics. If his father was 'the wisest fool in Christendom', Charles himself was Christendom's sorriest statesman. James had lectured his faithful Commons on the high and mighty mysteries of monarchy while his faithful Commons laughed behind their hands at the sight of the mighty monarch in garments padded against the assassin's knife. They had kept him short of money while nagging him for his failure to send forces to the aid of their religious compatriots in the Thirty Years War, and he was justifiably outraged by their close-fisted impertinence. But King James, while he talked big, acted on the whole with sense and moderation. Charles ranted far less and acted impulsively. When he reproached his faithful Commons it was rather in the tone of a long-suffering schoolmaster. Within a very few years, Charles made it as plain as a pike-staff that 'the divinity that doth hedge a king' may very well lack grass-roots in the liberties of the subject. The axe which took off his head on a frosty January day in 1649 levelled that hedge once and for all. Daylight was let in upon monarchy at the moment when Charles Stuart stepped out on to the scaffold through the little window of Inigo Jones's banqueting-hall opposite Downing Street. It is true that

> He nothing common did, or mean,
> Upon that memorable scene...

145

Rather it might be said that, as far as concerns the long history of the British monarchy, he inaugurated the age of the common-place.

King Charles always liked to be on the windy side of the law, and his law officers generally contrived to put him there. But while he won all the tricks, Parliament won the rubber. The five knights whom he imprisoned over a forced loan in 1627 were found by his Chief Justice to have been rightly detained *per speciale mandatum domini regis* (by special command of the lord king), but next year Parliament secured the King's acceptance of the Petition of Right, which purported, somewhat unhistorically, to re-state the principle of Magna Carta that taxes may not be levied without parliamentary consent nor the subject detained without cause shown. When, within a week or two, the House of Commons tried to make out that the Petition covered the levying of Tonnage and Poundage,[1] Charles was correct in describing this as a false construction of what he had granted in the Petition. He sent them home, and that year his friend and minister the Duke of Buckingham was assassinated.[2] At that point, Thomas Wentworth[3] left the opposition for the King's side in disgust at what he deemed to be Parliament's sharp practice. Charles never forgave or forgot the murder of Buckingham. It produced in him a trauma which disabled him from ever again putting complete faith in his fellow men. He decided to rule without Parliament, and for eleven years he succeeded.

'The Eleven Years' Tyranny' is a misnomer if it implies that England lived out these years (1629–40) in the shadow of an iron despotism, or indeed of anything like a regime of material and spiritual impoverishment. Looking back from the darkness of exile, Clarendon, the great historian of the Rebellion, believed

[1] Import duties.

[2] He was stabbed by John Felton, a distressed soldier, who attributed his sufferings to the Duke's mismanagement of an expedition for the relief of the French Protestants at La Rochelle.

[3] Thomas Wentworth, later Earl of Strafford, served the King as President of the Council of the North, and as Lord Deputy of Ireland. Charles never gave him his whole confidence, but he came to symbolize every aspect of tyranny to the parliamentary opposition which he had deserted for the royal service.

himself to discern *imperium et libertas* 'as well reconciled as possible' at that time, a time when 'England enjoyed the greatest measure of felicity that it had ever known'. The country was rich, the Church flourishing with learned and extraordinary men, trade increasing so that England was the exchange of Christendom. Peace was made with both France and Spain in 1630; Wentworth was governing Ireland; Laud was populating North America by making England too unbearable for religious dissentients, Puritans settling in Massachusetts and Catholics in Maryland; Vermuyden and his Dutchmen were draining the fens in the teeth of opposition by the angry fenmen. Some other things were happening, too, things that Clarendon omits to mention. Puritans and Parliament-men were recruiting their martyrs. In 1632 Sir John Eliot died in the Tower of a consumption brought on by his incarceration at the King's pleasure for his part in passing the three Resolutions which bear his name[1] while the Speaker was held down in his chair. Eliot's cruel story was long to rankle in the hearts of the King's enemies. So was the infliction of savage physical punishment upon men of the learned professions, Prynne, Burton and Bastwick, in Palace Yard, at the behest of the Star Chamber, for libelling bishops and contemning Laud's ecclesiastical regime. Those who profess to discover in Strafford, Laud and their royal master some association with the noble cause of benevolent despotism, or even the incipient Welfare State, need look little farther than these episodes for the reverse of the medal.

The King won his case against John Hampden, who had refused to pay Ship Money in 1647–8,[2] but it is not too much to say that the moral victory lay with Hampden. His courage and resolution aroused public spirit throughout the country, not least

[1] The Three Resolutions declared anyone to be an enemy of the kingdom who should (*a*) bring in innovations in religion, (*b*) advise the levying of Tonnage and Poundage without parliamentary grant, (*c*) voluntarily pay such illegal taxes.

[2] Ship Money was a long-standing levy on maritime counties and towns for the supply and maintenance of ships for the defence of the coasts against pirates; now it was being levied on *inland* counties, the King having obtained the opinion of his judges that it was lawful so to do.

in the country-houses where gentlemen long deprived of their sounding-board in the House of Commons were counting the days until the King's need for money should bring them once more to Westminster. Country-house politics may be said to have been born during the Eleven Years. When elections were again held in the autumn of 1640, a good deal of preparatory work had been done. Not only John Hampden but John Pym (soon to be known as 'King Pym')[1] and many another 'patriotic missionary' had been riding round England on a kind of 'resistance circuit' of the Puritan country-houses, canvassing for their faction. 'Contemporary men had no notion', Thomas Carlyle was to write, 200 years later, 'what an enormous work they were going on with; how could anybody know that this was to be the *Long Parliament*, and to cut his Majesty's head off, among other feats? A very *spirited election*, I dare believe.'

It was not the English, however, but the Scots who had brought it to pass. Without the Scots, there might have been a nation-wide passive resistance to ship-money; but when danger threatened from abroad (and Scotland was abroad, still) everything was suddenly put to the touch. The Scots in their presbyterian, not to say nationalist, wrath, refused to adopt a new Prayer Book based on that of the English Church in place of John Knox's Book of Common Order. Not only did they refuse to adopt it. They drew up and signed a National Covenant (1638) in which they described the liturgy of the English Church as blasphemous, devilish and profane, an offspring of papistry, damned and confuted by the Word of God and the Kirk of Scotland. They swore to live and die in their own religion, and, after King Charles had tried to bring them to compromise, their General Assembly formally abolished Episcopacy (1638). The two Bishops' Wars that followed (in 1639 and 1640) issued in the Scots victory at Newburn and the occupation of Durham and Northumberland by a Scots army for whose maintenance Charles was to pay as long as it remained on English soil. In effect, when the Great Council of Peers advised the King to call a Parliament, the game was up. The Parliament was to last

[1] See below, p. 155 n. 1.

for thirteen years, and to carry through a revolution. There was to be no Tennis-court Oath as in France, no Declaration of the Rights of Man as in America, nor anything resembling a *coup d'état*. There was to be, and then only after much heart-searching, a Civil War.

When Charles I set up his standard at Nottingham on a windy August day in 1642, it was blown down again the same night. However, John Pynnegar, yeoman, aged about thirty-seven, of the parish of Heanor in the neighbouring county of Derbyshire, was ready to swear that he saw it flying on one of the towers of the castle, and that he saw the King there, too. John Pynnegar was to have been a witness when the King years later stood his trial for levying war upon his subjects, although the King's refusal to plead meant that the witnesses to his unlawful acts could only be examined *ex abundanti*, 'for the further satisfaction of themselves'. The fact that they attended the trial with their sworn affidavits bears testimony to the legalistic habits of the English even when they set about killing their king. It was comparable to the conduct of Henry VIII when he indicted an archbishop who had been dead for 400 years for pretending to be a saint.

A cool observer in August 1642 might have been pardoned for thinking that the revolution was over before the sword was drawn: a revolution carried through by due process of law. The Statute Book already registered the abolition of both the Court of Star Chamber and the Court of High Commission; the illegality of Ship Money and the irregularity of the King's manner of raising Tonnage and Poundage; a whole host of corrective legislation about the royal forests, knighthood fines,[1] and 'ecclesiastical innovations'. The King had abjured his prerogative to summon, prorogue or dissolve Parliament at will, and had given his assent to a Statute requiring Parliament to meet triennally, with a minimum life of fifty days, along with a number of devices for securing these desirable ends should the King neglect to keep his royal word, provisions highly offensive to the

---

[1] A device for raising money by imposing fines on gentlemen who, being qualified for doing so, had failed to take up their proper rank and title.

royal honour, and duly struck out of the Act in 1664, with apologetic reference to their having been inserted at a time 'very uncareful for the dignity of the Crown or the security of the people'. Charles had also consented that the present Parliament could not be dissolved, prorogued or adjourned without its own consent. He had given up to parliamentary vengeance his most feared and hated servant, the Earl of Strafford. These were the King's concessions to Parliament which Dr Johnson thought the best example of the sheer incredibility of English history. All the legislation which had received the royal assent before the King drew the sword remained on the Statute Book, perfectly valid and intact, when the monarchy was restored in 1660. A revolution had been carried through under the forms of law before the war was fought. Why was it necessary to fight? Why did it take twenty years of bloodshed and chaos to fix the English political system in the form to which most men believed it had been successfully reduced in the summer of 1641?

In such a case, Kant once said, we are led to suspect something twisted in the question. And the fact is that, had the issue been purely a constitutional one, there need have been no war, for the King never had a party until moderate men were driven to his side by threats to overthrow the Church by such radical reforming measures as the Root and Branch bill. The war was fought on issues which went far beyond the constitutional sphere, questions which far transcended politics. The unsolved problem in 1642 was the problem of religion. Not simply the Laudian Prayer Book or the Anglican liturgy, but the religious concept of society, of hierarchy, of human life itself. This was not, of course, to be settled by swords. It was to settle itself by the passage of time, by a silent reorientation of men's minds, by a subtle and secret modification of the psyche, something that amounted in the course of fifty years and more to an intellectual revolution. The men of the age of Charles I and Oliver Cromwell and John Milton were one kind of men. The men of the age of Isaac Newton and John Locke were another. Here, in a tract of time extending roughly from 1640 to 1688, is the only watershed of English history. Its slopes are noisy with the clash of swords, but its monuments, like the 'sepulchral urnes lately digged up in a field at Old Walsingham', have quietly rested under the drums and tramplings of three conquests.

It was possible for a man to ignore the drums and tramplings. Most men did. As Clarendon says, 'the number of those who desired to sit still was greater than those who desired to engage in either party'. If a man so desired, he might furbish up a bit of old armour, a corset or cuirass long set aside by his great-grandsire after Tewkesbury or Towton. A man of ancient family might put on a whole suit of ironmongery and go clanking about to earn the name of 'lobster'. Some looked very handsome, in what must, even then, have seemed like fancy-dress costume: Henry Ireton, whose splendid portrait may still be seen in the National Portrait Gallery in London, or Lieutenant-General Cromwell, the heavily built horseman on his weight-carrier, his orange scarf flowing from off his cuirass. Red or orange scarfs and sashes the women wrapped round their men-folk's waists as distinguishing emblems, but even so some bad mistakes were made, notably by the French gentlemen who came over to fight for the King and found themselves fighting for the Parliament. Like most English wars, the conflict began reluctantly, went on with a good deal of muddle, and never wholly lost an air of amiable incompetence. It was perhaps a tribute to the civil achievements of the Tudor century that it took so long to begin, and that when it was begun it was so often a matter of pulled punches. The Earl of Manchester let the King get away after the second battle of Newbury, though Cromwell said that he would slay him like any other man if he met him in battle. It was only Cromwell's New Model[1] soldiers who came near to turning the gentlemanly war into a war of

---

[1] The New Model Army came into being after the first phase of the war (1642–44) had shown, despite Parliament's victory at Marston Moor, that neither in generalship nor in organization were the parliamentary forces capable of winning decisively. Waller advocated a standing army 'merely of their own' to Parliament in 1645. The 'New Model Ordinance' was passed on 13 February. Cromwell was to give it its soul. It became the first, and probably the last, army of an ideology in English history. Not that it was a 'people's army', though Cromwell's 'russet-coated captains' figured largely in it. At first, more than half the infantry were pressed men; but 21 out of 37 of the senior officers were of gentle or noble birth.

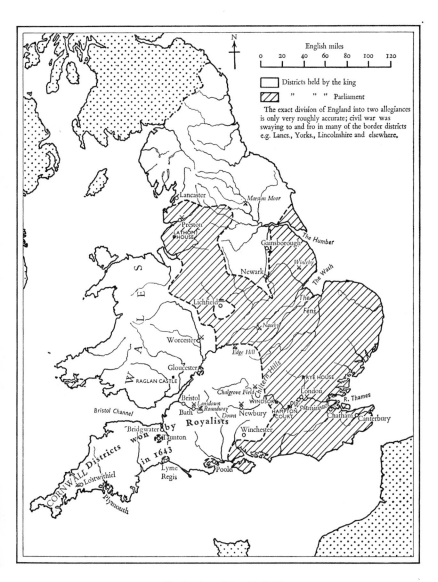

4 The battles of the Civil War

Protestant traditions, were almost solidly for Parliament. The King had his best resources in the west and north. How a man chose his side would depend on considerations of a complexity, even a mystery, that eludes categorical analysis, as might be expected of men who lived in a society of powerful local and personal loyalties, a society deeply engraved with hierarchical and aristocratic values. 'Fear God, Honour the King' was graven upon the battlements of many a manor-house and deep in the hearts of thousands of ordinary unthinking men. Many must have simply echoed the words of Sir Edmund Verney: 'I have eaten the King's bread...and will not do so base a thing as to forsake him,' even though, like Sir Edmund, they disapproved his every action. 'I have no reverence for bishops, for whom this quarrel subsists', Sir Edmund added. And there is an undoubted sense in which the Civil War could be called *bellum episcopale*.[1] Again, perhaps because it was an English war, it was considerably fought by the Scots.

If the King were to win he must win quickly, and it is not surprising that he won the first battles, coming as near to London as Turnham Green in the early weeks. The first months saw John Hampden's death after Chalgrove Field and Prince Rupert's descent upon Bristol, the defeat of the Fairfaxes in the north, and the onset of a great turning movement to envelop London from the south and west. The war might have ended that year. Only the Scots made it possible for it to continue. They were on English soil before it began. Their princes had been on the throne since the death of Queen Elizabeth. Their refusal of the King's religion had had a great deal to do with the war's breaking out. When the King had been at war with his English subjects for little more than twelve months, the Scots came in on the side of the Parliament by a 'Solemn League and Covenant' (25 September 1643), which provided for the setting up of a Committee of Both Kingdoms, the supply of an army of 20,000, and the

[1] The fact that it literally began with wars over Episcopacy in Scotland (p. 148 above) is only one fact in justification. Much more important is the fact of the King's devotion to the episcopal organization of the Church. The Church of England, its hierarchy and its philosophy, was what he died for. 'No bishop, no King' was sound sense whether as a warning or as a war-cry.

adoption as a war aim of the reform of the Church of England 'according to the Word of God and the example of the best reformed Churches', which meant, obviously, the Kirk of Scotland. Whether Pym[1] and the Parliament ever envisaged a Presbytery as a literal outcome of the war or not, they had restored the balance of military might. The God of the Big Battalions, it seemed, was a Scotsman after all. When, in May 1646, the King gave himself up after just three years of war, it was to the Scots at Newark that he made his surrender.

'You have done your work, my lads', Sir Jacob Astley said to Colonel Birch's men after the lost, and last, fight at Stow-on-the-Wold. 'Now you may go home and play.' He added, without unusual prescience: 'Unless you will fall out with one another.'

Over the next two years the country saw a triangular contest between King, Parliament and Army. The critical moment was that in which Cornet Joyce took the King away from Holmby House with 500 troopers for his warrant on a June night in 1647. Charles's charming behaviour to his captors suggests that he was, somewhat late in the day, learning something of the Tudor style. He had at least a chance of becoming that dangerously attractive figure, the Injured Man, though it was to need the headsman's axe to transform the Man of Blood into the Royal Martyr. The army had him in its pocket, and the officers of the High Command at any rate were anxious to come to terms with him. Men like Cromwell and Ireton, spiritual stepsons of the Patriot Queen of the golden days of their youth, were anxious to go on believing

[1] John Pym (1584–1643) died in the year of the treaty with the Scots (the Solemn League and Covenant). He had been a Member of the Commons since 1614, and had become the leader of the opposition at the time of the attack on Strafford in 1641–2. He had 'the greatest influence upon the House of Commons of any man', Clarendon says, and there was a moment in which the King had intended to make him Chancellor of the Exchequer. It was a tragedy that Pym never came to work with moderate royalists like Clarendon, for he was the leader of the middle party in the Commons, and it was through the middle party (as Professor Hexter has shown in his *The Reign of King Pym*, Harvard, 1941) that he ruled the House. Having forged the weapon of the Civil War House of Commons and carried through the military alliance with the Scots, he died leaving the House of Commons no successor of his moderation or experience. He was buried in Westminster Abbey.

that the late unhappy conflict had been only a slipped stitch in the seamless robe of their country's history. Their *Heads of Proposals* provided generously for the safety, honour and freedom of His Majesty's person, his Queen and his Royal Issue, with foreign policy, appointments, finance and religion in the hands of a Council of State and the two Houses of Parliament for a period of ten years. It was to be an honourable treaty providing for hostages and guarantees for a limited period, but leaving the traditional forms of government untouched, much like the baronial Provisions of Oxford[1] of the thirteenth century or the putting of certain aspects of monarchical authority into commission. The men who made these proposals were really the current counterpart of the *conciliarii nati*, or the gentlemen of England who had sought to bridle King John, and Henry III, and Edward II. But they had reckoned without such men as Buffcoat, Trooper Sexby, and the best of the rank and file who had fought the war.

These men were somewhat of the kidney of modern shop-stewards who have little trust in the trade-union hierarchy. 'There are many thousands of us soldiers that have ventured our lives; we have little propriety in the kingdom as to our estates, yet we have had a birthright', Trooper Sexby said. Rainsborough, a poor man, as he protested, wished plainly to know 'what the soldier hath fought for all this while'. It was beginning to appear 'that he hath fought to enslave himself, to give power to men of riches, men of estates, to make him a perpetual slave'. He ventured to predict that 'when these gentlemen fall out among themselves, they shall press the poor scrubs to come and kill one another for them'. It was up to the rank and file that the grandees should not 'through fraudulent accommodations' deprive the poor scrubs of the fruit of their victories. Men like Sexby and Rainsborough plainly suspected that men like Lieutenant-General Cromwell and his son-in-law, Colonel Henry Ireton, and their ladies, were trying on their coronets for a new peerage under the restored King. It was rumoured that they had knelt and kissed the King's hand in their talks with him. This was not what the army had fought for.

[1] See above, p. 81.

So they drew up their own proposals, which they called the Agreement of the People, wherein it was explicitly avowed that 'the power of this, and all future Representatives of this Nation, is inferior only to theirs who choose them'. Indeed, certain matters were to be reserved from the scope of the representative body altogether, matters which were declared to constitute 'our native rights...fundamental to our common right, liberty, and safety...' They include compulsion to serve in any foreign war, inquiry into past conduct 'in relation to the late wars or public differences', and matters of religion. On this last the Agreement is especially explicit: 'That matters of religion and the ways of God's worship are not to be entrusted by us to any human power.' Religious liberty, however, is not to be extended to Popery or Prelacy. A second Agreement was shortly to lay down a schedule of a reconstituted constituency system in accordance with modern changes in population density. Parliaments are to be chosen every ten years, and elections to be held on a certain day. Electors are to be adult denizens assessed ordinarily to the relief of the poor, excluding persons receiving alms, servants, and persons receiving wages from any particular person. Candidates are to be 'men of courage, fearing God and hating covetousness ...' Such provisions amply dispose of the frequent loose assertion that the Levellers[1] were advocates of universal manhood suffrage.

Perhaps because it was the work of men who were unlikely ever to be called upon to put it into effect, the Agreement of the People was to the last degree philosophical, with its reserved native rights, and its strict limitations upon the authority of the representative body. It partakes less of the nature of a written constitution, such as the Heads of Proposals, than of a manifesto or a Declaration of Rights akin to those similarly promulgated by the revolutionary peoples of France and America a century and

---

[1] The left wing of the army. A royalist journalist of 1647 tells us that it was the King who nicknamed them 'Levellers', this being 'a most apt title for such a despicable and desperate knot to be known by'. These desperadoes 'endeavour to cast down and level the enclosures of nobility, gentry and propriety, and to make us all even, so that every Jack shall vie with a gentleman and every gentleman be made a Jack'. Parliament, and Oliver Cromwell, abhorred them no less.

more later. Within a hundred years or slightly longer the English were to grow fond, perhaps over-fond, of boasting of their peculiar pragmatism, of their exclusive attachment to the *real* rights they enjoyed at common law, of their wholesome contempt for what they liked to call French rhetoric. Their contempt was the offspring of that very English characteristic, wisdom after the event, for they had had their revolution earlier, and they had grown content with it, and generally complacent about it. They had, they believed, nothing to learn from Frenchmen or Americans, and they could get on unperturbed with the revolution which now engaged their minds and energies more keenly: the industrial one. Such was, at least in part, the ironic legacy of the Levellers.

The Agreement of the People was read before the Council of the Army at Putney parish church on 29 October 1647, the beginning of that South Bank colloquy which lasted for a fortnight and is (thanks to the survival of the *Clarke Papers*[1]) as present to us as the Parliamentary Debates before the institution of Hansard, or Elliot's *Debates* on the adoption of the Federal Constitution of the United States in 1787. An astonishing spectacle it is, the officers and the rank and file of a victorious army sitting down in a parish church (the handiest extemporized debating-hall in those days) to thrash out their differences, boldly, rationally, and with almost perfect courtesy. There could be no finer tribute to the quality of the army that Oliver Cromwell had made, even if, as the days wore on, it became plain that the Leveller element within it was, albeit affectionately, concerned to get rid of Oliver Cromwell. The future Lord Protector, here among his men, cut a more sympathetic figure than he was ever to do from his high seat resembling a throne. The atmosphere was tense enough at times, but the Lieutenant-General, and his skilled debater of a son-in-law, listened patiently to Buffcoat and Trooper as they made it clear what they thought of such 'fraudulent accommodations' as the Heads of Proposals. As Trooper Sexby put it, looking straight into the faces of the grandees, their 'credits

[1] *The Clarke Papers*, ed. C. H. Frith, was published by the Camden Society, 1891–9.

and reputation had been much blasted'. It was not Sexby, however, but one whose identity has come down to us concealed
under the name of a 'Bedfordshire man' who simply said that
the engagements between the army and the King must be can-
celled if they were unjust, must be broken if they promised to the
King what rightfully belonged to the people. It was left to Colonel
Rainsborough to deliver himself of what has been rightly described as 'the straightest and simplest claim for equality ever
made in English history'. The Colonel said:

'For really I think that the poorest he that is in England hath a life
to live, as the greatest he; and therefore truly, Sir, I think it's clear
that every man that is to live under a government ought first by his
own consent to put himself under that government; and I do think
that the poorest man in England is not at all bound in a strict sense
to that government that he hath not had a voice to put himself under;
insomuch that I should doubt whether he was an Englishman...'

Neither the blasted Heads of Proposals nor the pristine Agreement of the People were to be the title-deeds of the English
Republic; but the utterances of the largely anonymous soldiers
gathered in that prayer-meeting cum revolutionary convention
on the South Bank of the Thames in the winter of 1647 remain
everlastingly lodged in the folklore of the English-speaking
democracies of two hemispheres. It may be too much to say that
the revolt of the army inaugurated the entry of a new class into
English politics. It is perhaps too little to say that the Putney
Debates record an immense educational experience. Certainly
they should help to cure that condescending habit of mind which
has afflicted historians of English popular movements from the
Levellers to the Luddites.

9

The Withdrawing Roar

The Sea of Faith
Was once, too, at the full, and round earth's shore
Lay like the folds of a bright girdle furled;
But now I only hear
Its melancholy, long, withdrawing roar,
Retreating to the breath
Of the night-wind down the vast edges drear
And naked shingles of the world.

MATTHEW ARNOLD, *Dover Beach*

The Levellers were contemned, and condemned, by both King and Parliament. The King proceeded to condemn himself by raising a second civil war, and the Parliament, which had legislated itself into eternal life as early as 1641, was sent packing by the Lord-General Oliver Cromwell in April 1653. As the Lord-General himself put it on that celebrated occasion, 'Not a dog barked'. From the day when he returned from his expeditions to subdue the Irish and the Scots, stained with the blood of Drogheda and crowned with the laurels of Dunbar and Worcester, to lay the subjugated realms at the feet of the Commons, it was unlikely that the Tudor country squire would go back to Huntingdon and plant the bergamot. He and his troopers were the sole effective power in the state. From the day when he turned out the Rump, as the remnant of the Long Parliament was called, he was acclaimed as 'brave Oliver', for the people of England were very like the man they acclaimed: they scarcely knew what they wanted, but they knew very well that they hated the selfish Presbyterian oligarchy which had come to dominate the Long Parliament, and which behaved not a whit less oppressively than the Laudian bishops or the priests of Rome.[1] At least, Oliver had

[1] Parliament had steadily become more Presbyterian, and exclusive, since the negotiation of the Solemn League and Covenant with the Scots in 1643. At the end of 1647 it had attempted to impose the Covenant on the officers of

the integrity and the inflexible courage to govern, and he was soon to make the name of England feared and respected once more in Europe. They were to hate the Lord Protector's 'Saints', too, but while Oliver lived it could not be denied that he was, as he preferred to call himself, 'a good constable set to keep the peace of the parish'. Keep it he did, holding the fort until his country should settle back into its traditional ways and its tried institutions.

The assembly of nominees which put power into Cromwell's hands and by so doing inaugurated the 'Protectorate' is remembered as Barebone's Parliament, so called after Praisegod Barebone, one of its more saintly members. This body produced the 'Instrument of Government', a written Constitution which provided for a Lord Protector and a Council of State and a single House of Legislature based on a property franchise from 'persons of known integrity, fearing God, and of good conversation' above the age of twenty-one. But Cromwell could no more govern with the parliaments of the Protectorate than Charles I could govern with his. The trouble with the Puritans was the Puritan activity of mind. They could never let anything alone. They not only quarrelled with the Protector, they insisted on debating the Instrument of Government itself. Were they not concerned to build the New Jerusalem? Oliver, however, was concerned to govern England in the aftermath of a civil war. He was an Elizabethan and was not content to stop at Elizabethan 'chidings' like the great Queen. He resorted to 'purgings' and exclusion. He had recourse to a regime of major-generals ruling over eleven military districts, and although the major-generals were not particularly tyrannical, neither they nor their general-issimo were ever to be forgotten or forgiven by the English people. 'Our rest we expect elsewhere,' the Lord Protector said shortly before he died; 'that will be durable.' His failure was innate and personal, a matter of both temperament and experience. He had never been what in England is called 'a good

the army, after which the army expelled Presbyterian members favourable to coming to terms with the King ('Pride's Purge'). Cromwell's turning out of the Rump was the conclusion of this process.

House of Commons man'. In the great days of Pym and Eliot he had been for the most part a dumb back-bencher, only liable to break forth into passionate articulation on the subject of God's people and the Whore of Babylon, much as John Milton poured forth his snarling and volcanic prose at the self-same provocation. He never served his apprenticeship in the arts of management, which alone can direct and make fruitful the disparate energies of a legislative assembly. Parliamentary government, largely because in a free country it must always be party government, partakes without degradation of the nature of a game; a game not more, and no less, base than a game of cricket. Cromwell, who had played football when he was at Sidney Sussex College, Cambridge, was yet temperamentally incapable of grasping the notion that anything in the nature of a game was involved in running government in partnership with a House of Commons. Politics to him were but an aspect, and an inferior aspect, of something else, as they had been to his medieval ancestors and as they were to be to his ideological descendants in the twentieth century. Unfortunately he was called to the tasks of government in the first dawn of the Whig epoch which intervened between the two, the epoch which gave us Liberalism, amateurism and cricket, and he was at sea.

He was, too, a conservative in an age of revolution. All his instincts, all his mental attitudes, were those of an Elizabethan country gentleman, a man of moderate fortune who became a genius of cavalry warfare in his forties, never ceasing to love all country sports, hawking and the cry of hounds, and stringed instruments and the game of bowls. As he said wearily: 'I would have been glad to have lived under my woodside, to have kept a flock of sheep, rather than undertake such a government as this.' No doubt he would have been happier, as England would certainly have been the poorer, if he had gone to America as he had twice meditated doing before the war, once under Laud's regime, and again when the Grand Remonstrance seemed likely to fail. There he would have made an exemplary founding father of the future republic, a pattern for the embattled farmers of the age of Washington. He would certainly have made a more convincing representative figure of a revolution with its eyes on the past than of the revolutionary England of the Levellers. When Cromwell said 'Thy Kingdom come', there was always the unspoken rider 'but not quite yet'. He scarcely qualified at any time as a builder of the New Jerusalem. He was far too baffled, too puzzled by the world as it had gone on in its wickedness since the death of the great Queen, besides being too immediately concerned with the quotidian tasks of 'a good constable set to keep the peace of the parish', too familiarly aligned—so one likes to imagine— with the conscience-stricken gentry of Anton Chekhov. In the perspective of the mind of the mid-twentieth century he remains a somewhat Blimpish figure, a steeple-hatted Whig progenitor of John Locke, or a good cavalry officer in the army of moral re-armament, who, as John Lilburne once said, 'will weep, howl and repent even while he doth smite you under the fifth rib'. The world has gone far beyond him, though the world must inevitably be the poorer if it fails to understand him. For he strove to establish religious toleration in an intolerant age, and if he was a dictator he was a reluctant one, and the only one to be com-mended by the Victorian Liberals. It was a Victorian prime min-ister who paid for his statue to be erected outside the entrance to the House of Commons. There he stands, invested with the Bible and the sword, the saviour of British parliamentary institutions who turned one Parliament out of doors and never succeeded in ruling with another. In Trevelyan's paraphrase of Marvell, he had 'locked behind himself the magic doors which close at the touch of force, but which force cannot reopen'. Marvell's own lines have the authentic flat-footed rhythm of a universal truth:

> The same arts that did gain
> A power, must it maintain.

As Cromwell lay dying a great storm swept over the land, the greatest England had known for a hundred years, levelling trees like harvest swathes, sinking ships offshore, tumbling roofs and chimneys and church steeples, 'howling over Thames-side palace stones…echoing dying Cromwell…' Did the dying dictator, as was his wont, look for a sign in the roaring tumult of the

universe at that hour? If so, it was not to be found there, in the old palace of the kings, but far away, beyond Grantham, near Woolsthorpe Manor, where the boy Isaac Newton was jumping against the wind under a tumbling strawstack, making his first recorded experiment in the course of discovering a law-abiding universe. The sign that Cromwell sought,
Universal order, where should he find it?
Not here, falling into death, but rising in life,
The young life of the mind of Newton…a youth strives
To right with mind matters beyond the reach of hands.[1]

The heroic age of the English revolution died with Cromwell, and its prosaic age, the age of the mathematicians and the grave men of science, was about to begin. It is probably not too much to say with the nineteenth-century historian John Richard Green that 'modern England' began with the restoration of the monarchy under Charles II in 1660. The twin forces that were to govern men's lives increasingly from henceforth were the forces of science and industry, and in the larger perspectives of history the most significant event of the years immediately following upon the Restoration was Charles II's incorporation of the Royal Society of London in 1662 'to promote the welfare of the arts and sciences'. It is an event which may be said to mark that 'transference of interests' from the final truths of theology to the provisional explanations of empirical science, a transference which reveals to us the peculiar character of the modern mind. Green went so far as to say that 'between modern thought and the thought of men before the Restoration there is a great gulf fixed', and that while it would have been difficult for a man in 1874 (the year of Green's Short History) to hold a fruitful conversation with Burghley or with Oliver Cromwell, yet Sir Humphry Davy could have talked with Sir Isaac Newton, or Jeremy Bentham with John Locke, without any sense of severance. We are no longer prepared to use such clear-cut or dramatic terms as Green, but we are conscious that after the Restoration 'the England around us becomes our own England', at any rate the England of Queen Victoria if not quite that of Queen Elizabeth II.

[1] Robert Gittings, 'Newton' (in *Wentworth Place*, p. 195).

The king who incorporated the Royal Society of London in 1662 deserves commemoration for little else. In extending royal patronage to the men of science, the King was incorporating a group of men who had been associating in London for philosophical discussion, under the inspiration of the pioneer of empirical method, Francis Bacon, since the 1640s: members of what Sir Robert Boyle had called 'the Invisible College'. Gresham's College, too, substantially housed by the benefaction of Sir Thomas Gresham since 1598 in the heart of the City, served as a nucleus, and even lodged the Royal Society when it was incorporated. The King's contribution, aside from the invaluable stamp of royal approval, was the building of the Royal Observatory at Greenwich in 1675 and the gift of Chelsea Hospital estate a few years earlier, a gift for which he paid the Society £1,300 in order to recover it. Charles attended an occasional meeting of the Society, notably on the evening of 3 May 1661, when he was shown the rings of Saturn and Jupiter's satellites through 'His Majesty's great telescope'. He seems to have had a laboratory of his own, though he liked to make game of the learned men of the Society for trying to weigh air.

On the whole, however, Charles II is better remembered for what he was than for what he did. He gave the lead in what was, after the heroics of the last generation, a salutary lightness of heart and a not altogether unwholesome indifference to principle. The tall and swarthy man who set foot on Dover beach on 25 May 1660 was a grateful embodiment of the comic spirit, lacking nostalgia for the sea of faith once at the full and girdling earth's shores, nor finding much to regret in its 'melancholy, long, withdrawing roar'. The tragedians were going off at the turn of the tide, the clowns were coming on for an hour, and the English were ready to rejoice. The theatres were open again, the maypoles went up, and the hearts of men delighted once more in their customary sins. For years the monarchy had been like an amputated limb which aches in its absence. To cure the ache, and to save a great deal of trouble, 1660 was counted as the thirteenth year of Carolus Secundus. While the bells rocked the steeples and the guns thundered from the river and the crowds roared themselves hoarse all the way from Dover to Whitehall, the King was heard to say that he doubted whether his prolonged absence from felicity had been wholly his own fault. He died in his bed after twenty-five years of happy, idle, inglorious restoration. All things considered, it was a remarkable performance.

The Church came back with the King, having never really been away, although the establishment had had a thin time during the Interregnum. In 1660 the temporal authority of ecclesiastical persons, taken away in 1641, was formally restored, so that the bishops could return to the House of Lords and the ecclesiastical courts could resume their functions, although the notorious Court of High Commission (which Puritans had likened to the Holy Office, the Roman Inquisition) remained abolished. Vastly more important than any such constitutional legislation was the formulation of a penal code enabling the Church to restrict and repress its rivals in the Sects. This re-establishment of the supremacy of the Anglican parson was effected by making it difficult for anyone who failed to subscribe to the Thirty-nine Articles of the Church of England and the Book of Common Prayer to preach, to teach, or even to reside in the urban areas of England. Rejection of the doctrines of transubstantiation and presbytery alike was the object of the exercise known collectively, and inaccurately, as the 'Clarendon Code'. It was to remain in many of its essentials an integral part of English law until the nineteenth century, though it was later tempered by the compromising practice known as 'Occasional Conformity' and by magisterial laxity in its enforcement as, with the passage of time and the cooling of doctrinal passions, the restored regime gained confidence in itself. It continued to embody the Church–State complex, as celebrated by Richard Hooker in his *Laws of Ecclesiastical Polity* in the reign of Queen Elizabeth, long after it had ceased to bear much relation to the facts of English life. The notion that two, or more, religions could live together in one state without confusion, treason or sedition was remarkably late in gaining acceptance in the modern world. Some have thought that it only gained acceptance when religion ceased to be a matter of belief and became a 'mere matter of opinion'. Opinion, or at any rate its printed expression, was at this period regulated, for the only time in England (apart from time of war), by a statutory censorship in the form of a Licensing Act. The operation of the Act was limited to a duration of two years. It was renewed at intervals only until 1695, when it appears to have been allowed to lapse without any particular protest or regret.

The Anglican Church at this time had every prospect of becoming a persecuting Church after the manner of the Roman Catholic Church with its monopolistic position in France and elsewhere. This was in no small part prevented, paradoxically enough, by the presence of a Roman Catholic or a crypto-Catholic ruler, James II, on the English throne, and his anomalous position as lawful head of the Church of England. Both Charles II and James II issued 'Declarations of Indulgence' to suspend the laws against Nonconformists, and certainly after the promulgation of the Clarendon Code indulgence might be thought to have been called for. Charles's declaration could perhaps be interpreted as an endeavour after that liberty of conscience which he had promised in the Declaration of Breda before his return. In both cases, however, it was plain enough that the Kings were less concerned with the liberties of their Protestant nonconformist subjects than with the privileges they wished to extend to their co-religionists of the Roman faith. This became perfectly plain in the case of James II, whose Declaration of Indulgence in 1688 was declined by his Protestant nonconformist subjects, largely through the influence of the Marquis of Halifax's *Letter to a Dissenter* under the text *Timeo Danaos et dona ferentes*. The Protestant dissenters of London were thus induced to stand aside, along with the Anglican clergy, seven of whose bishops were unavailingly indicted for libel for petitioning against the King's command that his gracious act of indulgence should be read in their churches. The acquittal of the seven was the flash-point of the Revolution of 1688.

After the Revolution the Protestant dissenters were rewarded by the exiguous terms of the Toleration Act of 1689. The Act embodied no principle of toleration, but simply gave a very limited exemption from statutory penalties to Protestant Non-conformists, explicitly excluding from its benefits Roman Catholics, Unitarians, Jews, and all who had no religious creed. It was the Stock Exchange and the Bank of England that did most to forward religious toleration in England, as Voltaire remarked after his stay in London in the reign of George I, when he was delighted to observe the way in which Englishmen of all religions, after attending their denominational churches on a Sunday, went freely and without quarrelling to these places of commercial intercourse on a Monday. As early as 1669 a Parliamentary Committee on Trade had been prepared to advocate 'some ease and relaxation in ecclesiastical matters' as 'likely to assist in the improvement of the trade of the kingdom'. The sentiment may be taken as a sign of the times, embodying as it does a consideration which was to become typical of the new climate of opinion.

Men were fond of citing the example of the Dutch, a busy, rich, commercial people who, it was perhaps somewhat too readily assumed, flourished because they enjoyed religious freedom. They seemed to provide the success story of the century, filling much the same role in English imaginations as the Americans were to fill in a later age. From the opening of the century Holland had become the protagonist in the world drama of colonial expansion, the first to realize the true meaning of colonies and the development of the home trade, snatching from Portugal the control of the Eastern Archipelago and threatening, through the efficiency of her mercantile marine, to absorb the whole carrying trade of the world. Observers, and would-be rivals, were more than a trifle mystified by the enormously profitable achievements of this small people with so few apparent natural advantages and a constitution that passed the wit of man (at any rate of Englishmen) to understand. How had it been done, how was it still being done? Sir William Temple's *Observations on the United Provinces* (composed after his return in 1670 from his ambassadorship at the Hague) afforded some valuable enlightenment, but on the whole the English remained fixed in their favourite posture of puzzled animosity, a posture which did not preclude them from that sincerest form of flattery, imitation. They fought the Dutch in a whole succession of 'Dutch Wars' under the Commonwealth and under Charles II, principally in defence of the Acts of Navigation of 1652 and 1660 which were designed to exclude the Dutch from the carrying trade to and from English ports, Acts which were for long to prove ineffective because the Dutch were deeply entrenched and the British mercantile marine was inadequate to compete. In the meantime England learnt a great deal about financial techniques from Amsterdam, and developed her early banking system from Dutch patterns. In 1688 she was to go to the United Provinces for a Protestant king, William III, to replace the intolerable Papist, James II. After that she went steadily into the enterprises planned by William III for the defeat of Louis XIV. The War of the Spanish Succession made the fortunes of Great Britain as a world power. At its conclusion, the Dutch accused her of treating them as a defeated enemy instead of a victorious ally. There was some truth in this, but the little republic had not the staying power to emerge as a successful contestant in a great continental war, and her fate was sealed after the Peace of Utrecht in 1713. She had been the rival, ally and victim of England, all within a century.

The quality of life in England on the eve of the Glorious Revolution was not wholly represented by the profligacy of Whitehall, Westminster and Drury Lane. Even in the darkest years, 1665–7, the years of the plague and the Fire of London, when the Dutch sailed into the Medway, and it might have seemed that England's sun was setting in a blazing inferno of the Divine Wrath, some fine and memorable things were happening. John Milton, old and blind in a world that had fallen in ruin about him, brought out his *Paradise Lost* in 1667, while the brave folk of Eyam shut themselves up in their tiny village among the Derbyshire hills, prepared to die in their fetid solitude rather than run away and carry the plague to the rest of the countryside. Although, when the Fire of London was out, a priceless opportunity was missed to rebuild the city after the plans of Sir Christopher Wren, which would have made London the finest capital in Europe for ever and a day, some handsome town houses were built by Nicholas Barbon (son of Praisegod Barebone of immortal memory[1]), notably in Red Lion Square and Bedford Row. It was not until after the Treaty of Utrecht in 1713 that the famous Georgian phase of urban house-building began, but Nicholas Barbon deserves to be remembered as a pioneer or precursor of a great age. His best memorial is in Devereux Court, hard by Essex Street and the Temple.

Great poetry, great courage, and some pioneer building were accompanied by quiet foundation-laying in science and technology. The names of the first generation of the Fellows of the Royal Society read like a roll-call of the modern mind. There is the Hon. Robert Boyle, 'youngest son of the first Earl of Cork, and the Father of Modern Chemistry'; Sir William Petty, founder of population statistics and 'political arithmetic'; Dr John Wilkins, Bishop of Chester and brother-in-law of Oliver Cromwell, who had published his treatise, *Mathematical Magic*, on mechanics and machines, as early as 1648, and ten years earlier his *Discovery of a New World*, on the moon; Robert Hooke, the professional experimentalist, who, it was said, could do almost everything; Christopher Wren, scientist and architect, who, in designing the Sheldonian theatre at Oxford, inaugurated in 1669 a building which Sir John Summerson has said 'of all buildings in the world most exactly reflects the early image of that Society and embodies its philosophy'. John Evelyn, another member of the Royal Society, who was present at the inauguration of Wren's building, tells us that Dr South, the University Orator, made a speech on that occasion which was 'not without some malicious and undecent reflections on the Royal Society as underminers of the University, which was very foolish and untrue, as well as unseasonable...' Not everybody, it is evident, was prepared to applaud the Society, pioneer of empiricism, close observation, and experiment as advocated by its intellectual ancestor, Sir Francis Bacon. To a don like Dr South, even the Royal Society had something of the aspect of a conspiracy in the 1660s. 'Underminers of the University', he said.

Sir Thomas Browne was still writing his jewelled prose, and was not to leave the scene until 1682. In 1667 'fat Tom

---

[1] See above, p. 161.

Sprat' (later Bishop of Rochester, and one of the seven bishops who stood up to James II), writing the first history of the Royal Society, delivered a grave warning against 'the luxury and redundance of speech'. He concluded that 'eloquence ought to be banished out of all civil societies as a thing fatal to peace and good manners'. Sir Thomas Browne could write of botany in terms of 'the elegant co-ordination of vegetables', or 'the quincunciall, lozenge, or net-work plantations of the ancients, artificially, naturally, mystically considered'. The Royal Society, however, was resolved 'to separate the knowledge of nature from the colours of rhetoric, the devices of fancy, or the delightful deceit of fables', and to promote the reformation of natural philosophy 'not by a glorious pomp of words; but by the silent, effective, and unanswerable arguments of real productions...They have exacted from all their Members, positive expressions, clear senses; a native easiness; bringing all things as near the mathematical plainness as they can; and preferring the language of artisans, countrymen, and merchants before that of wits or scholars.' Setting its face against the old sumptuous and elaborate prose, with its 'amplifications, digressions, and swellings of style', it demanded of its members 'a close, naked, natural way of speaking'. A line was being firmly drawn between science and literature, and the physician of Norwich whose experimental adventures had included a diet of spiders and bees was never to be admitted. When, a few years later, one of the Society's more distinguished members, John Locke, set down his 'thoughts concerning Education', he thought it necessary to warn parents against a proclivity for poetry in their sons, for, he said, 'it is very seldom seen that anyone discovers mines of gold or silver in Parnassus'. He was prepared to bracket poetry with gaming. They usually went together, and were 'alike in this, too, that they seldom bring any advantage but to those who have nothing else to live on'. It is clear that by 1688 or thereabouts the English mind was well on the way to that 'dissociation of sensibility' to which the late Thomas Stearns Eliot used to relate so many of the woes of the modern world. This, and not the plot which brought in Dutch William, was perhaps the real Revolution of 1688, heralded—like so much else—by John Locke. And it was far from 'Glorious'.

As generally happens in sad and bad times, some good came out of evil. The year after the Popish Plot[1] saw the passage (by counting one fat peer as twelve, Bishop Burnet tells us[2]) of the Habeas Corpus Amendment Act, which vastly improved the effectiveness of that ancient procedure which enables the subject under arrest to secure speedy trial or release from detention: except in case of detention for debt, or in civil cases. A number of defects still awaited attention until a further amendment was made in 1816, but after 1679 neither judges nor jailers could refuse to issue or to receive the Writ of Habeas Corpus without incurring very heavy penalties. Perhaps, though it is by no means certain, another benefit may be said to have followed upon the Exclusion Crisis of 1680: the naming,[3] but not precisely the origination, of Whigs and Tories. During these years, too, there came about a sharper application of the principle of appropriation of parliamentary supply, or the voting of funds, to specific purposes. Here again it may be said that good came out of evil, for the proviso which improved the procedure in 1665 came from what Clarendon calls the 'restless brain' of Sir George Downing, one of the tellers of the Exchequer. This improvement in the conduct of public finance was symptomatic of the process by which, in

[1] The Popish Plot, for the murder of Charles II and the setting up of his Catholic brother, James, Duke of York, was discovered, and to a large extent invented, by a murky character named Titus Oates. It caused much suffering to innocent people, and helped to perpetuate the 'No Popery' neurosis, one of whose consequences was the bringing forward of the Exclusion Bill in 1679 for the exclusion of James from the succession, a campaign that went on for several years. Exclusion only triumphed by James II's own conduct and the Revolution of 1688.

[2] Gilbert Burnet (1643–1715), *History of His own Times* (1723), vol. II, p. 263.

[3] Those who petitioned the King to call a Parliament in 1680, thus enabling an Exclusion Bill to be promoted, have traditionally been supposed the original 'Whigs' (contraction of Whiggam, a Covenanters' cry in urging on their horses ?), while those who abhorred such interference with the royal prerogative acquired the nickname 'Tories', a name for a species of wild Irish. The names stuck long after their original meaning, if any, was forgotten. Roughly speaking they denote 'prerogative men', those who abhorred any meddling with the king's prerogative (Tories), and 'anti-prerogative men', those who were less particular (Whigs).

the second half of the seventeenth century, the Lord Treasurer developed as the leading minister of the Crown, and the Exchequer as the most important administrative department. Ultimately, and considerably owing to the long reign of Sir Robert Walpole, the office of First Lord of the Treasury was to become synonymous with the office of Prime Minister.

The greatest of the 'plots' of the seventeenth century was that which issued in the Revolution of 1688, when a number of nobility and gentry invited the Prince of Orange to liberate the country from the intolerable misgovernment of James II. If there was a revolutionary involved in this affair, it was the King, who aimed to subvert the constitution by a number of actions in the interest of his religion. True to the tradition of the Stuarts, he did not so much break the letter of the law as violate its spirit. Probably his sole illegality was his revival of the Court of High Commission despite the fourth and final clause of the statute 17, Car. I, cap. II, which specified that 'no new Court shall be erected...which shall or may have the like power, jurisdiction or authority as the said High Commission Court', although James typically called his revived court of 1686 an 'Ecclesiastical Commission'. The power to dispense with or to suspend the operation of statutes had never been forbidden by law but was evidently subversive, more especially the dispensing power (as the Declaration of Rights was to put it) 'as it hath been assumed and exercised of late'; that is, to enable the king to appoint his fellow religionists to commissions in the army. His maintenance of a camp of some 13,000 men on Hounslow Heath to overawe London amounted to political suicide, though Parliament had been prepared to grant James supply for large numbers of soldiers after the suppression of Monmouth's Rising at the beginning of his reign.[1] He steadily lost every important piece on the board: his bishops with the Trial of the Seven who petitioned against his Declaration of Indulgence; his knights and his castles when the

---

[1] James, Duke of Monmouth, an illegitimate son of Charles II, landed at Lyme Regis in the summer of 1685 to lead a Protestant rising against his uncle, James II. The West Country rebels were broken at Sedgemoor, which was followed by the 'Bloody Assize' of Judge Jeffreys.

army left him, headed by John Churchill, Colonel Kirke, and many other officers, at the time of the landing of the Prince of Orange; and finally his crown, when he dropped down the Thames in a vessel that had been specially left for his use two nights before Christmas 1688. Checkmate had been certain from the moment when a son was born to his Queen in June, holding out the intolerable prospect of a Roman Catholic succession. One Popish king was enough.

The Revolution of 1688 completed that of 1640. By setting up a salaried king on terms laid down in the Bill of Rights (and its appendix, the Act of Settlement of 1701[1]), it killed divine hereditary kingship stone dead. For Edmund Burke to declare a hundred years later that the Revolution was 'only a little one' was rather like the serving-maid's apology for her illegitimate baby, and not all the casuistry of Whig publicists in their role as conservatives over the next century and a half could conceal the fact that there had been a revolutionary break in English constitutional history. Even Maitland found it necessary to protest his innocence of Jacobite leanings when he arrived at this point in his Lectures on Constitutional History. 'It seems to me', he concluded, 'that we must treat the Revolution as a revolution: a very necessary and wisely conducted revolution, but still a revolution. We cannot work it into our constitutional law.' For the work of the Convention which brought William and Mary, James II's Protestant daughter and son-in-law, to the throne and passed the Bill of Rights was only declared legal retrospectively by the Parliament which was duly summoned by the writs of the new King and Queen. The apologists who try to smooth over the breach are engaged in the familiar English activity of 'building bridges behind us', seeking 'to join up again, as though it mattered to us to maintain the contact with the past'. The clauses of the Bill of Rights amount to little more, and to nothing less, than a restatement of the 'Auntient Rights and Liberties' of the people of England in the form of a point-by-point condemnation of everything that James II had done as 'utterly and directly contrary to the knowne Lawes and Statutes and Freedome of the

[1] See below, chapter 10, pp. 182–4.

Realm'. There are no general philosophical principles; and a number of matters that were to be burning issues in the near future, such as the responsibility of ministers and the king's control of foreign policy, are not touched on. Only after some dozen years of experience of William III were they tackled, most ineffectively, in the Act of Settlement. The foremost matter, although it is easy to forget the fact today, was the exclusion from the Crown forever of anyone holding communion with the See of Rome or anyone who shall marry such a person (amended in the Act of Settlement to the positive requirement of communion with the Church of England).

The Revolution was to be described as 'Glorious' because it was bloodless. One king had been replaced by another, and the country had gone on with its business as usual, while an Anglo-Dutch army had marched in arms from the Tamar to the Thames. Perhaps it was at this point in time, and not in August 1914, that the maxim 'Business as usual' became the national device. The point is that there was business, the multifarious business of a rich and inveterately commercial-minded community, to carry on. Nothing serves as quite so sure a guarantee of stability as a widely dispersed system of property. There were great disparities in wealth, but the type of the Englishman, as the titles of the early news-sheets indicate, was thought to be the craftsman and the freeholder. Little or nothing had yet been done to disinherit either. From top to bottom of society men were deeply pre-occupied in making money, than which, as Dr Johnson said, there are few more innocent occupations. At any rate, a society so preoccupied is unlikely to be a society of professional politi-cians. Politics would be only a part of the activity or the interest even of the few men who did govern the state. In the summer of 1688 the Earl of Devonshire was busily engaged in the building of his fine new house at Chatsworth. He had recently thought it better for his skin to keep himself out of the way of national politics in the capital, and Derbyshire was always a good place to frequent in troubled times—except, as it later proved, in 1745. Now, in the year 1688, his lordship was prepared to break off his building operations while he took part in the Revolution. They still show 'Revolution House' in the little village of Whittington, near Chesterfield, where the fourth Earl plotted for William of Orange with his fellow noblemen. His lordship set his hand to the written invitation to the Prince along with the signatures of other Whiggish notables, and a few weeks later, when 'the Protestant wind' had brought Prince William into Torbay and thence on his victorious, bloodless march to London, he was back on his building site. The reward of a dukedom at the hands of the new King made it doubly desirable to complete his handsome 'Palace in the Peak'. The whole episode gives much the same impression as the man of business who puts up a notice on his office door to say 'Back in ten minutes'. Of course there were lesser men of business who had regarded the situation with more trepidation than the Earl. We hear of a London master joiner who sent his family down to Derbyshire early in 1688, where, in the same year, Mrs Richardson gave birth to the infant Samuel, who was to learn from the girls of Smalley village that knowledge of the female heart which went into *Pamela* in 1740. Evacuation to Smalley in order to elude the rather transient perils of the 'Glorious Revolution' had its part to play in founding the English novel. Once more, as so often in seventeenth-century England, good came out of evil.

The English Revolution very often appears like that, an episode, a parenthesis, a sentence in brackets. Sir John Seeley once said that the British Empire was acquired in a fit of absence of mind. There is a similarly somnambulant quality about this, the most celebrated of English revolutions. Of course, its engineers had very good luck, for no one had a mind to interfere. Louis XIV offered assistance to James, but it was declined, and the Pope took a poor view of James's lunatic course. Most important of all, there was an excellent supply of great men of property who were prepared to stake their heads on the success of the event. Little wonder that they did the business with speed and efficiency. Every one of them knew that his head would fall if it failed. It did not fail. The nation could boast that it had changed its king with scarcely more ado than a man changes his hat. If it could do this, was there anything that it could not do? The English got into the habit after this of talking about revolutions with a certain levity. They even called their great political families 'the Revolution families'. Cashiering kings for misbehaviour became a commonplace of political theory because it had been a fact of political experience. Only when, in the later years of the eighteenth century, a different kind of revolution appeared in the world, did the English change their tune. It was then that the 'Whig trumpeter', Edmund Burke, gave it out that revolutions were very well when conducted by Whig gentlemen, and not otherwise. It was one of those things, like parliamentary government and cricket, it seems, in which the English had the sole copyright.

John Locke did not write his two *Treatises on Civil Government* (1690) after the Revolution of 1688 to justify the event. He was enunciating Whig political principles evolved in the Exclusion Bill crisis, and earlier, touching them up a trifle here and there in order to serve the cause of 'Our Great Restorer', which is his title for King William in his Preface. After all, he had been family physician to the household of the Earl of Shaftesbury, friend and adviser of the putative father of the Whigs. What John Locke chiefly supplied was a wholesome counterblast to the *Leviathan* of Thomas Hobbes. Hobbes was perpetually horrified by what he called 'the dissolute condition of masterlesse men', and convinced that dissolution of government must involve the dissolution of society, or anarchy. The history of the English Revolution had refuted him in this, and Locke opened the final chapter of his *Second Treatise* with the famous sentence: 'He that will, with any clearness, speak of the dissolution of government, ought in the first place to distinguish between the dissolution of the society and the dissolution of the government.' As for the argument that absolutism is the best guarantee of the subject's health and security: 'This is to think that men are so foolish that they take care to avoid what mischiefs may be done them by polecats or foxes, but are content, nay, think it safety, to be devoured by lions.' And then again: 'He that thinks absolute power purifies men's blood, and corrects the baseness of human nature, need read but the history of this, or any other age, to be convinced to the contrary.' Locke did not share Hobbes's fear and suspicion of men's everlasting inclination towards disorder. They (and he evidently means his countrymen) are rather too inclined to be patient under misgovernment than to rush into revolution.

People are not so easily got out of their old forms as some are apt to suggest...This slowness and aversion in the people to quit their old constitutions has in the many revolutions that have been seen in this kingdom, in this and former ages, still kept us to, or after some interval of fruitless attempts, still brought us back again to our old legislative of kings, lords, and commons; and whatever provocations have made the crown be taken from some of our princes' heads, they never carried the people so far as to place it in another line.

Tom Paine was to point out, a good deal later, that the crown could have been put on the head of Judge Jeffreys instead of James II's Protestant son-in-law. It was not the kind of point to interest John Locke. He preferred Burke's 'small and temporary deviation'. Few things are more striking when we read Locke's thoughts on revolution in England in 1690 than their resemblance to the thoughts of Burke when holding up the English Revolution as an example to the French in 1790.

Locke achieved the myth of the English Revolution of 1688, the sanctity of the constitution as the Revolution left it, and the foundation of a conservatism which was to petrify English political thinking for the greater part of the eighteenth century. Hobbes had been the Tamburlaine of philosophy, it has been said, and his thought a kind of conquering, subduing march, while Locke was more like his own William, 'our Great Restorer'. The two men justly represent the two halves of their century and of the revolution it accomplished. By Locke's time it was the day and hour to put away the swords and drums. Men were shrinking to life size once more, and Locke was—as he said in his epitaph— 'happy in his mediocrity', a word which meant moderation rather than commonplace. His was the quiet voice of the humble heart finding utterance after the tumult of a century. In him we hear, at last, the long, withdrawing roar of waters at the ebb.

10

The Century of Success

The English entered the eighteenth century as the successful people, and the century has been justly remembered as 'the English century'. They seemed, at least until the revolt of the American colonies, to possess the secret of success in government, in arms, in commerce and industry. All the world went to school to England for lessons in how to succeed. Their constitution was supposed to enshrine the secret of reconciling law and liberty, and, although it was reserved for Englishmen of the next century to talk of their form of government in terms of that 'far-off divine event towards which the whole creation moves', they were already assured by such influential observers as the Baron de Montesquieu that they were well on the way to it. The dominant philosophy of the age was the offspring of Newton and Locke, and was soon to be christened by Voltaire 'the English philosophy', and commended for adoption by all civilized peoples, and more especially the French. Their economy was proclaimed by the vast forest of masts in the Thames and by the handsome houses and equipages of the London merchants. With his country-house and his city opulence the English merchant was the financial equal of any baron. By close study of the Dutch and their financial techniques, the English had stabilized their economy, and their politics, with the foundation in 1694 of the Bank of England. They had also, with somewhat less confidence, founded a National Debt in the previous year. Both these institutions may be said to have had the effect of tying a large class of investors to the fortunes of the Revolution Settlement and the new dynasty. They were presently to invent not only spinning-jennies and the steam-engine, but the novel, the news-letter and the circulating library.

One war, known as the War of the Spanish Succession (1702–13), inaugurated an empire overseas by the acquisition of

Newfoundland, Nova Scotia, Hudson Bay, Gibraltar and Minorca; another, called the Seven Years War (1756–63), gave them mastery over Canada and India, precious islands in the Caribbean, a foothold in Africa, and even a mahogany concession in Honduras. All things considered, it was not remarkable that the English had a superstition about the number seven, as Tom Paine observed, with their wars, their terms of apprenticeship, leases, and transportation of felons. By 1763 men were talking of a British empire to rival that of the ancient Romans, whose splendid elegy Gibbon was to embark on some ten years later. Half a century earlier their Parliament had become the Parliament of Great Britain with the Act of Union with Scotland (1707), and the Union Jack now lacked only the red cross of St Patrick. Dr Arne's *Rule, Britannia!* had been adopted as a party song for those who were opposed to continental campaigns and thought Britain should confine herself to maritime and colonial warfare. During the Seven Years War it became a second national anthem. In 1771–2 Lord Chief Justice Mansfield ordered the discharge of James Somersett, a Negro slave, from the Court of King's Bench on a Writ of Habeas Corpus, with the famous words 'the black must be discharged', on the grounds that such an odious thing as slavery was contrary to the positive law of England and that a slave becomes a free man when his foot touches English soil. Not everyone was quite so sure. As the *Black Dwarf*, a Radical journal, remarked of his fellow countrymen: 'They sit in their armchairs singing *Rule Britannia* while the chains are riveting about their necks.'

The triumph of free institutions during the liberal epoch of modern history which comprises the eighteenth and nineteenth centuries was inaugurated by the victory of England over France, planned by William III and achieved by his true successor, John Churchill, Duke of Marlborough, in the reign of Queen Anne. William, 'our Great Restorer', came to England in order to further his life's work; this was, in the first place, to save his own country, the Netherlands, and then, incidentally, to save Europe, from being swallowed up by Louis XIV. He knew that France, by far the wealthiest and strongest power in the Western world, could only be curbed by the enlistment of England in the ranks of her enemies, a prospect which was unlikely to come to reality while the Roman Catholic or crypto-Catholic cousins of King Louis, Charles II and James II, occupied the throne, and determined the European alignment, of England. William cared nothing for Whigs and Tories, save as a couple of factions whose contemptible sham-fight over trivialities he must somehow manage in order to harness the sinews of a rich and energetic nation to the chariot he proposed to drive into the field of the forthcoming European wars. At the age of twenty-two he had become Stadtholder of Holland, the very year when the King of France had overrun and annexed four of the seven United Provinces of the Netherlands. The young Stadtholder had narrowly saved Holland itself by the drastic expedient of cutting the dykes to preserve Amsterdam and The Hague from the on-coming French legions. Thereafter he had built up an army recruited from all over Protestant Europe, and engineered a net-work of anti-French alliances which became the League of Augs-burg in 1686. All this had taken four years. It was to secure the adherence of England to his anti-French coalition that he came here in 1688. In the following year he brought his new kingdom into a Grand Alliance comprising Holland and the Empire. On 17 May England declared war on France. The War of the Grand Alliance was to last twelve years and to form the prelude to the War of the Spanish Succession which would occupy nearly the whole of the reign of Queen Anne (1702–14).

William was not a genius of war, but he was brave in battle and indomitable in defeat. Perhaps he suited the English the better for his recognizable capacity to turn a military reverse into a tactical withdrawal and to take punishment while hanging on to the ropes for the next assault, *reculer pour mieux sauter*. After the French took Namur he was beaten at Steinjirk in 1692, and again at Landen in 1693, yet he had retaken Namur by the end of 1695. 'Brave! Brave, by heaven!' cried Uncle Toby, recalling the King at Landen where he rode along the line to lead the charge against Conti; 'he deserves a crown!' To which Corporal Trim, who had been left upon the stricken field, added: 'As richly as a thief a halter!' For Trim was an Irishman and could remember the Boyne[1] and much else. The King's best fortunes in arms had been mostly in Ireland against the ex-King James, as his worst were on Sambre and Meuse. After Londonderry and Limerick, 'the City of the violated Treaty', no Irishman, whatsoever his religion and his loyalty to the Dutchman, could quite forgive King William. Aside from his chequered fortunes in the Low Countries, he was a skilled and tireless diplomatist, always envisaging the larger issue, prepared to suffer every set-back without deviating by a hair's breadth from the pursuit of his overmastering end. He looked what he was—as his portraits at Kensington Palace show him—a man of sorrows, often a sick man, a genius of endurance. The English never loved him, but they admired his obdurate courage and his inflexible singleness of purpose. He better deserved the title 'Guillaume le Taciturne' than his more attractive ancestor, and was also worthy of far more of their gratitude. He scorned popularity, and although he gave everything for their freedom and their future greatness, many of them went on drinking toasts after his death to 'the little gentleman in black velvet' who brought him to his death when his horse stumbled over a molehill.

At the end of his reign Parliament passed a vote of censure upon him in the form of an Act of Settlement, and shortly afterwards the Commons committed to prison five gentlemen of the County of Kent who had petitioned the House to grant the King ('whose great Actions for this Nation are writ in the Hearts of his Subjects') sufficient Bills of supply so 'that His Majesty may be enabled powerfully to assist his Allies before it is too late'. The settlement of the crown upon the Princess Sophia of Hanover, and her heirs being Protestants, was all that William could have wished, since Queen Mary, his wife, had died without issue in 1694, while her sister, the Princess Anne (later Queen Anne), had lost her last surviving child in 1700. The Princess Sophia, granddaughter of James I, was the nearest Protestant heir. But before thus settling the succession, Parliament laid down eight pro-

[1] Where William III had routed James in 1690. James thereafter fled to France. 'The Boyne' became the symbolic term for all the ills of Catholic Ireland vis-à-vis Protestant England.

visions, at least three of which reflected adversely upon William's conduct as a foreign king. In the first place the Act of Settlement forbade the engagement of the nation in any war for the defence of dominions or territories not belonging to the crown of England, and forbade any future sovereign to go out of the British dominions without Parliament's permission. As an adverse comment upon William's conduct in transacting high matters of state (especially in foreign policy) on his own initiative or with the knowledge and consent of a few trusted advisers, it was laid down that in future all matters relating to the well-governing of the kingdom which are properly cognizable by the Privy Council should be transacted there, and that all resolutions taken thereupon should be signed by such of the Privy Council as advise and consent to the same. While such provisions might be relied upon to provide evidence against a Minister in the event of his impeachment, they also militated against the development of the nascent Cabinet. Fortunately they were repealed in 1705 before they could ever come into force. Another clause of the Act of Settlement even more drastically calculated to impede the growth of a modern practice of Cabinet, or ministerial, responsibility prohibited any person holding an office or place of profit under the King, or receiving a pension from the Crown, from serving as a Member of the House of Commons. This again was modified by the Statute of 1705 so as to allow a Member to hold an office or place of profit providing that he secured re-election, an arrangement which ensured until very recent times that the formation of every Administration was followed by a crop of by-elections. The provision that no one not a native of the realm should be permitted to accept office or serve in Parliament was an obvious shot at King William's Dutch friends and favourites. Two excellent and abiding provisions forbade the Royal Pardon from serving as a bar to impeachment or to the trial of Ministers for treason by the House of Lords on their prosecution by the House of Commons. This species of royal obstructiveness had made it difficult for the Commons to punish Charles II's favourite, Danby, and William III's advisers (Lord Somers in particular) who had given him their assistance in negotiating the Partition

Treaties of 1698 and 1700, embodying arrangements for the frustration of Louis XIV's designs on the Spanish Empire at the death of Charles II of Spain: the achievement which completed his life work *vis-à-vis* that aggressive monarch.[1] The Act of Settlement also set the seal upon the seventeenth-century endeavours to secure an independent judiciary by requiring judges' patents to be made *quamdiu se bene gesserint* (during good behaviour), and their salaries 'ascertained and established', while it was provided that a judge might be removed from office upon an address of both Houses of Parliament.

The Act of Settlement represents the completion of the Revolution of 1688, or so the constitutional historians, who are very proud of it, would tell us. It reflects the rootedly oppositional habit of the House of Commons after nearly a century of struggle with the Stuart kings. It is implied in every line that the business of the House of Commons is neither to govern nor to produce a government, but to oppose the king's ministers; not to support them, or to criticize them, or to overthrow them by votes of no confidence on the floor of the House, but to exclude them, and if necessary impeach them as maleficent individuals. The servants of the Crown were readily identified with 'placemen'— royal agents or creatures or yes-men, conspirators against the House's independence and the people's liberties. Whigs and Tories alike assumed almost instinctively an 'anti-Court' attitude, an attitude proudly associated with the 'Country Party' of the reign of Charles II, and recognizably present even in the reign of George III: morally self-righteous, taking for granted the sycophantic avarice of all courtiers and the inherent corruption of all professional politicians, and implying always that the virtue and patriotism of England were the preserve of the country gentlemen. The attitude long outlived the age of the Stuarts, and it delayed the growth of properly 'parliamentary' government, in the sense of cabinet government based on a disciplined party majority, until the reign of Queen Victoria. Indeed, in the larger historical perspective, such an in-and-out-party parliamentary system of government may well appear to have been a phenomenon of

[1] See above, p. 180.

rather less than a century of British history. Perhaps because it made possible the classic parliamentary duel of Mr Gladstone and Mr Disraeli it has been readily assumed to be the norm of parliamentary history, a kind of Platonic Idea towards which everything before it was tending to approximate and away from which everything since has been drifting.

King William sought to rule above parties, to employ mixed ministries, which often meant that he was trying to rule through ministers whose party colouring, and principles, were in opposition to those of the House of Commons on which the king must depend for his supplies, and more especially for the upkeep of his armed forces. Neither he nor his servants, least of all the House of Commons, could be expected to understand that parliamentary ministries were the only guarantee of a minimum of smooth and effective government. Only at the end of his reign was he enabled, by tailoring his ministry to a Tory pattern in order to achieve some consonance with a Tory House of Commons, to secure parliamentary authorization to the European alliances and alignments requisite to the next and vital stage of the contest with France. The settlement of the succession in the Protestant House of Hanover after the death of Anne may properly be regarded as an integral part of these arrangements, and both political parties were, before William died, sufficiently reconciled to support both the Grand Alliance and an ultimate Hanoverian succession. Even as he died in 1701, the five gentlemen of Kent who had begged in their petition to the House of Commons for national unity and a generous supply for the King in order that he might be 'enabled powerfully to assist his Allies before it is too late', were recalling his 'great Actions for this Nation', actions which 'can never, without the blackest Ingratitude, be forgot': these gentlemen were being committed to prison for venturing to present a petition so 'scandalous, insolent and seditious; tending to destroy the Constitution of Parliaments, and to subvert the established Government of this Realm'. His Majesty's Commons were not to be told their duty by country gentlemen begging 'that this House will have Regard to the Voice of the People'. Parliament had already passed a Tumultuous Petitioning Act in 1661 to repel 'pressure from without', and for many generations to come—from the Yorkshire Association in 1780 to the Chartist Convention of 1839—Parliament was to take a jealous attitude to anyone who presumed to instruct it. In 1715 it was to pass a Septennial Act which extended the life of Parliament from three to seven years without any reference whatever to 'the voice of the people', and in wilful subversion—as a dissentient minority of peers pointed out—of so essential a part of our constitution as the right of the people to rid themselves of representatives deemed to have betrayed their trust, 'and to choose better men in their places'.

The parliamentary high-handedness against which John Wilkes was to make his stand half a century later was already in evidence, and some were inclined to say that the tyranny of kings had now given place to the tyranny of parliaments. 'In truth,' Macaulay writes of the House of Commons which sought to get through the House of Lords a Resumption Bill for divesting the King's friends of their rewards in land in both England and Ireland, by 'tacking' it to a money-bill, 'in truth the House was despotic, and was fast contracting the vices of a despot'. In commenting upon their Lordships' objection to 'tacking', one member went so far as to say: 'They object to tacking, do they? How would they like to have bills of supply with bills of attainder tacked to them?' 'An atrocious threat,' Macaulay exclaims, 'worthy of the tribune of the French Convention in the worst days of the Jacobin tyranny.' The insolent temper and oppositional habit of the House of Commons at this time were never more frankly expressed than by the gentlemen who rebutted the charge of 'flying in the King's face' by the assertion: 'Our business is to fly in the King's face. We were sent here to fly in the King's face.'

William's anxiety to secure the Protestant succession in the House of Hanover by Act of Parliament before he died was perhaps enhanced by his knowledge that the Princess Anne, his immediate heir, harboured a good deal of daughterly feeling for her father, James II, and her half-brother in exile at Saint Germains. Whether or not she ever sought to persuade William ideologies, thereby making it extremely unlikely that such a thing would ever be allowed to happen again.

'Push of pike' was the mode of fighting for foot-soldiers, though pikes had other uses, notable for pulling down ripe fruit and hooking clean linen off clothes-lines and splitting faggots. 'I cannot conceive what these fellows are doing with their weapons,' one commander groaned. The weather, too, was typical of the island for this peculiarly English war: wild winds in August, mild and foggy winters, plenty of rain at any time, blazing sunshine for the decisive battle of Naseby. There were few real atrocities, though tempers were lost when Catholic met Puritan head-on, as at Bolton, or a garrison had to be overcome by storm, as at Basing House. When Fairfax court-martialled and shot the Cavalier officers Lucas and Lisle in the dry-moat at Colchester castle, there was sufficient outcry to show how rare it was, and the 'Victims' were memorialized on the spot. More typical, from first to last, was the Parliamentarian Sir William Waller's message to the Royalist Sir Ralph Hopton on the eve of the battles of Lansdown and Roundway Down in July 1643: 'My affections to you are so unchangeable that hostility itself cannot violate my friendship. We are both upon the stage, and we must act the parts assigned to us in this tragedy. Let us do it in a way of honour and without personal animosities.' A war of two small minorities of gentlemen might well remain a gentlemanly war. In the age of the Thirty Years War it must have appeared a family tiff, at least until the King intrigued with the Scots to start a second round, thereby earning for himself the title 'The Man of Blood'. The conduct of hostilities deteriorated after that. Cromwell began to ship prisoners to the Barbadoes. Few of the ruins attributed to him, however, were his work, and when the fighting was over the country was hardly defaced by deep or lasting scars. Even the memorial to the decisive action of the war, at Naseby, was put up in the wrong place, as if men had forgotten or did not wish to remember too well.

The divisions between the parties to the English Civil War were neither class divisions nor those of physical geography. Certainly London and the south-east, areas of trade and strong of the feasibility of James III's succeeding herself in due course cannot be certainly known. Nevertheless, she came to the throne in 1702 as the securely Protestant child of her father's first marriage, with Anne Hyde, and as an ardent devotee of the Church of England. This assured her of the whole-hearted support of the Tories, who at this time were very far from being the Jacobite enthusiasts that many of them were to show themselves to be at her death in 1714. Even Henry St John, the future Viscount Bolingbroke and would-be engineer of the succession of James III, was in 1701 talking of going over to Hanover and making interest with 'those that are like to wear the crown of England', both for the service of his country and—as he was bold enough to add—the advancement of his own fortune ('investing in futures', as it were). When Queen Anne lay dying, and 'fortune turned rotten before it was ripe', Bolingbroke was first minister of the Crown for just three days before the Queen handed the white wand of the Lord Treasurer to the Earl of Shrewsbury. In the following year Henry St John left hurriedly for France, where he became secretary of state to the Stuart family, married a niece of Madame de Maintenon, and composed some masterpieces of Augustan prose, notably on the study of history, on party, on patriotism, and on 'The Idea of a Patriot King'. The Prime Minister, Robert Walpole, allowed him to return to England in 1723, but not to resume his seat in the House of Lords. He kept up his vitriolic attacks on the great Minister to the end, chiefly in the opposition paper, *The Craftsman*, and when in 1756 Edmund Burke published his *Vindication of Natural Society* as the work of 'a Late Noble Writer' it was widely thought to be a posthumous piece of Viscount Bolingbroke, of whose marble style it was an excellent parody. 'Who now reads Bolingbroke, who ever read him through?' Burke was to ask a little later. The answer must be, not George III but Benjamin Disraeli, who was to enshrine him in the Pantheon of the Tory Party. Perhaps the clever scoundrel was better remembered as the friend who taught Alexander Pope the distorted Lockeian philosophy of the *Essay on Man* at Twickenham. After all, the *Essay* was dedicated to him.

> Awake, my St John! leave all meaner things
> To low ambition, and the pride of Kings...

But 1732 was a little late in the day.

What do the English remember of Queen Anne? First, of course, that she is dead: a statement which was to become a proverb (meaning 'old news'). Secondly, perhaps, that she presided over a charming style of architecture which the barbarians of a later age were to describe as 'ghastly good taste'. Some few, perhaps, recall her as Pope's 'great Anna' of *The Rape of the Lock*:

> Here thou, great ANNA! whom three realms obey,
> Dost sometimes counsel take—and sometimes Tea.

Finally there is 'Brandy Nan' whom Henry Esmond saw in Windsor Great Park, 'tearing down the Park slopes after her stag-hounds, and driving her one-horse chaise—a hot, red-faced woman, not in the least resembling the statue of her which turns its stone back upon St Paul's. She was, William Makepeace Thackeray told the Victorians in 1852, 'neither better bred nor wiser than you and me, though we knelt to hand her a letter or a washhand basin,' adding with the inverted snobbery of which he was a master, 'Why should History go on kneeling to the end of time?...I would rather have History familiar than heroic...' Another master in the same *genre*, Walter Bagehot, said of her: 'A smaller person has never been placed by the caprices of fate amid great affairs than "the good Queen Anne".' For, he declared, 'her comprehension was as limited as her affections'. She chose a minister according to whether he wore a tie-wig or a full-bottomed one, and changed her party-political affiliations with her ladies-in-waiting. The great historian who has written the history of her reign in the present century has corrected this travesty. 'Only those who have not followed recent historical writing will be surprised to find', the late G. M. Trevelyan wrote in the Preface to *Blenheim*, 'that I think Anne had a policy of her own, independent of her favourites,' and he closes his third and final volume with the judgement that the last Stuart to rule the island was 'for all her simplicity, the wisest and most triumphant of her race'. In the perspective of the general incompetence of the Stuarts, this may not be very high praise, but it is just and decent.

The Age of Queen Anne, like that of George III and of Queen Victoria, is one in which the glory of the monarchs owes almost everything to the glory of the society over which they presided, the reflected luminosity of great men and great events. The story of Queen Anne's reign, as Trevelyan wrote in the long and lovely sentence which opens his great *History*, 'moves among brilliant societies and reveals distant landscapes'.

Whoever writes of the England of that day must show Marlborough's many-coloured columns winding along the banks of Rhine, Danube and Maas; English fleets heaving on Mediterranean and Biscayan waters, or coasting the West Indian islands and the misty Newfoundland shore; Gibraltar's rock rising into azure above unwonted smoke and uproar; envoys posting over land and ocean with Godolphin's gold and Marlborough's persuasive counsel to half the Courts of Europe from Lisbon to Moscow; nearer home, the fashionable arena of sedan chairs and glass coaches between St James's Palace and the Parliament House, the battle ground of political and literary intrigue in the days of Swift, Addison and Pope—with Wren's dome in the distance still rising to its completion above the masts of the river, and beyond it the Tower, the workshop of Newton as Master of the Mint.

This little nation of some five and a half million people, which yet had 'Wren for its architect, Newton for its scientist, Locke for its philosopher, Bentley for its scholar, Pope for its poet, Addison for its essayist, Bolingbroke for its orator, Swift for its pamphleteer, and Marlborough to win its battles, had the recipe for genius'.

The Age of Queen Anne established the nation upon the path of its modern destiny, and the salvoes of cannon which proclaimed the accession of the House of Hanover at her death, echoing the guns of Blenheim, proclaimed 'the triumph of English liberty, religion and law'. No victory in the long tale of European conflict was ever more decisive than Marlborough's at Blenheim (1704). It broke 'the exorbitant power of France' for generations to come and established the tone of eighteenth-century civilization with a chord on the cor anglais that not even the cannonade of Valmy or the crash of Austerlitz was to subdue. The genius of Marlborough and the 'tow-row-row' of the British Grenadiers from Blenheim to Malplaquet, seconded by Rooke and Cloudesley Shovell at Gibraltar, changed the path of destiny not only for England but for the world, because the people who came out upon the uplands of the eighteenth century at the close of the War of the Spanish Succession constituted a greater nation than that of Harry the King, or Elizabeth, or Cromwell, a nation which, for all its Whig and Tory shadow-boxing, was united under one law and one Parliament from the Hebrides to the Straits of Dover, secure in the possession of free institutions and a pathway upon the waters that lead to the uttermost ends of the earth. Old men who remembered the banners taken at Worcester fight being laid up in Westminster Hall in 1651 rejoiced that the trophies of Blenheim bore no native devices but only those of the King of France and the Elector of Bavaria. 'Mons. Tallard and two other Generals are in my coach', Marlborough wrote to his wife Sarah from the saddle at the end of the day. Marshal Tallard was on his way to honourable captivity at Nottingham where he was to teach the local gentry how to grow celery and to lay out gardens after the fashion of Versailles.

> But what they fought each other for
> I never could make out...

There was little or no excuse for the ignorance, or the stupidity, of Old Caspar in Southey's poem. The littlest Whig in England knew better, were it only by hind-sight, for the terms of the Treaty of Utrecht (1713) were to underwrite Great Britain's title to the rank of a great power steadily advancing to eminence for the next two centuries. The very title, 'Great Britain', was indeed inaugurated by the war which sped the formation of the Union with Scotland and the foundation of the British Parliament in 1707. The Scots received a proportionate representation in both Houses of the single Parliament of the 'United Kingdom', and, while retaining their own Church, their own judiciary, and their own law, were liberated from all the commercial restrictions which had hitherto applied to them as subjects of a separate, or 'foreign', realm. They were given assistance in paying off the Scots national debt and indemnification for the losses that many Scots had suffered as shareholders in the Darien Company, or 'The Company for Trading with Africa and the Indies' (1698–1700) founded by Scottish merchants on the pestiferous Isthmus of Darien and ruined (at least in part) by the machinations of the English. No doubt the Scots regarded such economic or commercial equality as they received by the Union as resembling the equality at which Voltaire mocked when he spoke of the equality of rich and poor alike to sleep on doorsteps. They had neither the capital nor the business organization to reap the benefits held out to them by the Union. Their disappointment with what to most Scots appeared to be a cruel mockery soon found expression in a wholesale recourse to smuggling, which became almost the national industry of the Scots for more than a generation. In the long run, as all the world knows, they were to apply their energies and intelligence to staffing both the British Empire and the enterprises of the forthcoming Industrial Revolution. Not an outpost of empire, not a factory, not an ocean-going craft on the commercial waterways of the British-speaking world but held a North Briton as District Officer, or overseer, or chief engineer. A race of maritime leopards, or vikings, plundering the earth from their island lair, Oswald Spengler once called the English; skilled enough to get subject peoples to do the dangerous and dirty work for them. After the Jacobite rising behind the Young Pretender in 1745, the Scots clan-chiefs lost their heritable jurisdictions, and for a time even the tartan was proscribed. Marshal Wade had already driven his great roads into the Highlands, and Pitt was to harness the magnificent fighting qualities of the clansmen in the Scottish Regiments of the Crown. The English, afflicted perhaps by the well-known difficulty men have in forgiving any one whom they have injured, for long suffered from that anti-Scots phobia which found its bitterest political expression in their hatred of Lord Bute and its classic comedy in Dr Johnson's baiting of James Boswell. But Scotland was by that time well on its way to the Scottish Enlightenment of Hume, and Robertson, and Adam Smith, with Edinburgh rising into the intellectual and architectural glories of the 'Athens of the North' whose latter-day conquest of the Sassenachs finally came with Sir Walter Scott and the Waverley novels.

The War of the Spanish Succession might have ended in 1706, when Louis XIV was prepared to come to terms, had not the Whigs decided on a policy of 'No peace without Spain!' This meant that England would fight until she could be certain of securing suitably rich commercial advantages from King Louis's ally. It is not true that the Whigs as commercial men were intent on serving the turn of trade and commerce at the expense of the Tory country gentlemen who paid the land-tax. For one thing, there was no such neat alignment of economics and party politics, and for another the Tories were as eager to fight the war *à outrance* as anyone when it became pretty clear in 1708 that they were winning it. Rather than abandon Spain, Lord Peterborough, the hero of Barcelona (which he had captured with great dash and adroitness in 1706), told them, when he came back to England, that the country should be prepared to submit to a land-tax of nineteen shillings in the pound. They grumbled, of course, but they were proud to pay now that they could see rich returns for their money, which they had not seen in the days of King William's inconclusive campaigns on the Maas. Only one Peer, Lord Scarborough, was ready to oppose the country's committing itself so far as to seek the partition of the Spanish empire in 1707. The English imagination was still bright with the vision of El Dorado which had haunted Raleigh and the English adventurers a century earlier. Two years before the peace of Utrecht, Robert Harley, Lord Oxford, secured the incorporation of a South Sea Company, in anticipation of the untold riches that would be harvested after the war. The first shareholders were state creditors, persons who had lent the government their money. By this assignation to the South Sea Company of the consolidated National Debt with a guaranteed interest of 6 per cent it became much more than a party-political concern to secure all, and if possible more than all, the benefits promised by the Spaniards in the *Asiento* contract: a transfer from France to Great Britain of the monopoly of the South American slave-trade for thirty years. As so often happens in negotiating a peace treaty, the prospective advantages were already pledged before the final act was drawn, and the Dutch complaint that they had a claim to a fair share of the Asiento benefits was incapable of being met. The South Sea Company, it might be imagined by dabblers in divine retribution, would in future labour under the curse which afflicts, however belatedly, those who traffic in human flesh and blood. But when the South Sea Bubble burst in 1720, it was not on account of the defalcations of the Directors at South Sea House (the company was on the whole well and honestly managed) but on account of the inflation of share prices in general by the mushroom growth of companies with little or no capital resources, a bubble structure that would be blown away with the first gale of diminished confidence that blew. Walpole, becoming First Lord of the Treasury and Chancellor of the Exchequer, proved to be the pilot who weathered the storm. His success in coping with this, the first great crisis to strike a people who had yet to learn the rudiments of sound financial speculation, was not due to his being a financial wizard but to his consummate skill in political manœuvre. He managed the situation in the terms he knew best: in terms of politics. His personal salvation amidst the shoals of the great storm he owed to the services of his own stockbroker, or financial man of business, Robert Jacombe.

If Walpole was not the first prime minister, it is very certain that no one else was, for he held for more than twenty years (1721–42) the essential position of a prime minister in a monarchical constitution: that is to say that he held the Commons because he had the royal favour, and he was indispensable to the King because he alone could manage the Commons. He was, in short, the King's minister in the House of Commons, and he represented the House of Commons with (or to) the King. It was not a matter of his becoming Mayor of the Palace, because the Hanoverian kings could not speak English. They could speak French perfectly well, and so could everyone else who was anybody in that century. If the Hanoverians had lost control, it would have been because they did not care to keep it. But they did not lose it. They were always the real masters of their own affairs in everything that mattered to them, and Walpole knew it, as did everyone else. Walpole had to persuade the royal master that he wanted what Walpole wanted, something best achieved in the case of George II through Walpole's clever and faithful ally, Queen Caroline. At the same time, Walpole showed the royal master that he was indispensable because he alone could manage the Commons, and for that purpose he built up and nourished with exceeding care his influence in East Anglia. There, by means of friends and kinsmen, he had the most substantial basis of his authority in an age and a society where all politics was ultimately local politics.

With Walpole and his 'Robinocracy', the country entered upon the long flat plain of the Hanoverian Age, the happiest if not the noblest era of its modern history. Before it lay a vista of stepped roofs and Dutch gardens, Palladian façades and ornamental waters, neatly hedged fields and fat sheep, turnips and marl-pits, with quiet market-towns in the middle distance and dense woodland closing the horizon. Over all arch the clear skies of East Anglia, the high roof of Walpole's country. This is the time of moderate men, and in such a vista moderate men look big enough, even if they generally act small. The representative figure in the landscape is Daniel Defoe, a busy journalist and a Dissenter who had drawn the sword for the Duke of Monmouth in youth, though no one knows what he had done with it since then, unless he had beaten it into a steel pen to write on *Public Credit* and an *Essay on Loans* (both in 1710), a *General History of Trade* (1713), and *Robinson Crusoe* (1719). Robinson Crusoe is the characteristic image of this world: 'isolated economic man, pitting his lonely strength successfully against Nature, in a remote part of the earth, and carrying on a little missionary activity as a sideline'. The last great novel before *Robinson Crusoe* had been *Don Quixote* (1605), the chivalric satire of a soldier of Spain; the next was to be *Pamela* (1741), by 'the little printer' of Salisbury Court, Fleet Street, a Dissenter like Defoe. The novel is the invention of moderate men, the art form of the middle classes and urban life, but there is a whole world between Richardson and Cervantes, and the chivalric ethic of the Knight of La Mancha was already as antique as the myth of King Arthur. Before the century was out, the ethic of business was to find its apotheosis in the Felicific Calculus of Jeremy Bentham, and Bentham's grandfather had been a high-class pawnbroker of the City of London under Charles II. 'The age of chivalry is gone', Edmund Burke declared when he recalled Marie Antoinette in 1790. 'That of sophisters, economists, and calculators has succeeded...' By that time, Walpole had been dead for nearly half a century, and men (especially Irish men) were talking nonsense once more.

'Pudding-time' became the sobriquet of the age of Walpole when men presently began to thirst once more after noble causes and lofty ideals. 'Soul dead, stomach well-alive' was the verdict of Thomas Carlyle, the Victorian lecturer on hero-worship. It was certainly an age of great coarseness of fibre in both public and private life, robust, greedy to excess of food and drink, prone to brutal sports, often careless of pain inflicted upon the weaker creation in both child and dumb animal. They had ceased to burn witches (the Parliament of Great Britain repealed the law permitting their capital punishment in 1736), but they still burnt wives who murdered their husbands (a woman at Dorchester, 1705, and Catherine Hayes, 1726) under a law that was not repealed until 1790. They strung up women and children, as well as men, for petty theft, and they enjoyed a pleasant afternoon's entertainment by gazing at the lunatics in Bedlam. It was also the first age of genuine philanthropy, with men like James Oglethorpe and John Howard the prison reformers, and of commencing religious revival, with John Wesley (1703–91) and Selina Countess of Huntingdon (1707–91). The age of Fielding's Parson Trulliber and Hoadley, the real-life absentee Bishop of Bangor, was also the age of William Law and his 'Serious Call to a Devout and Holy Life', a work which Dr Johnson said was the first occasion of his thinking in earnest of religion and which even impressed Edward Gibbon. The late Norman Sykes with his *Church and State in the Eighteenth Century* (1934) and Gladys Jones with her fine study of the Charity School Movement (1938) have effectively

modified the caricature that once passed for a portrait of religious and social unconcern in the age of Walpole.

The key note of the age was peace. Not simply the *quieta non
movere* associated with Walpole himself, but the peaceable social
tone which developed with the passing of the ages of aristocratic
rebellion, armed retainers, private castles, and the bad old practice
of decapitating fallen statesmen. Men fought duels behind locked
doors, or at dawn in remote places out of town, and the warfare
of the pen in the age of slashing Bentley and venomous Pope was
to pass unmitigated into the age of Junius and Wilkes. But, when
a gentleman went abroad now, he no longer travelled with a
private army but in a coach attended by two footmen and a page.
He might be held up by foot-pads, but he generally came safe
home again. The country was becoming linked increasingly in a
common consciousness by the public courier and the newsletter.
By the reign of Queen Anne civil life had definitely become
civilian, and urban life was becoming urbane with its coffee-
house wits and its polite journalism. A light and pellucid style was
encouraged by such conditions, as we have it in Addison's *Spec-
tator* and Johnson's *Rambler*. A man is unlikely to wear his heart
on his sleeve in a coffee-house, and such resorts certainly tended
to generate an excess of hard, worldly wisdom. There were 3,000
coffee-houses in London by 1708. Indeed, urbanity was the ideal
everywhere. The editor of the *Gentleman's Magazine* called himself Mr Urban. And if the wits tended to repeat themselves unduly
it was probably because they never could remember next day
what they had said the night before when high-flown with wine.

Even the country-house was really a town-house set down in
the country, which was what the 'Queen Anne style' encouraged
with its pink brick boxes and large white-framed windows. By
the early years of the eighteenth century the country gentleman
was trying hard to compete with his town cousin in the matter
of sash-windows and wainscot, plaster ceilings and marble fire-
places. The diamond panes and tapestries of the old manor-houses
were coming to be regarded as deplorably rustic. Many a country
squire failed to stand the pace in terms of expense and was
tempted to sell out to a rich man who wanted to buy land not so

much as an investment in its fruits as in order to acquire all that went with it in terms of social prestige and political power. Such people were, as Professor Habakkuk has said, buying up the perquisites of a neighbourhood. 'When they looked over the fields they wanted to see their own land and nothing but their own land.' Later generations have tended to a certain prudery in this matter of the eighteenth-century equivalence of political power with property, more especially landed property. The attitude is unhistorical. English institutions were, and are, descended from feudalism, which equated public law with private law, so that jurisdiction was property, office was property, the kingship itself was property. Defoe once argued, no doubt with his tongue in his cheek, that the freeholders, as owners of the soil, 'might give notice to quit to the rest of the population'. Such a proprietary political system could only work if the ruling class were moved, by self-interest perhaps, to spontaneous activity, prompted by public spirit and a sense of personal dignity. All political power, as Professor Plumb has shown us in his masterly analysis of the basis of Walpole's authority, was based on local power and influence. The key position was that of the lord lieutenant who presided over county sessions, grand juries and county meetings.

To dismiss English politics in the eighteenth century with a glib and indignant reference to 'bribery and corruption' was a habit of the retrospective moralism of the Victorian Age. Perhaps Sir Lewis Namier and his disciples have tended to carry us too far in an opposite direction, but they have at least taught us to attend to the political and social realities that lie behind the pejorative labels, and good authorities have assured us that a Parliament chosen by universal suffrage in the middle of the eighteenth century would have been very little different in composition from the Parliaments chosen by the minority groups which then dominated the political scene. In fact, the eighteenth-century Parliament was as good an example as any in history of an age and a people getting the kind of government it deserved. It carried the country through one of the most brilliantly successful periods of British history with surprisingly little dislocation or distress, the period which saw the founding of the first British Empire and loss of America, the first and most critical experience of financial speculation, and the birth of the modern forms of industry and agriculture. It has been argued that at least the old system had the merit of bringing young men into Parliament while their wits still shone with the brilliance of youth, though few would wish to deny that it also made straight the path for hordes of nonentities. The number of great political figures who came into Parliament through pocket boroughs[1] and patronage could be counted on the fingers of both hands, and such men quickly went on to secure the suffrage of more numerous constituencies. But there is no need to apologize at all profusely for a system which produced the Pitts, father and son, and Burke, and Fox, Wilberforce, Canning, Palmerston, and Peel. Even Mr Gladstone first entered Parliament, in 1832, for the close borough[2] of Newark, which belonged to the fourth and latest Duke of Newcastle, the noble lord who had already made sure of what Lord Morley called 'an unpleasing immortality in our political history' by his celebrated defence of the borough-mongering[3] system on the ground that a man 'had a right to do as he liked with his own'.

[1] An urban constituency in personal possession, i.e. in some one's pocket.
[2] An urban constituency of very few voters, and these under the sway of some magnate or group.
[3] Commerce in borough-seats, or buying and selling of same.

11

The first British Empire

When Walpole resigned in 1742 there was no question of the
Whigs giving place to the Tories. The great Tory party of the
age of Queen Anne had gone to pieces on the rocks and shoals of
Jacobitism.[1] Nearly half a century of Whig rule, together with
the cult of peace and prosperity during the long reign of Sir
Robert, had done its work. 'Robinocracy' had made England
safe for Whiggery for another fifty years. It was fully that length
of time before the younger Pitt laid the foundations of a new and
effective Toryism by bringing about a coalition between Old
Whigs of the 1688 tradition, now led by the Duke of Portland,
and Edmund Burke and his own personal followers, or 'Pittites',
in order to fight the French Revolution in arms.

Meanwhile the country got on very well with Whigs in office
and Whigs in opposition. They only differed in that 'Whigs
out of place' talked a good deal about corruption, placemen,
standing armies, profligate public expenditure, and the subjection
of British interests to those of the King's Electorate of Hanover.
Year in, year out, 'gentlemen out of place' thundered for an
effective Place Bill[2] while in opposition, and conveniently forgot
about it when they had the places. They could generally elicit
a principle of opposition from the question how much, or how
little, the country ought to do in Germany, and when this controversy slept—as the late Richard Pares put it—there was
nothing left to divide about, indeed to think about, but who

---

[1] The Jacobites were the adherents of James II after his abdication, or of his
descendants, out of belief in the principle of divine hereditary right of kings.
They were Tories because the 'exclusionists' were Whigs. For the origin of
party names see above, chapter 9, p. 172.

[2] A bill designed to exclude certain office-holders from the House of Commons,
generally persons who had received their office through patronage wielded
by the Administration, in order corruptly to influence the votes of the House.
Many bills of this intention were brought in during the century, but few were
successful and fewer still were effective.

should have the 'places'. To govern in the mid-eighteenth century did not mean to legislate but to keep the peace at home, to make war abroad, and to raise the taxes with as little inconvenience as possible to the tiny minority who had to pay them. It was with only a faint air of incredulity that David Hume could say, 'We are. . .to look upon all the vast apparatus of our government as having ultimately no other object or purpose but the distribution of justice, or, in other words, the support of the twelve judges'. Not until the age of revolutions set in (American, French, industrial) was there again anything to divide Englishmen at the roots.

All government was 'minimal government'. The day-by-day government of the country rested where it had always rested, and more especially since the end of the equivocal paternalism of the Stuarts and the abolition of the courts and councils associated with it. Such changes as were brought about for the public weal were nearly always promoted by philanthropy, local initiative, or voluntarist associations on the part of the multitude of gentlemen whose private and personal interests as landlords or men of business were sufficiently identified with the service of the public. The same was true of the country's interests overseas. The rise of British power in India was for the most part the achievement of the servants of the East India Company, while in North America the English fought the French as traders, trappers and settlers fighting for their own hand against the attempt of the French Governor of Canada to block their advance into the west. When General Braddock was sent to their aid in 1755 (while His Britannic Majesty was still officially at peace with the King of France) he was promptly defeated. When Clive won India the most the British government could fairly claim to have contributed was the dispatch of meagre royal forces to co-operate with those of the Company in defence of its possessions, and the operations of a squadron of the Royal Navy off the coast of Coromandel. Not even William Pitt ever allowed India to distract him from the conquest of Canada. He knew he could leave the task to 'John Company' and its 'Heaven-born General', Robert Clive. The first British Empire, which emerged from the Seven Years War in 1763, was not an empire in the classical sense of territorial conquest, but a by-product of the private enterprise of traders and men of business on the make in search of markets, trade-routes, and concessions. It was the typical 'empire' of a 'nation of shop-keepers', even if Adam Smith had not yet bestowed that honourable title upon his fellow subjects. Enemies have sometimes called it a 'concessionary empire', a commercial dominion wrested from weaker bargainers in the world's mart. It was not a matter of trade following the flag, but of the flag (often somewhat reluctantly) following trade. Perhaps this shopkeeping, left-handed, haphazard, and by no means unequivocal character of the achievement gave rise to the famous Victorian boast (or was it an apology?) that the British Empire was acquired in a fit of absence of mind.

At the time, however, Englishmen entertained few doubts as to what they were doing. They knew perfectly well that the successive contests called the War of Jenkins' Ear, the War of the Austrian Succession, and the Seven Years War were all aspects, or phases, of the second Hundred Years War between Great Britain and France, a war which in its larger perspective went on from the heyday of Louis XIV to the fall of Napoleon, from Blenheim to Waterloo. The stakes were no longer the Duchy of Normandy and the French possessions of the House of Anjou, but the trade and, in consequence, the empire of the world. The second Hundred Years War differed from the first not only in its range and the magnitude of its ends, but in its presiding spirit. Henry V had said of his wars on his death-bed: 'I protest before God that I was not drawn into them by any ambitions for domination or vainglory or worldly honour.' Robert Clive, cross-examined by a parliamentary commission late in his career of conquest, complained that he was treated like a sheep-stealer. 'By God, Mr Chairman,' he protested, 'at this moment I stand astonished at my own moderation!' As for Mr Pitt, Lord Hardwicke once said he had seen a draft note in his hand, concerning peace negotiations with France in 1761, couched in 'a very haughty and dictatorial style more strongly than any which I remember to have seen of Louis XIV in the height of his glory and presumption'. 'It looks as if we intended to finish the conquest of the world next campaign,' wrote Horace Walpole when Wolfe at Quebec added Canada to India. To the Ministers of the Crown the long tale of conquests seems to have been a prolonged geography lesson. 'Pray where is Annapolis?' asked the Duke of Newcastle when told that Annapolis must be defended. The Prime Minister was likewise astounded when he learnt that Cape Breton was an island. 'Ha! Are you sure of that?...Egad, I'll go directly and tell the King that Cape Breton is an island.' But, after all, what are private secretaries for? 'Come upstairs and show me where these places are', a Victorian statesman is said to have requested when he became Secretary for the Colonies.

The principal defect of English statesmanship in the age of the Pelhams,[1] the successors of Walpole, was not so much ignorance of geography, or economics, or even foreign languages, as it was a failure in imagination. 'Since Granville was turned out,' Tobias Smollett made a character in *Humphry Clinker* complain in 1760, 'there has been no minister in this nation worth the meal that whitened his periwig.' The shining exception was William Pitt, and Pitt, coming in as Secretary of State in 1757, had to run in double harness with the Duke of Newcastle, the 'Minister for Loaves and Fishes', or Minister for Majorities, the great cement-mixer who, while the Great Commoner held the hearts of the people, held Administrations together by the judicious handling of 'influence'. The greatest war-leader in British history before Winston Churchill, Pitt possessed not only a visionary grasp of the overall strategy of a world conflict but the greatness of soul which made men think that there was something finer in him than his words. When he said that he knew he could save his country and no one else could, men took it not merely as a personal opinion but as a fact of nature. The idol of the people and the god of the City of London, men discerned in him the features of another kind of leader than his contemporaries and

---

[1] Thomas and Henry Pelham, the former better remembered as the Duke of Newcastle and the elder Pitt's partner in the great war-winning ministry of the Seven Years War, represented the Walpole tradition. They replaced Lord Carteret (1742–44) on disagreeing with his foreign policy. Carteret became Earl Granville.

predecessors of the high chevelure and the Revolution Families, the kind of leader who belonged, if not by formal choice or conscious predilection, to the nation. Never since the days of Cromwell had a British statesman dared, or cared, to elicit a historic principle from a clash of arms. It would, of course, be absurd to invest Pitt with the symbols characteristic of a Cromwell or a Gustavus Vasa. Not the Bible but a ledger, not the sword but a subsidy roll, were the outward signs of his inward sovereignty; and at his back there march not the soldier saints but the Common Councilmen of the City of London. He stood at the head of a busy commercial community. He had decided that the House of Bourbon should no longer pasture in the fattest places of the earth, which he undoubtedly believed God had made for his Englishmen. When the Lord Mayor laid the foundation-stone of the new Blackfriars' Bridge in 1760, it was inscribed as

A MONUMENT TO THIS CITY'S AFFECTION TO THE MAN WHO
BY THE STRENGTH OF HIS GENIUS
AND THE STEADFASTNESS OF HIS MIND
AND A CERTAIN KIND OF HAPPY CONTAGION OF HIS
PROBITY AND SPIRIT
RECOVERED, AUGMENTED AND SECURED
THE BRITISH EMPIRE
IN ASIA, AFRICA AND AMERICA
AND RESTORED THE ANCIENT REPUTATION AND INFLUENCE
OF THIS COUNTRY AMONGST THE NATIONS OF EUROPE

Pitt was an eccentric genius (not inappropriately was *Tristram Shandy*, the most eccentric novel of the century, dedicated to him) and a man of enormous, indeed terrifying, *gravitas*. His defects were the reverse of his war-winning qualities. He resigned in 1761 because his colleagues refused to go to war with France's ally, Spain. The war had lasted, in its full maritime and colonial phase, for nearly five years, and had put a heavy strain on the country's resources. This, the first truly global war, had been a gigantic foray under arms for the riches of world trade and command of the overseas trade-routes. The Peace settlement of 1763 not only recognized British authority in Canada, India, and large areas of the West Indies; it also assured Britain a footing in Africa (Senegal) and the western Mediterranean (Minorca), and in general may be said to have secured the original objects of the war and 'satisfied the reasonable ambitions of all Englishmen but those who lived by war or war-mongering'. A trade recession was threatening, and even Pitt's friends in the City were prepared to pause for digestion. But when Pitt was gone, to suffer temporary eclipse under the title of Earl of Chatham, it seemed to many that the glory had departed, and for the next twenty years and more the country was to be afflicted by the visionless politics of a swarm of little men, culminating in the loss of that empire in North America that the Great Commoner had done so much to secure. He was to die on his gout-crutches, storming in the House of Lords against George III and Lord North's mean and disastrous treatment of the American colonies.

The young man who became King George III in 1760 was perfectly well aware that he would never be King of England while Pitt ruled in the hearts of his people. The pitiful tragedy was that if there was a man in England who really shared the patriot moralism of George III it was Pitt. For George III was never less than a Patriot King even if there is no evidence that he ever read Bolingbroke's essay. He was anxious to play his proper and essential part in the 'mixed constitution' as it subsisted in the century following the Glorious Revolution, that 'matchless device' for which, Lord North tells us, the King was prepared to live on bread and water. If that delicate mechanism of mixed and balanced parts were to work at all it was important that its monarchical element should play its part boldly and responsibly, for the King was still the mainspring of the balance, the 'governor' of the machine. It was no doubt unfortunate that at this moment in time, when constitutional development was precariously swinging over from a predominantly monarchical to a predominantly parliamentary character, the throne should have been occupied by a young man of such neurotically self-mistrustful disposition, intensely suspicious of his grandfather's servants, indeed of politicians in general, and pitifully anxious to hang on to a handsome nonentity like John, Earl of Bute, his chief minister.

Neither at this time, nor at any other, was George III prepared 'to turn out one set of men in order to put another in their place'. All ministries for many years to come were coalitions, hybrid collections of the clan-followers of leading noblemen, mostly of Whiggish complexion. Ministerial history was kaleido-scopic, administrations changing their hue chameleon-like within the Whig spectrum. The King's jealous preservation of his independence was only the royal version of that boasted by the country gentlemen or of Burke's classic doctrine of the proper independence of a Member of Parliament. There were to be times when he talked of abdication if any malign set of politicians pushed their perverted designs 'indecently and unconstitutionally' so far as to force themselves into his counsels. 'Storming the closet' was the contemporary term for this wicked procedure, and it was the King's perennial nightmare. George III for many years modelled and remodelled his governments in an endeavour to place in authority, second only to himself, a man who would serve him faithfully as a bulwark against this kind of assault. He may have been 'a conscientious bull in a china-shop', but he was a brave bull, indeed a pattern of John Bull, for which his people honoured him. 'The good old King', they called him as the years wore on. 'A very honest kind-hearted gentleman (added my uncle); he's too good for the times. A king of England should have a spice of the devil in his composition.' That was Smollett's Squire Timothy Bramble speaking in 1771.

George III was, in fact, very much a man of his times, a product of his age and country. A new seriousness had begun to over-take the English after the mid point of the century as the age of Hogarth gave way to the age of Wesley, and the innate moralism, not to say religiosity, of the race found free play once more. With Wesley, the country was in for a religious revival more socially momentous than any in its history. With the Pitts, father and son, the new moralism was to transform the world of politics. It is not too much to say that with the accession of George III care and conscience, domestic virtue and laborious ways were in the process of capturing the throne itself. No enligh-tened despot ascended the throne in 1760. There occurred rather the encounter of a moralistic king with a moralistic people, the shadowy initiation of a spectacle which was to become familiar in the nineteenth century England of Queen Victoria. Only a blind determination to remain on the plane of constitutional history can obscure the importance of the accession to the throne of George III.

That he grew up something of a prig and dangerously isolated from the aristocratic world of the men with whom he would inevitably have to work as King of England was to prove a misfortune. 'The private and lifeless solitude' of his youth, as Horace Walpole called it, no doubt left him 'blameless', as Dr Johnson observed, but at the same time it left him a prey to every fear and fantasy that may flow from 'the immaturity of juvenile years and the ignorance of princely education'. He was indubitably a 'good' young man. The trouble was that he knew it, and was all too ready to equate his own actions and intentions with the cause of 'religion and virtue'. He came to see himself as God's good man sent to redeem his country from the grasp of the vicious and the clever, terms which in his mind were all too often synonymous. In his preference for morals over mind, for persons over ideas, and in his assurance that he was himself the virtuous man contending with clever wickedness on behalf of a nation debauched by long years of servitude to 'the dirty arts' of politicians, George III really was a new kind of monarch to wear the crown of England, and his accession marks a great change in both the public and private affairs of his people. Nobody with an eye for character could fail to perceive that something important happened to the British monarchy in 1760. It would not be too much to say that George III's accession inaugurated an ill-fated rehearsal for that of Queen Victoria.

The King's personal tragedy was the tragedy of good intentions. That he saw himself as a latter-day St George at war with the Dragon of Corruption may seem absurd, but it is none the less true. It is even likely that for a moment he saw himself as a figure of historic tragedy, thwarted and betrayed by the failure of other men to rise to his own moral eminence. When Lord Bute resigned in favour of George Grenville in the spring of

1763, the sad young king wrote to his 'D. friend' in language which suggests that he felt the eye of History upon him. He deplored the forfeiture of their joint claims to immortality, to the everlasting respect of a grateful posterity. He clung to the mantle of St George long after it had become clear that the virtuous young king had assumed the role of 'chief of the borough-mongering gentlemen of England'. The illusions of mankind are no less important to the historian than are the realities that defeat them. Only thus is revealed the true irony which haunts all human endeavour, the commonplace tragedy which transcends the claims of the conventionally heroic upon our compassion. Slowly, sadly, the king learnt that the 'dirty arts' he detested were an indispensable part of the political landscape in which he lived and reigned, and that no one, however pure in heart, could maintain a government for a fortnight without them. It is hardly surprising that he succumbed within a very few short and disordered years to the exigencies of his day and generation, or that his health broke down for a while in 1789 and for the rest of his life in 1810. If the historian understands the King's dilemma better than the King, that is principally because he has the advantage of having read the works of Sir Lewis Namier.

When George Grenville, a pedantic, lawyerly man, highly respected by the House of Commons, took charge of the King's affairs in succession to Lord Bute in 1763, there were soon to be heard the first faint but ominous crepitations of revolution beyond the seas. Grenville's Stamp Act, levying a duty on stamped paper, passed unobtrusively enough through a Parliament athirst for an American revenue. It was thought that the colonists should help to foot the bill for the war which had removed the French menace in North America and to maintain an army of 10,000 men against the resurgence of French power and the depredations of the Indian tribes, very real dangers with Choiseul's expansion of the French navy and the Pontiac rising of 1763. Grenville wanted £60,000 from the Americans as a contribution to the total of £350,000 per annum required for the maintenance of a defence force in North America. The National Debt stood at £140,000,000 in 1763, and it weighed to the extent of £18 per head on Englishmen as compared with 18s. per head per annum on the colonists. Country gentlemen paying a land-tax of 4s. in the £ thought themselves to be the most highly taxed people in the world, and American taxation was sweet music in their ears. There was no question of the British Parliament's right to tax the colonies. If they did not send representatives to Parliament, nor did a great many other tax-paying people in the King's dominions. The Solicitor-General had given a perfectly clear and correct ruling on that as long ago as 1724. And when Lord Rockingham repealed the Stamp Act in 1766, the repeal was accompanied by a Declaratory Act reasserting the theoretical right of Parliament to tax the colonies. But as Burke was to declare in his great speech on Conciliation with America in 1775, 'it is not what a lawyer tells me I *may* do; but what humanity, reason and justice tell me I ought to do...' Few things in parliamentary history are more ironical than the spectacle of Mr Burke, who was making a useful income as London Agent for the colony of New York, staring into the faces of the serried ranks of country gentlemen and thundering night after night upon the poor plundered colonists. Until then they never realized how much they hated the Americans, and how right they were to hate them.

Grenville's Stamp Act was one item in a whole series of measures by which he proposed to increase the revenue from America: most of them were directed to the reduction of smuggling and the cost of collection of duties. It was costing £8,000 to collect £2,000 worth of customs duties in American ports, and about £750,000 worth of merchandise was smuggled in and out of North America per annum. Grenville was undertaking to save £130,000 by economical and administrative reform, even if the improved collection did wear 'the air of hostile combination'. As for the stamp duty itself, he summoned the colonial agents in London and asked them to propose alternative suggestions. They failed to do so, and only then did he go ahead. That it aroused large-scale opposition was not because it was 'the last straw' but rather because it was, along with all his other measures, in such strong contrast with the policy of 'salutary neglect' which had prevailed *vis-à-vis* the colonies for a hundred years. It was particularly ill conceived as a revenue-raising measure in that it was calculated especially to aggravate the most lively and vocal element in colonial society—those people who had occasion to require stamp-bearing paper, attorneys, journalists, publicans, all persons who had a hand in shaping public opinion.

It was tainted also in American eyes because of its point of origin in the Parliament at Westminster, that assembly of corrupt and needy aristocrats towards whom Americans were already assuming a typically 'Honest-John', or 'Holier-than-thou' attitude. 'If I must be enslaved,' wrote one who called himself 'Winchester Farmer' in 1774, 'let it be by a KING at least, and not by a parcel of upstart lawless committee-men.' This attitude was much favoured by English Whigs of the opposition who thought to shoulder off responsibility for clumsy and unimaginative statesmanship by calling the ensuing conflict 'the King's War'. Nor was the King concerned to forgo the compliment implied. He made it clear at all times that he was resolved to fight the battle of the legislature, and when the Americans drew up their Declaration of Independence they found it expedient to arouse world sympathy by drawing their indictment against the King. One tyrant made better reading, and produced a more concentrated portrait of tyranny, than 600 Westminster politicians. Not that tyranny was involved at anyone's hand. Neither at this time, nor in the past, had the colonies suffered any real oppression from the rule of the British Crown and Parliament. What they had suffered, and still suffered, was the subjugation of their interests in many particulars to the interests of the English merchants trading in the New World. Under the old colonial system, which had been in force since the time of the Navigation Acts of 1651 and 1660, the monopoly of colonial trade in the interests of British merchants and manufacturers was held to be the *raison d'être* of the empire. Plantations and colonies were conceived as ministering unto the wealth and strength of the mother country by providing her with raw materials and consuming her manufactures. Nor were the colonists in all respects the losers by this apparently one-sided arrangement, for the same legislation which gave British merchants the monopoly of trade assured the colonial producers a virtual monopoly of protected markets within the British dominions for their goods. On top of this, the lax administration of the Acts of Trade left many doors open to extensive and highly lucrative smuggling, more especially during the long years when Walpole winked both eyes at colonial liberties. What hurt the colonists in George Grenville's time was his lawyer-like endeavours to stop up the innumerable breathing-holes. Nor were the Americans prepared to go on suffering British prohibition upon industry in the New World. Such prohibition was not in effect particularly harassing, but it main-tained the psychological irritation of the colonists, who were not likely much longer to rest content with their rank as very junior partners in every enterprise contributing to imperial prosperity.

As regards sovereignty, the Americans were agnostics. They had stopped thinking with John Locke, for whom all government was limited government. They were not simply opposed to the Stamp Act or the imposition of taxation without representation. They refused to be taxed by anyone, and they wanted America to themselves. They had shown their consciousness of what later was to be called America's 'Manifest Destiny' in their inimical attitude to the Royal Proclamation of 1763 imposing limits upon their westward expansion. By the Quebec Act of 1774 the British government sealed its infamy in American eyes by con-tinuing the undemocratic government of the old French province by an appointed governor and council, by extending the frontier to the Ohio River and the Mississippi, by restoring French civil law, and (most sinister of all to New England Puritans!) pledging the British government to religious toleration for the Roman Catholics of Quebec. The fear that 'hordes of Popish slaves' in Canada would infect the liberal, enlightened, New England Dissenters (the sons of Protestant freedom who had left England to get away from the crypto-Popery of Laud), possibly—nay, probably—instituting the Inquisition in Philadelphia with a St Bartholomew's massacre to follow after, was perhaps less in-fluential than the prospective ruin of Philadelphia merchants (among whom were such men as George Washington and Patrick

Henry) by the extension of the southern boundary of Quebec to the Ohio River. Once more, western land speculators felt the stranglehold laid upon them previously by the Proclamation of 1763. The Americans wanted to substitute their own aristocratic leadership for that of aristocratic England. Out of the two and a half million people living in the thirteen colonies it is doubtful whether one in ten at any time took any active part in throwing off allegiance to King George III. From first to last, the American Revolution was, like all revolutions, the work of an active minority, a native governing class of merchants and landowners whose interests were threatened by the new imperial policy at Westminster and especially by the barrier to westward expansion imposed by the Proclamation of 1763 and the Quebec Act of 1774. If there were any elements of historic inevitability in the story, they were provided by two thousand miles of ocean, a whole world of geography, and a century and a half of disparate historical experience. It is the part of statesmanship to overcome the ponderables of space and time in the interests of a universal humanity, and the failure of the English-speaking peoples in the crisis of these years was a failure in statesmanship.

The King was unfortunate in his ministers throughout. Grenville was an excellent man of business, but he lacked flexibility, and was inclined, as Burke once said, 'to think the substance of business not to be much more important than the forms in which it is conducted'. As a lawyer he was bred to a profession inapt to open and liberalize the mind in proportion to its understanding. Besides, he was a bore, and inclined to lecture. 'When he has wearied me for two hours,' the King complained, 'he looks at his watch to see if he may not tire me for one hour more.' Before long the King was to declare that he would rather see the Devil in his Closet than George Grenville, and it was during Grenville's administration that the King suffered the first short attack of the illness that was to incapacitate him in his later years. He sought for the return of Chatham, the man who could best hold the hearts of his people both at home and across the Atlantic, but the fallen statesman found it impossible to envisage serving the King in company with men who, in his view, had betrayed king and country and 'the Great Commoner' in the year 1763. The Rockingham Whigs lasted very nearly twelve months, and papered over the cracks in the rift with the American colonists by repealing the Stamp Act, but the King hardly thought of the Marquess as more than a *locum tenens*. When at length in July 1766 Chatham consented to take over in their train and formed the 'Tessellated Pavement without cement', or a ministry drawn from every party or connection, he soon became too ill to lead it or control it. The task fell into the nerveless hands of Augustus Fitzroy, Duke of Grafton, and it was in this period of Chatham's illness and Grafton's ineffective deputyship that Charles Townshend, the Chancellor of the Exchequer, inaugurated his fatuous policy 'to tax and to please' the Americans, a policy which simply served to madden them with import duties and to provoke the Boston Tea Party. Grafton also had to deal with the 'Wilkes and Middlesex' furore,[1] not to mention the virulent onslaughts of the *Letters of Junius*.

It is hardly to be wondered at that the King imagined, and hoped, that he had found salvation in Frederick North, elder son of the first Lord Guilford, a young man in his middle thirties distinguished by sweetness of temper, readiness and skill in debate, and first-rate abilities in the management of public finance, though, like another great financier, Pitt the Younger, singularly incompetent in managing his own. He had no 'tail'; there were never many 'Northites' clamouring behind him for the spoils of office. His family had never adjusted itself to the post-1715 situation, and had remained devoted to the House of Stuart for as long as, and longer than, such devotion remained a viable political allegiance. His father, the first Lord Guilford, had belonged intimately to the Court of Frederick, Prince of Wales, George III's father, and that amiable prince had indeed stood godfather to the young Frederick North, his namesake. In fact, so closely did the Hon. Frederick North resemble George III in physical features that there was a good deal of base, and baseless, speculation on the theme of their possible common paternity during Lord North's long tenure of the Treasury.

For whatever reasons George III clung to Lord North, none of them need have been either obscure or esoteric in origin. Cling he did for twelve years, the most decisive years of the century for the future of the English-speaking world (1770-82). This was not because North served simply as the King's puppet; at any rate that was not what the King wished North to be. North once described himself as holding 'the place next the director of Publick Affairs at this time', a just and accurate description of a prime minister in the then stage of development of the Constitution. The King, as his letters to North in these years show, was constantly begging him to show more spirit and energy, to 'prepare a plan' against the expected attacks of the opposition, indeed to exert himself as the first-rate parliamentarian he was, and as he had shown himself to be in overcoming the most menacing oppositional forces in the first year of his ministry; a triumph which historians are still trying to explain, and which will remain inexplicable as long as 'the cult of personality' remains under interdict. North was, for a politician of those days, a poor man, generally encumbered by debts, and mentally harassed in consequence. The King was generous to him, and as a man of honour North felt deeply indebted to the Royal Master in every sense of the word. His ill health, and his lack of conviction that the King's American policy was either well considered or viable, made him hanker after resignation year after year, but always his final sense of obligation to the King, along with the King's limpet-like attachment to the man who had served, and indeed saved, him so brilliantly in 1770, kept him in office until the fall of Yorktown in 1782.

Thrashing the colonists into submission had never been a likely proposition, not because fighting a war at a distance of two thousand miles was inherently any more impossible in the 1770s than it had been in the 1750s, but because Lord North was not a Pitt, and Generals Howe and Cornwallis belonged to an entirely inferior order of commanders in the field to Robert Clive and James Wolfe. Most important of all, the Colonial Office was under Lord George Germain, a soldier who had been declared incompetent and unworthy to serve His Majesty after his inertia at the battle of Minden in 1759. It was Lord George who failed to send vital instructions to General William Howe, instructions which would have prevented the surrender of 7,000 men, half of them Germans, at Saratoga Springs in 1777. Whether or no the British forces were equipped with muskets that could not be fired downhill because the bullets rolled out of the barrels before they could be discharged by powder, they hardly deserved any better fate than defeat by the American farmers who at least knew, and loved, what they were fighting for. After the fiasco of Saratoga Springs the French entered the contest on the side of the rebels. By 1778 Spain was in the anti-British coalition. Holland joined in 1780, and in the following year Prussia and Austria joined the Armed Neutrality of the North which had been formed by the Baltic Powers to concert resistance to British interference with neutral shipping on the high seas. Nor was Ireland any slower than usual in making England's difficulties her opportunity. The Irish Volunteers brought Protestant support for the Irish Parliament's demand for free trade, and before the war ended Grattan's Parliament had in 1782 secured Irish legislative independence. Great Britain, it seemed, was without a friend in the world, and by 1779 the British Isles were in imminent danger of invasion by the combined fleets of France and Spain. The Anglo-French war had flared up again in both India and the West Indies. Admiral Rodney beat the Spaniards off Cape St Vincent in 1780, but within twelve months the French were in the Chesapeake and bringing about the surrender of Howe at Yorktown. At the news Lord North is supposed to have thrown up his hands and thanked God that it was all over. This was true of his Administration, but it was not true of the war. Next year the French went on capturing islands in the West Indies until Rodney defeated De Grasse, while their fleet under De Suffren brought Admiral Hughes to action time after time off the coast of Coromandel. In 1782, Eliott compelled the Spaniards to raise the siege of Gibraltar after a magnificent defence of the Rock for three years. It was at the end of that year that Great Britain acknowledged the independence of the United States of America, and Lord Shelburne's Ministry, wherein young

William Pitt served as Chancellor of the Exchequer and leader of the Commons at the age of twenty-three, negotiated the Peace of Versailles with a world of enemies. The feats of Rodney and Eliott in the last stages of the war enabled Britain to negotiate from a position of much greater advantage than had at one time seemed possible. As regards France and the West Indies, which were all that really mattered, the treaty was practically a restatement and confirmation of the terms of the Peace of Paris twenty years before.

Englishmen were under no delusion about what had hit them. They did not suppose for a moment that they had been defeated by 'the embattled farmers'. That was a delusion they left to the school-books of the young Republic and to the Liberals of Victorian England. They knew very well that they had been defeated by the French Navy, and that this was a reverse in the course of the second Hundred Years' War. The French had been playing with fire, and when the 'Athletes of Liberty', headed by that rich and vain young man, the Marquis de Lafayette, carried the virus of revolt back to the enfeebled body politic of France, the English watched the result, if not with satisfaction, at least with a sense that justice was being done. France, it was felt, deserved all that was coming to her, and one of the earliest things that came was her diplomatic defeat in the United Provinces in 1787 where she unwisely gambled on ousting British influence in secret support of the Dutch Patriot party in opposition to the House of Orange. Napoleon always held that this further attempt to fish in troubled waters was a prime cause of the French Revolution. Certainly Great Britain's diplomatic defeat of France's last adventure in the politics of revolt, combined with Pitt's outmanœuvring of Vergennes over the Free-Trade Treaty in the previous year, did much to discredit Louis XVI's government in its last years.

The loss of the American colonies might have been expected to afford the mother country a salutary lesson in the government of dependent peoples. And certainly there were some who took the American affair as a judgement upon an unnatural parent who had forsaken or betrayed her nobler birthright, and many had applauded the Americans as fighting the battle of old England on the soil of the new, liberty-loving descendants of Hampden and Sidney and Locke striving to deliver freedom to a new birth. 'We cannot, I fear, falsify the pedigree of this fierce people,' Burke had declared at the height of the struggle, 'and persuade them that they are not sprung from a nation in whose veins the blood of freedom circulates.' Burke spoke also from the heart of eighteenth-century humanitarianism. The issue had never been, to him, one of contending theories of law, but rather one of humanity, morality, magnanimity, generosity, all the nobler parts of social intercourse which (he would say) begin where law ends. 'The question with me is, not whether you have a right to render your people miserable,' he told the House of Commons when they contended upon the right to tax the colonies; 'but whether it is not your interest to make them happy.'

When, twenty years later, war and revolution came within sight of their native shores, some were to ask themselves whether the revolution in France were not *le fléau de Dieu*, the flail of an outraged Deity. So the young Coleridge, watching the Bristol Channel from Quantock Head for the sails of the French invasion fleet, beat his breast:

> We have offended, Oh! my countrymen!
> We have offended very grievously,
> And been most tyrannous...Therefore evil days
> Are coming on us...And what if all-avenging Providence,
> Strong and retributive, should make us know
> The meaning of our words, force us to feel
> The desolation and the agony
> Of our fierce doings?

This repentant mood which afflicted many sensitive minds as the eighteenth century turned to the nineteenth was not wholly the product of panic fear as Europe crackled into the smoke and flame of the revolutionary era. It may be detected, somewhat ambiguously as yet, perhaps, in the impeachment of Warren Hastings on charges of misgovernment and injustice as Governor General of India which began in 1787 and lasted until 1795. The younger Pitt, coming to power on the morrow of the surrender at Yorktown and the British acknowledgement of American independence, had opened his career as an imperial statesman with his India Bill of 1784, directing his energies to the great eastern dominion which owed so much to his father's conquering career, and his father's 'Heaven-born General', Robert Clive. Pitt's India Bill, replacing the measure brought forward in the previous year by the Unnatural Coalition of Fox and North, and frustrated by the personal influence of George III in the House of Lords, subjected the East India Company to a Board of Control appointed by the Crown instead of Commissioners named by the ministry of the day. This detailed and cumbrous measure of eighty-five clauses, instituting an elaborate system of checks and counter-checks necessitated by the double nature of a government of India shared between Crown appointees and servants of a private company, constituted the instrument by which India was to be governed (with some amendments) until the Mutiny in 1858. In effect, Pitt enjoyed every bit as much patronage in India as the Fox–North bill had sought to secure for the Unnatural Coalition. Henry Dundas, president of the Board of Control, who was Pitt's close personal friend and bottle-companion, saw to that.

Authority in India really lay in the governor-generalship of Bengal instituted by North's Regulating Act of 1773. The Governor General from 1774 to 1785 was Warren Hastings, who in these years laid down the permanent principles of British rule in India. In fact, Hastings did more for the Indians than any other Englishman of the century, but he was to be represented as a tyrant and a monster of cruelty because he was resolute, vigorous, and high-handed in emergency, a benevolent despot, in fact, exercising what amounted to absolute authority over peoples who understood no other. When his enemies in India (of whom Philip Francis, the probable author of the *Letters of Junius*, was the most malevolent) came home to enlist Edmund Burke for Hastings' impeachment, it was Pitt who played the decisive part in determining that the great pro-consul should be put on trial. As so often, Pitt's reasons were clouded by over-subtle argumentation. The impeachment of Warren Hastings for his unjust actions in governing India was the martyrdom of a great governor general, perhaps the greatest who ever bore rule in the sub-continent, in the cause of Great Britain's moral title to rule in the East. Burke's maniacal conduct of the prosecution leaves a bad taste in the mouth now that we know more than we used to know of the financial dealings of the house of Burke, but we can never regret that, with all his savage exaggeration of the great governor-general's offences, he lavished his burning elo-quence in the cause of Britain's responsibility before God and man for the well-being of the people of India. We have the testimony of some of those people, the inhabitants of Murshed-abad in Bengal who wrote: 'Thousands reaping the benefits [of his rule] offer up their prayers for the prosperity of England and for the success of the Company.' Yet it is hardly too much to say that the doctrine of imperial trusteeship was born of Burke's speeches in Westminster Hall. When he declared that 'all political power which is set over men...ought to be in some way exer-cised for their benefit', he was proclaiming the moral charter of the new Empire, and making possible the future Common-wealth. One empire had perished with the loss of America, but the impeachment of Warren Hastings was not the least of the measures which made it possible for another empire to be born.

12

The Age of Everything

It was the best of times, it was the worst of times, it was the age of
wisdom, it was the age of foolishness, it was the epoch of belief, it
was the epoch of incredulity, it was the season of Light, it was the
season of Darkness, it was the spring of hope, it was the winter of despair, we had everything before us, we had nothing before us, we were
all going direct to Heaven, we were all going direct the other way—
in short the period was so far like the present period, that some of its
noisiest authorities insisted on its being received, for good or for evil,
in the superlative degree of comparison only.

CHARLES DICKENS, A Tale of Two Cities, chapter 1

William Cobbett, who was, it seems, born in the year of the
Stamp Act (1765), and who certainly lived to see the Reform Bill
of 1832, always said that he could not recall that country people
(by which he must have meant most English people) ever knew or
thought anything about politics in the 'dark ages' when he was a
boy. 'The shouts of victory or the murmur at a defeat would
now-and-then break in upon our tranquillity for a moment; but
I do not remember ever having seen a newspaper in the house...'
After the American War had gone on for a time, however: 'We
became a little better acquainted with subjects of this kind.' His
father was a partisan of the Americans, and would drink to their
success even while his neighbours were celebrating the British
success at Long Island. In general, it seems to have been the young,
the generous, the romantic who rejoiced with the rebels, very
much as they were to do a few years later at the vision of 'France
standing on the top of golden hours'. Even Robert Stewart, the
future Lord Castlereagh, was signing himself 'a true American'
in 1777. Politics had begun to mean something once more; something to do with ideas and emotions, even with principles;
something other than the perennial question whether (as Dickens
put it in *Bleak House*) Lord Boodle should have the Home
Department or whether Lord Coodle should have the Exchequer.

The awakening had much to do with the birth of English Radicalism, even though the name was not to be adopted for another fifty years. The inception of a movement for parliamentary reform owed more to the American than to the French Revolution, for people came to believe that the dispute with the colonies had had a good deal to do with representation, or the lack of it, and the friends of America readily became the advocates of representative reform in England. Parliament's treatment of John Wilkes, one of its own Members, had already sparked off the movement in 1769, for Wilkes valiantly contested his expulsion from the House of Commons in consequence of his libel on the King in number 45 of *The North Briton*, and the obscene libel of the *Essay on Woman*. It was his vindication of the rights of the electors of his constituency of Middlesex after his expulsion, and the seating of the defeated candidate in his place, that led to the formation of the first parliamentary reform association, the Supporters of the Bill of Rights, in 1769. The Americans recognized in Wilkes an ally against parliamentary tyranny and sent him live turtles and a 45 hogshead of tobacco when he was laid up in the King's Bench prison. The parliamentary opposition to Lord North also tried to make capital out of Wilkes's wrongs, but found him an embarrassing ally, partly on account of his disreputable morals, and even more on account of his popularity with the London mobs, the fellows who, as Lord Hardwicke told the Duke of Newcastle, 'would have hanged your Grace and me a few years ago, and would do so still if they had the power'. Even Burke, producing his *Thoughts on the Causes of the Present Discontents* in 1770, cut little ice with the radical politicians of the City. Mrs Catherine Macaulay, who belonged to the circle of the Supporters of the Bill of Rights, in her *Observations* on Burke's pamphlet, protested that the Whigs of the parliamentary opposition were only concerned to get back into office, and that it would scarcely serve the interest of the people to consolidate the position of another aristocratic clique. Only 'a more extended and equal power of election' could do that. The energetic if somewhat inchoate radical movement which existed in England before the French Revolution was a native growth, echoing sometimes the sentiments of the Republicans and the Levellers of the Commonwealth, but stirred into life mainly by the wasteful and incompetent handling of the nation's affairs during the American War. It found expression in such movements as the Yorkshire Association of 1780, which was concerned generally with profligate public finance and shameful mismanagement of public policy. Parliamentary reform, as a programme, was much less a product of abstract political doctrine than of practical utility in terms of cheaper government, lower taxes, or 'value for money'. There was a good deal of shame involved, too, shame that the great country of Chatham and the Seven Years War should have degenerated into the ineffectual polity that let itself be beaten by a crowd of American backwoodsmen and shopkeepers, not to mention the popish slaves of the King of France. National pride was very much involved in setting on foot 'The Age of Improvement', which is one of the many names that have been given to the last decades of the eighteenth century and the early decades of the nineteenth. Few things perhaps are more indicative of the injured feelings of the English after the American War than the rumour that the Ministers had offered Edward Gibbon a 'place' to refrain from following up his classic history with a *Decline and Fall of the British Empire*.

One reason why the English were not for long dismayed by the loss of the American colonies, or remained even longer unconcerned to learn from it the lessons of humility and the need for gentler ways, was their preoccupation with another revolution which was proceeding at home. Even while Pitt and Clive and Wolfe were founding the 'First British Empire' or making 'drum-and-fife history', the rough Peakland millwright, James Brindley, and the Barber of Bolton, Richard Arkwright, were laying the foundations of the Industrial Revolution that was shortly to make Great Britain the workshop of the world. In 1839 Thomas Carlyle was to apostrophize Richard Arkwright as the William the Conqueror *de Ses jours*: 'O reader, what a Historical Phenomenon is that bag-cheeked, potbellied, much-enduring, much-inventing barber! French Revolutions were a-brewing to resist the same in any measure, imperial Kaisers were impotent without the cotton and cloth of England; and it was this man that had to give England the power of cotton.' At Birmingham too, Matthew Boulton was announcing to the admiring visitors from all over the world who came to gaze upon his engineering works at Soho: 'I sell here, sir, what all the world desires to have—POWER.' Dr Johnson, visiting Derby with James Boswell in 1776, left Boswell to visit Soho alone. 'I wish that Johnson had been with us', Boswell wrote. 'The vastness and contrivance of some of the machinery would have matched his mighty mind.' Perhaps the Doctor shared some of the fears of Cobbett, who confessed that he never liked to see machines 'lest I should be tempted to endeavour to understand them'. However, Cobbett was writing in 1832, by which time the pristine glories of the new age were being overcast by the smoke and squalor of the age of Manchester and the industrial slums. In the 1770s and 1780s the country was still rejoicing in the heroic age of the Industrial Revolution when everything was a wonder and a wild amaze, and the pioneers were hailed as magicians, while their works were hailed as likely to eclipse the monuments of ancient Rome. When, in 1759, the Year of Victories, James Brindley constructed 'the greatest artificial curiosity in the world' in the form of an aqueduct 40 feet high over the river Irwell to carry coals from the Duke of Bridgewater's collieries at Worsley to the Mersey, so that men stood amazed to see water carried over water and barges sailing high in the air while others sailed along the river below, a writer in the *St James's Chronicle* called him a magician who could handle rocks 'as easily as you and I handle plum-pies' and could make 'the four elements subservient to his will'. What Brindley's magic achieved, in effect, was to halve the cost of coal at Manchester and lay the foundation of the mechanized cotton industry in Lancashire. Ten years later, when Arkwright set up his spinning-mills at Cromford, he initiated a fully fledged factory system based on power-driven machinery.

The 'much-inventing barber', as Carlyle called Arkwright, was not a great inventor but a genius of organization and a quite unscrupulous picker of other men's brains, notably those of James Hargreaves, who had, some time between 1764 and 1767, devised the spinning-jenny, which enabled half a dozen threads to be spun in the same time and by the same amount of labour as one had been spun before; and also of John Kay, the clock-maker of Warrington, who had produced a frame in 1768 which enabled a strong 'twist' to be spun by rollers driven by water-power. Arkwright's water-driven mill in Matlock Gorge, which exploited these inventions, was modelled on the famous water-powered silk-mill set up by the brothers Lombe on an islet in the Derwent at Derby as early as 1718. The Lombes' silk-mill, too, had been a wonder of the world in its day, with its six storeys and 460 windows, employing 600 workers, mainly children, and producing (according to Daniel Defoe) 73,726 yards of silk every time its single river-driven wheel went round, which (also according to Defoe) was three times a minute. The steam-engine, which was to replace water-power much later in the century, was as yet only employed in the form of a stationary engine for pumping water out of coal-mines. Thomas Savery had demonstrated his 'fire-engine' to the Royal Society in 1699. Thomas Newcomen's piston-driven beam-engine followed in 1708. The link between the coalfields and the metallurgical trades was coke-smelting of iron at Coalbrookdale by the Abraham Darby dynasty after 1709, a process which led on to the production of cast-iron cylinders for steam-engines a generation or more before the days of James Watt. In 1779 the third Abraham Darby threw an iron bridge across the Severn, the first of its kind in the world. The Carron Ironworks, which gave its name to the carronade, or handy quick-loading gun, the weapon that played a vital part in giving Nelson's men-of-war their superiority, was founded in the year before George III became king. The crucible and sand-mould method of making cast steel had come into action as early as 1742 at Sheffield.

All these things, and many more, were to amount to an 'Industrial Revolution', though the term only gained academic currency after the first Arnold Toynbee's book of that name in 1884. At the time, people more often appear to have thought about what was happening in terms of art and aesthetics. They had had Edmund Burke's *Philosophical Inquiry into our Ideas of the*

Sublime and the Beautiful since 1756. It appeared at the time when forge and furnace were beginning to blaze in the sky above the Severn valley. 'Whatever is fitted in any sort to excite the ideas of pain and danger; that is to say, whatever is in any sort terrible, is a source of the sublime,' the young professor of aesthetics wrote. Coalbrookdale under the administrations of the Darby dynasty possessed not only vastness, power and obscurity, but also another of Burke's ingredients, 'stenches'. Arthur Young, the agricultural traveller, twenty years later called the aspect of the place 'horribly sublime'. The artists were anxious to paint these sublimities. The Coalbrook Company inscribed Rooker's view of the dale to the King. The line runs on from Rooker to Robertson, de Loutherbourg, and the grand chiaroscuro of Wright of Derby (1734–97), attaining true glory in 1844 with Turner's 'Rain, Steam and Speed'. The age had its yardstick of imperial measurement ready in the eighteenth-century cult of ancient Rome, the uncovering of Herculaneum, and the writings of De Volney and Gibbon. When Arthur Young set eyes on Brindley's engineering feat at Barton Bridge in 1768, he was prepared to predict that 'it will exceed the noblest work of the Romans when masters of the world', and the Rev. John Dalton, writing *A Descriptive Poem to two Ladies on their returning from viewing the Mines near Whitehaven* in octosyllabic couplets, concluded with a paean to Thomas Savery, patentee of the stationary 'fire-engine' for pumping water out of coal-pits, containing the prophecy:

> Men's richest gift thy work will shine,
> Rome's aqueducts were poor to thine...

The employment of the name 'Industrial Revolution' for what happened in the world of industry in the reign of George III is like the use of the word 'Renaissance' for what happened in the world of art and letters in Western Europe in the fifteenth century. Even if employed as the name for a movement in time, it becomes less than helpful when we realize that many of the inventions that became effective in the later eighteenth century had been made long before, but rendered inoperative by the absence of other factors requisite for their profitable employment, or even deliberately suppressed. Silk-throwing machinery was in use in Italy as early as 1607, and was within reach of English technologists by 1620, but it was not brought into operation here until the reign of George I. Lee's invention of the stocking-frame seems to have been deliberately suppressed by the Elizabethan government's fears about creating unemployment. The most and the best that we can do is to ask why the main technical changes, and their accompanying social changes, came when and where they did.

The basic factor which made Britain the first home of modern industry was political. England went ahead earlier and faster than any other country of Western Europe, indeed of the world, because she had (or thought she had) solved earliest the problem of orderly government under a single all-powerful authority without outraging or alienating any considerable class, or interest, in society. The first really important steps towards a modern industrial form of society were taken after the Revolution of 1688. By 1694 she had a Bank of England, and within a very short time a movement was on foot to supply the country with private banks, great and small. It was not simply a matter of supplying capital for investment in new enterprises, for most of the enterprises of the age of developing industry were financed not directly by banks but by loans between friends (often enough Friends in the Quaker sense of the word), men of the same religious congregation who knew and trusted each other, men sharing the same 'Protestant virtues' (often 'Puritan' virtues) of frugality, thrift, plain living. Such a social and religious network of confidence, backed by the political or constitutional stability afforded by the Bank of England as 'the bankers' bank', made investment safer than anywhere else in Europe. Many a man built a small business into a large one by personal frugality, ploughing back early profits. Large numbers of respectable Dissenters, finding the public service closed to them by the religious tests, or at least discouraged by the fact that entry depended upon membership of institutions under the Anglican monopoly, readily turned to trade and industry, which made no such difficulties. The amount of exclusiveness which prevailed left them free for such activities and yet did not cause them to develop the worst characteristics of 'outsiders'.

The manpower situation was safe enough, because of the enormous increase of population, which steadily assumed the proportions of an 'explosion' between 1740 and 1820. This, the most astonishing feature of England in the 'Age of the Industrial Revolution', is also the most mysterious. The birth-rate rose slightly, but the mortality-rate declined steadily after the decline of excessive gin-drinking which followed the so-called Tippling Act of 1751, the increasing availability of better diet with the improvement of agriculture, the increased consumption of vegetables, and a certain improvement in the standards of personal cleanliness—notably through the production of more soap and plentiful cheap cotton clothes, along with the substitution of brick-and-tile urban houses for the ancient insect-ridden timber and thatch. Some improvement in paving, draining and water-supply helped to diminish the incidence of plague and ague and the multitude of infantile ailments which had been killing diseases in earlier times, though there was still only a fifty-fifty chance of surviving childhood in cities. Some improvements in medical science, including notably the slow spread of inoculation against smallpox, were saving more lives, and the first smallpox hospital was opened in 1746. Mostly, however, although hospitals and dispensaries were increasing, there is reason to believe that hospitalization of patients helped to spread more infection than it prevented or cured. If the great increase in population (a 40 per cent increase in the second half of the eighteenth century from six and a half to nine million, and a 50 per cent increase from nine to fourteen million in the first three decades of the nineteenth) were thought to have had much to do with the onset of an industrial revolution, it should be remembered that the rate of increase was fairly uniform throughout the kingdom and not proportionately excessive in the urban and industrial areas.

Increased population would account for very little unless taken in conjunction with certain factors uniquely at work in England. One of these was the comparative freedom of England from restraints imposed on enterprise by the survival of ancient forms of regulation or control. The removal of the regional courts and councils of Tudor times in the early seventeenth century left the field clear for the free play of private initiative. The supposedly infamous regime of *laissez-faire*, against which modern governments have levelled their batteries of state intervention, may have led to callous neglect of the poor and weak, but it certainly put a premium on the enterprise of the strong and energetic. There was, for one thing, a peculiarly lax patent-law, and stealing other men's inventions, as the career of Richard Arkwright shows, was relatively easy. There were some ancient trades, notably the wool trade, which suffered the strangling restrictions of statute law and gild regulation, but a new industry like the cotton trade could find free scope for immense and even headlong development in areas beyond the grasp of ancient fetters, which helps to account for that great industry finding its home in Lancashire. Most important of all, however, was the prevalence in England of an attitude of mind, for the Industrial Revolution was above all else something that went on in men's heads. Briefly, this may be described as the predominance of a scientific outlook upon the world. It would be difficult to trace much more than an episodic and tenuous connection between the Industrial Revolution and the foundation of the Royal Society, and yet the outlook which made possible the exploitation of nature, which was the point and purpose of the myriad achievements of the men who made the first great age of modern industry, was shaped by the experimental and empirical passions of the generations which lived their lives in the Society set on foot by Charles II in 1662. It is not the great mountain peaks of science that make the landscape, but the crowding foot-hills, the low-lying ranges from which those solemn eminences take their rise. To produce a Newton, an Einstein, a Rutherford, it is necessary to have a reserve of highly trained scientific workers, workers whose names may never be known to the general public at all. More than that, it is necessary for the scientific habit of mind to permeate the intelligence of men who are not scientists. That was what happened in England over the century following the foundation of the Royal Society.

The achievements of the Industrial Revolution were the offspring of the communion between the man of science and the craftsman. Their shared conviction was that by understanding nature man could control it. This conviction was more than a concern with spinning-jennies and cheap cotton shirts, though that was a heroic concern, too.

In the early or heroic age of industry there was a widespread desire to understand, as well as to admire, the technical achievements of the time. The Midland towns were alive with avid intellectual life, as we see it in the Lunar Society of Birmingham (1765), a group which included Matthew Boulton, James Watt, Erasmus Darwin, Josiah Wedgwood, Francis Galton, and many more, a company which was to constitute the vanguard of scientific thought in England for the next twenty-five years or 'the technological general staff of the Industrial Revolution'. Nor were they alone, for similar societies, generally called 'Literary and Philosophical', existed soon in Edinburgh, Newcastle, Manchester, Derby and Liverpool. By 1776, Boulton's Soho Works was as famous as Holkham Hall or Etruria or (later) Owen's New Lanark. Karl Marx himself, looking back on this stirring, busy, seminal time, while he hated its failure to distribute its fruits justly, could never say enough in praise of its productiveness. Ultimately, while the time saw a victory for the human understanding of, and control over, Nature, it saw also the beginning of a new attitude to the problems of society. There could have been no humanitarianism, and very little humanity, in the nineteenth century if Englishmen, and Scots, had not made the earth multiply and be fruitful in the eighteenth.

The fruitfulness of England's earth in terms of beef and mutton, corn and root-crops, increased no less rapidly than its mineral harvests in coal and iron. Already the enterprise of great landowners like Viscount Townshend of Rainham had set on foot the agricultural improvements that were to turn the sandy soils of eastern England into gold, and to fatten the pastures of the midland shires for Robert Bakewell's pedigree sheep. The temper and outlook of these great lords and country gentlemen were strongly akin to the temper and outlook of their commercial cousins of the counting-house and the Exchange. They saw their lands, quite literally, as fields for investment, every bit as susceptible of speculative skill and scientific management as the distant markets of their mercantile kinsmen; fields, moreover, that were conveniently situated at the doorsteps and under the windows of the great houses which served as the centres of social life in the countryside. For the English aristocracy, great and small, lived on their estates. The dull Court of the Hanoverian kings, the political monopoly of Walpole, and the passion for all forms of country sport and pastime, made these men the truly 'residing aristocracy' that Cobbett was to contrast so forcibly with the 'now-and-then residing gentry' who came to the country in increasing numbers at the close of the eighteenth century. Their inveterate business outlook may be perceived in Robert Bakewell's definition of a sheep as 'a machine for turning grass into mutton', in 'Turnip' Townshend's practice of writing the Norfolk crop-rotation into the leases of his tenant farmers, and in Coke of Norfolk's employment of the Palladian splendours of Holkham Hall as the setting for an enormously profitable agricultural show-ground.

Nothing less than aristocratic patronage and resources could have achieved the transformation of agricultural organization and techniques within the intensely conservative society of rural England at that time. The business activities of lords and gentlemen among the fields and heaths of the ancient countryside were to make good farming a fashion. They also made England into a land of large farms, enclosed fields and landless labourers at the very time when the peasant proprietorship of France was being born. While that old enemy became the land of *le petit propriétaire*, England was becoming a land that could support the large urban populations which made the machines and the goods of the industrial revolution. Cobbett was to talk about 'the big fish swallowing up the little fish' as the torrent of enclosure transformed his country from a patchwork of straggling allotment gardens into a chessboard of neatly hedged fields, of country houses screened by avenues of trees from the sight of tumbledown cottages. But there was, as the Radical H. G. Wells later noted, one good thing about what he called 'the Bladesover System', or the country-house and estate system of the nineteenth century: it abolished the peasant habit of mind, liberating us from 'the dream of living parasitically on hens and pigs'. About the park at Bladesover, among the fields and woods of Midhurst and Bromley in Kent, one might find at least some of the elements of a liberal education if only because there were some acres of land 'not given over to manure and food grubbing'. With all its faults, the England of the later eighteenth century was still a beautiful country. The smoke-streamers were still faint in the sky and the grunt of steam and the internal combustion engine had not broken the heart of rural quiet.

The decades which saw England's transition from the eighteenth to the nineteenth century, the sixty years between 1770 and 1830, have been variously labelled according to the peculiar interests of historians. To the economic historian they are the Age of the (first) Industrial Revolution. To the historian of literature they are the Age of the Romantic Revival. To the historian of government they are dominated by the movement for reform which culminated in the parliamentary Reform Act of 1832 and the Municipal Reform Act of 1835, establishing something faintly resembling a modern system of representative government. To the historian of democracy the story is that of emergent Radicalism, social unrest, Whig treachery and Tory reaction, with Wilkes at one end and the People's Charter at the other. The most innocuous label is undoubtedly 'The Age of Improvement', for whatever was happening was directly or indirectly concerned to improve the human condition in the sublunary world and (if only incidentally) the world to come. Perhaps it would be best to call it 'The Age of Everything', for verily everything seems to have been happening. Industrial and agrarian change, parliamentary reform, the *Lyrical Ballads*, Constable's landscapes, the Waverley Novels, Miss Austen's 'ivories', Mr Pickwick, Nash's London. The most far-reaching formative forces were the religious revival arising from the labours of John Wesley and the philosophic radicalism arising out of the labours of Jeremy Bentham. And out of it all, like a conscience-stricken mouse emerging from the mountains long in labour, was to come forth the Age of Queen Victoria, with the steam-locomotive, the chimneypot hat, *In Memoriam*, and the Great Exhibition.

Wesley and Bentham, of all eighteenth-century Englishmen, did most to shape the age that succeeded them. Wesley (1703–91) devoted himself to the conversion of England, travelling close on a quarter of a million miles on horseback, and preaching at least fifteen sermons a week, often in the open air, since the Anglican Church, of which he always professed himself a loyal member, closed its doors in horror of his enthusiastic 'rabble-rousing' style. He left England sown with Methodist chapels and with myriads of converts to a religion that was intensely personal, emotional, sometimes superstitious, and resolutely unintellectual. His appeal was to the poor, the forsaken, the misprized. In an increasingly mechanistic world, where working-people seemed to be losing their value as individual men and women, he taught the poor that even if they did not matter to men they mattered supremely to God. He brought a gleam of other-worldly hope to large numbers of men who might otherwise have sunk into sullen resignation or been driven into desperate courses. Teaching the poor to die quietly, Cobbett called it, and not to cut the throats of their betters. 'The opium of the people,' later radicals were to call it. Of course that was not the whole story. Methodism, by the very self-help, even self-government, which it encouraged in the religious life of the Little Bethels, had a long-term politically educative influence among the working-men who were nourished there. Wesley also had a lot to do with stirring the Established Church into evangelical life as time went on. The great Evangelical Revival in middle-class England, typified by Wilberforce and satirized by Thackeray, owed much to the dynamic of Wesley.

Jeremy Bentham, in a life of eighty-four years (he lived from 1748 to 1832), taught men to apply to laws and institutions the acid test of utility, in terms of 'the greatest happiness of the greatest number'. He was the great questioner of things established, the great 'debunker', a later age would say, the steady and prosy purveyor of a corrosive irreverence in a world encumbered with the social, political, and especially the legal, lumber of the ages. 'What is the use of it?' Bentham asked, and generally produced a negative answer resembling that of the wide-eyed child who pointed out that the emperor was wearing no clothes. He taught a whole generation of disciples a rationale of common sense, and in his mole-like way he accomplished for England much of what the Revolution and Napoleon did for France. In more moderate terms, it may be said that he brought England out of the age of humbug into the age of humdrum. The Utilitarians who sought to apply the Benthamite criterion were the opposite numbers in England of the *philosophes* in France before the Revolution, and their memorials were to be found in government Blue Books, in the new Poor Law of 1834, in a civil service recruited by competitive examination. In their day they were regarded as dangerous men, men to be watched, though their ranks were filled from the middle classes, and their most effective figure was the great pioneer of public health, Sir Edwin Chadwick. Their intellectual ancestry was French and Scottish, and the English never liked them. As John Stuart Mill protested, the description so often given of a Benthamite was that of a mere reasoning machine. Probably most Englishmen still think of a Benthamite in terms of the ignorant, but amusing, parody of the type by Charles Dickens in Mr Filer (*The Chimes*, 1844) and Mr Gradgrind (*Hard Times*, 1854): hard-hearted, calculating, insensible to the natural feelings of average humanity. Frigid and scholastic many of Bentham's disciples may have been, but Bentham's portrait reveals the humane and humorous face of an eighteenth-century philanthropist; and of his followers it may be said that, like the Fabian Society of a century later, they carried through a revolution by injecting their sense of rational social purpose into every section of our public life, and that 'by the straight and narrow paths they cut we are walking still'.

13

War and Peace

♪ When Revolution broke out in France in 1789 Bentham was not impressed. He had spoken scathingly in his *Principles of Legislation* of those who run after political liberty, or 'the most equal distribution which can be imagined of political power', people who would imperil all the happiness of a nation 'for the sake of transporting power into the hands of those whom an invincible ignorance will not permit to use it, except for their own destruction'. As for the Rights of Man, they were nonsense, 'nonsense on stilts', or, as Burke was to say, 'blurred paltry shreds of paper'. Indeed when the doctrine of the Rights of Man crossed the Channel most Englishmen thought to recognize in them the familiar and well-established Common Law rights of Englishmen tricked out in the gaudy plumage of Gallic rhetoric, and none the better for that. They were not unsympathetic with the French. They thought, and it was the opening theme of Burke's *Reflections*, that they were at last catching up with the English. The younger Pitt, who was now in charge of affairs, felt it his duty to applaud them, since they were apparently about to equip themselves with a constitution on the English model. A decent system of government might make France more formidable as a rival, but it should make her less obnoxious as a neighbour. In general it seemed that France would be fully preoccupied with her great task for years to come, so that on the whole there was little need to take serious note of the Revolution. It might be, as Burke for a moment thought, that the affair of the Bastille was simply 'the old Parisian ferocity' of the Fronde 'breaking out again in a shocking manner'. He added: 'What will be the event, it is hard, I think, to say.'

There were some, like Dr Richard Price and the gentlemen of the Society for Commemorating the Revolution of 1688, who were warmer in their welcome and wished to send fraternal messages to the French, who, it seemed to them, were about to complete the Glorious Revolution of 1688. Though that Revolution, as Dr Price said, 'was a great one, it was by no means a complete work'. It had left our Constitution in an imperfect state, particularly in respect of 'the INEQUALITY OF OUR REPRESENTATION', and the civil rights of the Protestant Dissenters. 'After sharing in the benefits of one Revolution I have been spared to be a witness of two other Revolutions, both glorious. And now methinks, I see the ardour for liberty catching and spreading; a general amendment in human affairs...' Dr Price's commemorative sermon at the Meeting House in the Old Jewry brought forth Burke's famous 'intervention' in the form of his *Reflections on the Revolution in France* in 1790, a book that was like a historical deed, conjuring up the horrid shape of things to come with all the prescience of what Sir Lewis Namier called Burke's 'malignant imagination'. It sold nearly 20,000 copies within twelve months, and George III had copies elegantly bound to give to his friends, for it was, he said, 'a book which every gentleman ought to read'. Pitt remained unmoved. When Tom Paine replied with *The Rights of Man* next year, he has been reported as saying: 'Tom Paine was quite in the right,' adding, 'What am I to do? As things are, if I were to encourage Tom Paine's opinions we should have a bloody revolution.' Perhaps it was France's preoccupation, as well as his own hope to be able to complete his great programme of financial reform, that led him to make his most famous, and most derided, prophecy in his Budget Speech of 17 February 1792: 'Unquestionably there never was a time in the history of this country when, from the situation of Europe, we might more reasonably expect fifteen years of peace than at the present moment.' This was certainly not the speech of a warmonger on the watch for a chance to take over France's colonies. Within something less than twelve months Great Britain was at war with France, principally over France's opening of the Scheldt and threat to the Low Countries. The war was declared by France, and it was to last with short intermission for twenty-two years.

It was still the second Hundred Years War, begun in the reign of William III, and the stakes were still world dominion in terms of trade and colonies; but the protagonists may now be seen to have represented antagonist philosophies. Great Britain, being the power already in possession of the richest regions of the extra-European world, was moved by the conservative principles appropriate to a possessor defending an ancient inheritance and the latter-day loot of empires, east and west. Certainly, in the War of the Revolution and the Napoleonic Wars Great Britain professed always to be at war in defence of liberty, and primarily in its aspect of national self-determination. France, on the other hand, now lived and moved and had her being in the revolutionary philosophy of 'Liberty, Equality and Fraternity', the greatest of these being Equality. She would liberate the peoples everywhere into the gospel of the Rights of Man—at the point of the bayonet. The war of the revolution, Burke said, was not 'France extending a foreign empire over other nations', but 'a sect aiming at universal empire, and beginning with the conquest of France'. From the centre of Europe thus secured, the Revolution could move outwards, like a crusade, to join forces with its friends in every country. Thus, as Pitt insisted, (Great Britain was not at war with France but with an armed doctrine.) It is very likely true that he never understood what that doctrine was. Coleridge observed in *The Character of Mr Pitt*, which he wrote for the *Morning Post* in 1800, that the French Revolution was 'a new event; the old routine of reasoning, the common trade of politics were to become obsolete'. Unprepared for it, Pitt half favoured, half condemned it, knowing neither what he favoured nor what he condemned. Yet he stood at the head of a nation which was, in Albert Sorel's words, 'the most redoubtable enemy of the French Revolution because she was the only country to oppose it with analogous forces: national principles and popular passions'. Her great captains were more men of passion than of principle. Nelson knew only that he hated Frenchmen, and taught his midshipmen that it was the duty of Englishmen to do so. Wellington disliked generalizations, and was content to describe the chief of his country's enemies as lacking the instincts of a gentleman. The nation, as so often, was to triumph despite its leaders.

Pitt's failure to understand the Revolution and the enormous energies released by the quasi-religious nature of its philosophy, led him to imagine that the war would be a short one.(He believed that France in her disorganized state was unlikely to be able to resist for long the trained and disciplined armies of the great land powers of Europe or to maintain the financial burdens of a prolonged contest. Great Britain's best service, he argued, along with most of his colleagues, would be to weaken France's resistance by depriving her of her sources of wealth from ocean trade and colonies. He had given much time to the rebuilding of British naval power after the failures of the American War, laying down twenty-four capital ships, raising the peace-time establishment of the navy from fifteen to eighteen thousand men, and expending £180,000 on strengthening the forts and naval defences of the West Indies.) Naval warfare, then, would engage Britain's main efforts, along with close military co-operation with her allies in Flanders. In the event, however, Pitt squandered resources in men and money on a number of projects against metropolitan France which served mainly to unite the French against the common enemy. Dispersion of forces—'too little and too late'—notably at Toulon and in La Vendée, is the principal criticism to be brought against his strategy in the early years of the war. In the long term, his most costly mistake was to continue his pre-war policy of building up the Sinking Fund for the reduction of the National Debt by raising money at high rates of interest, an error which reflects his misinterpretation of the war as one more eighteenth-century war, limited in its incident and its length. He had all his father's sublime self-confidence and none of his father's grasp of the lines and logistics of a world strategy. However, he showed some of his father's genius when, on his return to power in May 1804, he inspired the Third Coalition with Russia, Austria and Sweden which culminated in the victory of Trafalgar—and in Napoleon's crushing land victory at Austerlitz. Figuratively speaking, the war was a contest between a whale and an elephant, and, not until some years after Pitt's death after Austerlitz, did the great maritime power put an army into Portugal under Wellesley in 1808.

Pitt's greatest material contribution to his country's war-winning assets had been made by his policies of financial and economical reform before the war broke out, so that 'Pitt's gold' gained a legendary name as the cement of coalition after coalition in the subsequent years of danger and defeat. His contribution to the nation's morale was no less momentous. In his unwavering spirit he stood for the England of his most memorable speech: the England that saved herself by her exertions and Europe by her example. 'The pilot who weathered the storm' is a somewhat negative tribute to the endurance of a man who died at forty-seven in his country's service no less devotedly, though less dramatically, than Nelson at the same age. The poets never had much to say in his praise. Poetry was inveterately political in those days, and the poets were mostly Radicals, even Jacobins, while the Prime Minister was 'the Apostate Pitt', the erstwhile reformer who had postponed reformism for the duration. One does not repair one's house in the hurricane season, though a romantic poet may think it heroic to try. So the poets preferred the tribune, Charles James Fox. Wordsworth's lovely lines 'Loud is the vale! the Voice is up...' were written 'on reading in a newspaper that the dissolution of Mr Fox was hourly expected'. Only the Tory, Walter Scott, was raised up for a moment to something like poetry by the death of Mr Pitt:

> Now is the stately column broke,
> The beacon-fire is quenched in smoke,
> The trumpet's silver sound is still,
> The warder silent on the hill...

Like all Great Britain's wars until the twentieth century, the Napoleonic War was fought at a distance, and generally by professionals paid for their services. It has frequently been remarked that Jane Austen's young ladies were not surprised to find that their young gentlemen were not in uniform, though Miss Austen herself had two admirals among her brothers. The long struggle came harshly home to the labourer and the artisan when Napoleon's blockade, or 'Continental System', and our own retaliatory Orders in Council of 1807 began to affect the continental markets for British manufactures, and again when the American Non-Intercourse Act against the Orders in Council closed the market for a third of Britain's textiles. By 1812 exports were down by 33⅓ per cent, prices were 87 per cent above pre-war level, and the price of wheat was 160s. a quarter, so that the quartern loaf cost 1s. 8d. The enclosure movement was greatly accelerated by the needs of food production, and (as Cobbett bitterly observed) farm labourers were becoming known as 'the labouring *poor*'. Since 1795 the pauperizing expedient known as 'Speenhamland' had been subsidizing the labourer's wages out of the rates, and before the end of the war expenditure on poor-relief had risen from four to six millions. Machine-breaking was made a capital offence in 1812, and soon there were as many troops in the industrial Midlands and North as had gone to the Peninsula with Wellington. Pitt's Combination Acts, to prohibit associations for the alteration of the hours and wages of labour, had been on the statute-book since 1799–1800, though without much effect. Not only fear of secret combination of workmen but the sacrosanct free-trade political economy of Adam Smith lay behind these measures. By leaving the law of supply and demand to operate freely, it was argued, 'things would find their own level', a paraphrase which constituted, as Coleridge once said, 'an ironical definition of a storm'. When, in the first year of the peace, Lord Liverpool introduced a Corn Law (known as 'the Waterloo Corn Law') to arrest the collapse of agricultural prices by keep-ing out foreign corn until the home price reached 80s. a quarter, he apologized for this breach of *laissez-faire* principles with the plea that in 1814 he was faced with an exceptional situation. 'The general principle,' he said, 'supposing all nations, or at least the most considerable nations, to act upon it, was that in these cases the Legislature ought not to interfere, but should leave everything to find its own level.' Lord Sidmouth, his colleague at the Home Office, once wrote an *Ode to the Author of the Wealth of Nations*. There was comfort in Dr Johnson's couplet:

> How small, of all the ills that men endure,
> The part which Kings or States can cause or cure.

Perhaps that was one reason why, in the same year, they abolished the Income Tax which Pitt had first imposed in 1798 (inflicting the 'penal' rate of 2s. in the £ on incomes above £200 per annum), though it must be remembered that they were redeeming the promise of Mr Pitt that the tax would be for the duration of the war only, and Mr Pitt was their idol even more than Adam Smith.

In the House of Commons, the younger Pitt was to be referred to respectfully as 'Mr Pitt' long into the reign of Queen Victoria. He laid the impress of his upright and unbending spirit upon a whole generation of men who thought, with George Canning, that it would 'defy ingenuity...to trace any circle of greatness from which Mr Pitt shall be excluded'. He has never been exceeded by any other English statesman in the number of eminent men whom he trained and inspired. Canning himself, whose 'political allegiance was buried in his grave', was to be followed by Castlereagh, Liverpool and Wellesley. Perhaps it is not too much to say that Mr Pitt was the prototype of the ramrod figure with the poker-face and the stiff upper-lip which imposed itself upon Europe in the nineteenth century as the 'stock' English statesman. Certainly, as Canning's biographer wrote, 'servile imitation, obstinately pursued in the face of new conditions, is often the most insincere form of insult', and this was reflected in the long Tory ascendancy of the Liverpool Administration (1812–27) which saw the great war to its victorious conclusion and presided over the first troubled years of the peace. 'Apish Jupiters' the radical *Black Dwarf* once called them, anxious to wield the thunderbolts of their great predecessor but incapable; inheriting Pitt's errors without his genius; forgetful of his reformism but imitative of his repressive measures. Disraeli correctly recognized Pitt's claims to be remembered as a Tory in the first half of his career when he was concerned to combat borough-mongering, and to promote economy, French alliance, and commercial treaties, rather than in the latter part, which was 'pure Whiggism'—close Parliaments, war with France, national debt, and commercial restriction—'all prompted and inspired by the arch-Whig trumpeter, Mr Burke'. Disraeli's later concern to trace *le sang pur* of Toryism, however, must not blind us to the fact that the party which Pitt shaped out of the national resistance

to the French Revolution in arms was to be steadily transformed
in a liberal direction in the age of Lord Liverpool, more especially
after 1821 when Robert Peel replaced Sidmouth as Home
Secretary and George Canning replaced Castlereagh as Foreign
Secretary, while Mr Huskisson, as President of the Board of
Trade, embarked on the policy of tariff reduction which was to
culminate in the repeal of the Corn Laws in 1846. *Pace* Disraeli,
the infusion of liberalism into the Tory party in the ministry of
Lord Liverpool was to save its life as a national party in the days
of Sir Robert Peel, and even to make possible the career of
Disraeli himself after the mid century.

(European Liberals have never quite forgiven Great Britain for
her victory over Napoleon.) At St Helena the Emperor imposed
the legend of his liberal intentions for Europe, and did not fail
to blame the English for frustrating them. For some years after
Waterloo certain English intellectuals, Bentham, Hazlitt, Leigh
Hunt and others, were persuaded that the great battle had been
the victory of the forces of reaction, not least in their own
country. Hazlitt put on a crepe mourning-band. James Mill
wrote: 'Bentham and I have been mourning a victory which
must certainly prove unfavourable to a cosmopolite philosophy.'
As is not uncommon, war against a despotism produced a certain
despotic temper in those concerned to overthrow it. From the
time of Pitt's 'triumvirate' (Pitt, Dundas, Grenville) down to the
days when Liverpool–Castlereagh–Sidmouth–Eldon presented
the grim aspect of a multiple monster to the young Shelley and
Lord Byron, authority had become concentrated in fewer and
fewer hands under the stresses of war and the perils of peace.
(When the war was over, Great Britain found herself bracketed in
the popular mind with her war-time allies, the despotic powers
of Russia, Prussia, and the Austria of Metternich. 'Under our
presiding influence', one Whig gentleman wrote in his diary,
'the Monarchs are leagued against every exertion of popular
energy.' The taint of despotism seemed very black indeed when
Lord Castlereagh, representing his country at Congresses of
despotic monarchies concerned with preserving the peace,
and incidentally with suppressing liberal movements abroad,

made obligatorily polite allusions to the Tsar and his Holy Alliance. In private the Foreign Secretary might describe this Christian trade-union of kings as 'a piece of sublime mysticism and nonsense', but this could not save him from Liberal tirades against 'Castlereagh and the Holy Leaguers'. Not until Canning took his place and pointedly abstained from such associations did Great Britain enter into the role of 'friend of peoples struggling to be free', notably into Canning's benevolent attitude to the Spanish colonies in South America. At last she had entered into her favourite role in the age of Palmerston and Gladstone, freed at last from the suspicions and ambiguities engendered by her former association with the despotic monarchies.

There can be little doubt that Great Britain emerged from the long contest with Napoleon complacent to a fault. The 'Sacred Constitution' under which she rode out the storm could be even more readily identified with the Ark of the Covenant, and long-postponed reforms could be further delayed by respectful reference to the old order of things which had carried her through. The English had been shut up in their island with little intermission for nearly twenty years. The alacrity with which they rushed abroad in the brief breathing-space of the Peace of Amiens (25 May 1802 to 18 May 1803) and the positive stampede to the Continent in 1814–15 were evidence of their travel-starved condition. The gorgeous insularity of Mr Podsnap which Dickens was to satirize in *Our Mutual Friend* (1864–5) with the celebrated boast that 'this island was Blest, sir, to the Direct Exclusion of such Other Countries as—as there may happen to be' was no doubt a legacy of the beleaguered years of the early century as well as a product of Victorian pride in Victorian achievements. Nor is it altogether surprising that London, the only capital city in Europe which had not heard the drums of *la Grande Armée* or seen the Absolute riding by on a white horse, should have imagined herself to enjoy the favour of a special Providence, and cherished a grateful attachment to her splendid isolation. The Gordon Riots in 1780, the distant shadow of the guillotine in the 'nineties, the alarms and excursions of the immediate post-war years, all bequeathed a memory of 'the Mob' which haunted

Englishmen long into the new century. When in 1848 every European capital save London experienced insurrection, great or small, the English were reinforced in their gratitude to their private Providence. The mid-Victorian generations had little need of Alfred Tennyson's injunction not to imitate 'the red fool-fury of the Seine', to shun 'the falsehood of extremes', and in general to rest assured of the moral and physical supremacy of a people

> whom the roar of Hougoumont
> Left mightiest of all peoples under heaven.

In 1832 Lord Grey and the Whigs passed the Great Reform Bill, enfranchising the £10 householder in the towns and slightly remodelling the county freehold franchise, while inaugurating a redistribution of seats at the expense of the immemorial 'rotten boroughs'. This, the Duke of Wellington said at the time, was the first step down the slippery slope to 'a fierce democracy'. It was quite obvious to the Duke, and many more, that

> If I say A, I must say B,
> And so go on to C, and D,
> And so you see no end there'll be
> If once I have said A, and B.

A philosophic Tory like Coleridge deplored the Act's want of principle, in attempting to draw 'such a confessedly unmeaning and unjustifiable line of political empiricism as £10 house-holders'. Once the principle of representation of interests has been deserted in favour of a delegation of persons, he added, 'you can never, in reason, stop short of universal suffrage: and in that case I am sure that women have as good a right to vote as men'. To stop short, however, was the very meaning and purpose of the Act of 1832. Whigs and Tories alike were concerned to establish the myth that 1832 was 'a final and irrevocable settlement' (to use Sir Robert Peel's words), a myth that gained for Lord John Russell the nickname 'Finality Jack'. The Radicals, of course, only accepted the Act on the proverbial principle that half a loaf is better than no bread, and set about agitating for a further instal-ment of the democratic franchise by canvassing 'the People's

Charter'. But thirty-five years were to pass before a second Reform Act came upon the statute-book. The year 1832 was, indeed, an early example of that wise, instinctive 'concessionism' by which the higher classes of Victorian England turned a precipice into a gradual slope towards political democracy. As Walter Bagehot put it, in the year of the Second Reform Bill (1867): 'While they have the power they must remove, not only every actual grievance, but where it is possible, every seeming grievance, too; they must willingly concede every claim which they can safely concede, in order that they may not have to concede unwillingly some claim which would impair the safety of the country.' What would happen when they came to the point of no return? the point where they could not concede further without catastrophe to their pockets and their prospects? Harold Laski was to ask the question when the twentieth century had passed beyond its 'teens, and to answer it. This was the point in time when the upper classes would become Fascists and resort to violence in defence of their interests. The twentieth century has long passed its half-way mark, and they are still conceding.

All that was conceded in 1832 may be summed up in the statement that the Great Reform Bill marks the point at which the upper classes, aristocracy, gentry, or whatever, took the middle classes into partnership. It was a very one-sided partnership for a long time. The first reformed House of Commons differed hardly at all from its predecessors in social composition. It contained an overwhelming majority of country gentlemen and members (and auxiliaries) of the aristocracy. 'By their works ye shall know them.' During the five years between the passing of the Great Reform Bill and the accession of Queen Victoria it abolished slavery in the colonies with £20,000,000 in compensation for the slave-owners; it passed the first effective Factory Act for the protection of women and children only; it made the first state grant (£20,000) for the provision of primary education, but without committing itself to state control; it put an end to the 'Speenhamland' system; and it passed the Municipal Reform Act which put borough government on an elective basis wider than that pertaining to parliamentary constituencies, thus inaugurating local authorities that could be used for the well-being and amenities of the town-dwelling population henceforward: possibly a greater step in the long run towards social improvement than the Great Reform Bill itself.

It was in the year immediately preceding the Great Reform Bill that Thomas Carlyle noted the most characteristic feature of the era that was dawning. In an essay in the *Edinburgh Review* called 'Characteristics', the future Sage of Chelsea (still observing life from a farm in Dumfriesshire), wrote: 'The state of Society in our days is, of all possible states, the least an unconscious one: this is specially the Era when all manner of Inquiries into what was once the unfelt, involuntary sphere of man's existence, find their place, and, as it were, occupy the whole domain of thought. ...Never since the beginning of time was there, that we hear or read of, so intensely self-conscious a Society.' Never did a people subject itself to such prolonged and rigorous self-examination. Mostly, but not entirely, this self-examination was undertaken by Royal Commissions. 'Blue Books' containing the findings of these inquiries were on sale by 1835. The public read them, sometimes with startled horror. Novelists like Disraeli and Charles Kingsley turned them into novels. Such revelations on the many-sided 'Condition-of-England Question' came home to people with scarifying force at a time of crisis like that of the cholera outbreak of 1830, and especially the frightening suspicion that none of the measures taken to combat the crisis had had the least effect on its incidence or its departure. It was especially terrifying to discover that the cholera was no respecter of persons. It came very near to the victor of Waterloo himself when it struck down his 'amiable friend' Harriet Arbuthnot in August 1834. Perhaps, Carlyle observed, it was only by dying of typhus and infecting seventeen of her neighbours that a poor Irish widow could prove her sisterhood, or that we are veritably members one of another, in this age of the cash nexus. Certainly there were early Victorian cynics to maintain that the health of the poor would be better taken care of when it became clear that they were likely to infect their betters. 'The English think soap is civilization,' Treitschke is said to have remarked. They certainly came to think it was safety. 'The middle classes know', Lord Shaftesbury said, 'that the safety of their lives and property depend upon their having around them a peaceful, happy and moral population.' He might have added 'clean'. There could have been many worse grounds for the great Tory Evangelical's devotion to the well-being of his fellow creatures.

The heroic age of the Industrial Revolution was over, and men were counting the cost. Poets who had once celebrated its achievements with classical comparisons were taking up the theme of the Dark Satanic Mills. As early as 1803, Henry Kirke White was looking back at Nottingham from Clifton Grove with mixed feelings:

> ...where the town's blue turrets dimly rise,
> And manufacture taints the ambient skies,
> The pale mechanic leaves the labouring loom,
> The air-pent hold, the pestilential room,
> And rushes out, impatient to begin
> The stated course of customary sin...

Including, doubtless, the demon drink. Another poet had already commended Methodism as an alternative. This very enthusiasm, Coleridge was suggesting in 1796, 'does perhaps supersede the use of spirituous liquors and bring on the same pleasing tumult of the brain without injuring the health or exhausting the wages'. This from Coleridge, of all people! Not the least of the demons now to be combated were those of ugliness and boredom. The hideous brick walls that came to constitute man's industrial prison in the nineteenth century were going up everywhere, and the English became the first people to find themselves face to face with a phenomenon new to Western Europe—the industrial town. There had always been towns, and in sundry times and places they had been the principal nurseries of culture and of the higher consciousness of mankind. What happened in nineteenth-century England bore little or no relation to such traditions. Hordes of men, women and children were swiftly and quite literally swallowed up in the dark and barren fastnesses of an industrial wilderness without either prevision of, or provision for, the most elementary needs of an urban population in terms of health, amenity, or even law and order. The horrific scars which this transformation left upon the English landscape are not wholly healed even today, while the scars which it left on the mind and spirit of the people can be detected everywhere in the politics of Socialism. English literature from Charles Kingsley and Elizabeth Gaskell and Dickens down to Mark Rutherford and George Gissing and William Morris reflects the complex beastliness of the story. It was D. H. Lawrence, the miner's son from the industrial Midlands, who uttered the last great cry of shame upon his countrymen: 'It was ugliness which really betrayed the spirit of man in the nineteenth century...The human soul needs actual beauty even more than bread.'

The boredom of the new industrial life was perhaps more insidious even than its physical ugliness. Men had long suffered the 'sickening aversion' for their work which the Radical leader Francis Place, the breeches-maker of Charing Cross, tells of as a consequence of the deadly monotony even of domestic and rural labour. Daniel Defoe had spoken of his countrymen as the 'most lazy-diligent Nation in the world', prone to work very hard until they had collected a pocket full of money and then to go idle, and perhaps drunk, until all was gone. Such irregularity was incompatible with machine industry, which demands a steady rhythm in the worker, akin to the rhythm of the machine itself. This alien rhythm of the machine, now replacing the familiar even if equally laborious rhythm of nature, was the real tyranny of industrialism. It took several generations of Sunday Schools with their inculcation of the virtues especially valuable in the artisan and the machine-minder—punctuality, diligence, sobriety, thrift—to turn the people of the old crafts, the villages, and the cottage industries into good factory-hands. No wonder the mill-owner patronized the Sunday School, the school of the elementary virtues essential to industrial discipline. Such conditioning achieved its ends, taming the people of the older, wilder England for a different world.

Much of the trouble, of course, was due to the fact that although the English had towns they had remained a deeply rural people. They had never developed an urban tradition either of building or of living. Their big towns were, and some still are, collections of villages, like London itself. Just for a moment, at the beginning of the nineteenth century, they indulged in a real urban style. Regency London still survives in sufficient quantity in the neighbourhood of Regent's Park to show what could happen when a profligate prince and a masterly architect, eluding for an hour the limitations normally imposed by the 'man-in-the-street' through his elected representatives in the House of Commons, came together to construct an urban plan. Nash's London was the first and (it seems) the last fling of a truly urban style in the history of modern England. Close on its heels came the 'great divide' which the late C. S. Lewis once called 'the greatest of all divisions in the history of the West...the greatest change in the history of Western man'. The divide runs like a chasm, or a geological fault, across our historical landscape, somewhere between the world we live in and the world of Jane Austen and Sir Walter Scott, somewhere between the England of *Our Mutual Friend* (1865) and the world of Mr Pickwick (1837). The late Humphry House went so far as to say that between the two the very physical features and complexions of the characters in a Dickens novel seem to have changed as much as their clothes. A new style, a new quality of life, was developing, another kind of consciousness, a change not merely in the landscape but in the scope and tempo of individual living. House thought the change was brought about by the coming of the railways. Perhaps it was. Looking down on a passing train from a bridge over the London and Birmingham line near Rugby, Dr Arnold was jubilant. 'I rejoice to see it,' he cried, 'and to think that feudality is gone for ever.'

14

Victorian Ages

The term 'Victorian' was coined in the year 1851, the year of the Great Exhibition, but Victorianism existed long before and was by no means confined to the Queen's dominions. Much that we now identify as essentially Victorian may be discovered at Windsor Castle in the reign of the Queen's grandfather, where the King presided as a paragon of domestic virtue, and no less clearly on the confines of Clapham Common where dwelt the Evangelical families of the 'Sect'. In 1787 William Wilberforce, the most celebrated of the Claphamites, induced the King to issue a royal proclamation condemning vice (or, at any rate, as Sydney Smith said, vice among persons with incomes under £500 per annum) and founded a Vigilance Committee. Many believed the access of propriety among the well-to-do as the old King's reign went on was a consequence of the French Revolution, for, as Lady Bracknell said, 'we all know what that led to'. Bowdler's[1] *Family Shakespeare* appeared in 1818, and a strong moralistic tide is to be detected beneath the glittering surface of Regency England. A certain air of stuffiness, smugness, prudery, philistinism, not to mention humbug, still afflicts our nostrils at the mention of the word 'Victorian' despite the endeavours of recent historians to dispel it. It proceeds from any part of Europe where middle-class comfort prevailed, from the Germany of *Buddenbrooks* and the France of Stendhal and Balzac as strongly as the England of the Prince Consort. Not that it can be equated at all simply with the dominance of that complicated monster known

[1] Thomas Bowdler was pained that the works of the Bard contained blemishes which rendered them unsuitable for reading aloud in the family. His expurgated Shakespeare went into six editions in 1818, and he went on to treat similarly Gibbon's *Decline and Fall*, leaving out the whole of the fourteenth and fifteenth chapters. The Bowdlers certainly had a sincere appreciation of good literature, and did much to inaugurate the much ridiculed prudery of Victorian England.

as 'the middle class'. So-called 'Victorian attitudes' were the attitudes of whole societies. So widespread was the cult of *Gemütlichkeit* (comfortableness) in the German lands by the early decades of the nineteenth century that we might suspect much that we call 'Victorian' to have been brought here by Albert of Saxe-Coburg-Gotha. The Queen's husband was indeed the model Victorian, and a good deal of what we call Victorian might better be known, perhaps, as Albertian.

As for the Queen herself, she was born in 1819 and had lived her early years in the garish afterglow of the Regency. When she married Prince Albert, her husband was frequently distressed to discover in his young wife a considerable desire to frolic. What she chiefly loved in preference to her husband's learned discussions with his learned friends was to dance all night and ride out at dawn to see the sun rise over London. She was hardly beautiful, but she had a graceful carriage and sat well on a side-saddle. She had the face of a 'poppet' (=*poupée*, or doll), with slightly protrusive china-blue eyes, a neat little beak of a nose, and very fair hair flattened to a small round head. All her life she was to respond readily to the flattery of male persons, whether that of Lord Melbourne, 'Dear Lord M.', who, as her first prime minister, guided her first steps as Queen of England with avuncular eighteenth-century charm, or the somewhat fulsome flattery of Benjamin Disraeli, Lord Beaconsfield, who (privately) called her 'The Fairy'. There were other conquests of which she could know nothing. 'I have fallen hopelessly in love with the Queen', the young Charles Dickens wrote to a friend on the day after the royal nuptials in February 1840:

I am utterly lost in misery and can do nothing.

> My heart is at Windsor,
> My heart is not here,
> My heart is at Windsor,
> Following my dear.

Her last and most unlikely conquest was Lytton Strachey. Albert, of course, held her whole heart always, and it was Albert who, with his Germanic notions of monarchy, made her into the 'right-down, regular, royal Queen' who could, after a moment of hesitation, laugh at the Savoyards when they came to play *The Gondoliers* at Windsor.

The monarchy was indeed due for a revival after the unpopularity and disrespect brought upon it by Victoria's two egregious predecessors. When, in 1867, Walter Bagehot came to write his celebrated essay on *The English Constitution*, he could include two whole chapters on the monarchy, devoting a good deal of space to 'the use of the Queen' as the means to 'intelligible government'. For, as he put it, 'a vast number like their minds to dwell more upon her than upon anything else, and therefore she is inestimable,' and more especially to that half of the human race who care fifty times more for a marriage than a ministry. 'A *family* on the throne', Bagehot wrote, 'brings down the pride of sovereignty to the level of petty life. To state the matter shortly, Royalty is a government in which the attention of the nation is concentrated on one person doing interesting actions.' This keen observer, even in the year of the Second Reform Bill, could conclude that the monarchy 'gives a vast strength to the entire constitution by enlisting on its behalf the credulous obedience of enormous masses'. He found it a matter for congratulation that monarchy should act as 'a disguise' because 'the masses of Englishmen are not fit for an elective government...Its mystery is its life. We must not let in daylight upon magic.' Needless to say, however, the Queen's subjects took a somewhat patronizing view of the totemistic cults of their fellow subjects in more remote parts of the dominions of the Great White Queen. It was in 1916 that Sir Arthur Steel-Maitland wrote to *The Times*: 'Democracy will only be equal to its task if it can see through make-believes to reality.' Democracy and its task was still remote from the England of 1867.

There were several Victorian Ages. The Second Reform Act, of 1867, known as 'the leap in the dark' because it extended the suffrage to all householders in the towns and slightly widened the franchise in the counties, may be said to mark the end of the first, that robust and confident age whose typical phenomenon was the railway and whose apotheosis was the Great Exhibition. The railway age really began on the day in September 1830 when the Duke of Wellington formally opened the Liverpool and Manchester Railway. In 1830 there were fewer than 100 miles of railway track in the country, but by the end of 1850 there were some 6,000. The building of the great London termini reflects most notably the robust self-confidence of the nation at that time. A terminus such as Euston was built (1838) by men who knew themselves to be building for eternity as surely as the men who built the medieval cathedrals or the pyramids. There were six of these monuments of permanence in London by the middle of the 'Hungry 'Forties', the very time when Europe at large was experiencing another spate of revolutions and certain British prophets of doom (like Thomas Carlyle) were giving our institutions another five years to live. Scarcely twelve months after the erection of the masterpiece in Euston Square, a railway train carried a hundred London constables to Birmingham to disperse a Chartist rally at the Bull Ring. The Chartist Convention called this 'a wanton, flagrant, and unjust outrage...by a bloodthirsty and unconstitutional force from London'. The arrival of the London reinforcement by railway gave notice that the twenty-four-hour start which provincial disorder had for so long enjoyed over the peace-keeping forces of the capital was at last coming to an end.

The Chartist Movement[1] and the 'Hungry 'Forties' coincided with a revolution in transport which revealed the country to itself by linking its various regions and bringing the physical facts of life under the passing gaze of thousands who in earlier times might have remained as distantly ignorant of them as the people of China or Peru. The actual manner of financing the railways also served to promote the development of what Carlyle called 'organic filaments', by spreading the network of property far and wide in the ramifying interests of a multitude of small investors. The 'railway share' brought the habit of investment to

[1] Chartism takes its name from the 'People's Charter', a six-point programme for a democratic franchise, all of which except the demand for annual parliaments was to be instituted over the next hundred years. But Chartism is more properly the name for the working-class movement for social justice in general over half a century.

men at every social level, to the trustees of the widow and the orphan, the chapel and the school and the co-operative stores. The growing dominance of the railway time-table in people's lives ('Bradshaw' first appeared in 1839) no doubt had something to do with the increasing regularity of life and habit which was overtaking the ways of an older and wilder England, a society in which the male sex—for so long resplendent in wigs and ruffles, brocaded coats and silken raiment—was encasing itself in the sombre, hideous, industrial uniform known as 'morning dress'.

The *annus mirabilis* of these far-reaching changes in life's tempo and rhythm came in 1851 when the excursion trains unloaded their thousands of ordinary folk at the doors of the Great Exhibition in Hyde Park. The pundits had prophesied disorder, riot, even revolution in the capital with the arrival of these hordes of country cousins, not to mention international crooks and anarchists, in the city whose streets were paved with gold; but all passed off peacefully in a fume of ginger beer and a crumble of penny buns. It was more than an exhibition of the arts and industries of the new age. It was an exhibition of the growing respectability of the working-class world at whose hands these wonders had come. The 'swinish multitude', the 'great unwashed', the 'mobility': such terms were henceforth to become myths of historic memory, best forgotten. The future was to lie with the 'respectable artisan'. The year of the Great Exhibition saw the foundation of the Amalgamated Society of Engineers, that aristocracy of labour which Disraeli had dreamt of including as a 'Praetorian Guard' among the 'fancy franchises'[1] which appeared in the Conservative Reform Bill of 1867. What was happening was an early phase of that 'universalizing of the middle class' which in the end may prove to have been the greatest single social fact, if not the best description of English social history, in the nineteenth century: the pride and joy of lower middle-class

[1] 'Fancy franchises', or the admission of the more educated and skilled members of the working class, but not the working class *en masse*, to the suffrage, had figured in Disraeli's thinking and speaking on parliamentary reform as early as 1848, although he rejected, even ridiculed, the idea in his speech on the third reading of the Conservative Reform Bill of 1867.

poets and prophets like Martin Tupper (*Proverbial Philosophy*, 1838) and Samuel Smiles (*Self Help*, 1859) and the disdain of revolutionaries like Karl Marx, already at work in that hot-bed of revolution, the Reading-room of the British Museum. The first volume of *Das Kapital* appeared in 1867. It was a long and painful process, fraught with many an hour of danger and dismay for the owners of property. Tennyson's *Locksley Hall* in 1842 contained the lines:

Slowly comes a hungry people, as a lion creeping nigher
Glares at one that nods and winks behind a slowly-dying fire.

Such images of civilization under siege, of beasts advancing out of the darkness upon the camp-fires of the guardians of man's inheritance, were part of that apocalyptic view of history as a great succession of catastrophes which dominated men's minds long into modern times. 'Remember the proud fabric of the French monarchy...supported by the triple aristocracy of the church, the nobility and the parliament', Gibbon had written in 1792. 'They are crumbled into dust; they are vanished from the earth.' Burke's fearful prognostications on the French Revolution had embodied the belief that one mighty blow could overturn the world, a horrid vision which could trigger off the malevolent imagination of a desperado like Arthur Thistlewood of Cato Street fame.[1] Even Macaulay conjured up the vision of a future visitor from New Zealand sitting beside the Thames to sketch the ruins of St Paul's. In *Coningsby* (1844), Disraeli expressed the view that the English social system was in infinitely greater danger than that of France, and in the previous year Lord Shaftesbury had warned the House of Commons that 'no one who knew the facts could hope that twenty years could pass without some mighty convulsion, some displacement of the whole system of society'. How a society thus racked and haunted by premonitions of catastrophe, social revolution, even race suicide, was able to pass peacefully into the humdrum but hopeful world of the Parliamentary Labour Party and the Trades Union Congress

---

[1] The Cato Street conspiracy (1820) was a plot for the wholesale assassination of the Liverpool Cabinet.

is a question only to be answered by the total history of that society over the greater part of a century.

A crucial factor in the story must be the general downward trend of prices in the 1830s together with an unmistakable upward trend in the general standard of living immediately after the bitter years remembered as the Hungry 'Forties. Sir John Clapham's famous dismissal of the notion that everything was getting worse for the working man between the Great Reform Bill and the Great Exhibition as 'a myth that dies hard' is unlikely to solace anyone who chooses to look at all closely at conditions of life and labour in any one industry. Cheaper bread after the repeal of the Corn Laws in 1846 certainly helped. So far from wages being reduced as the price of bread fell, as the Jeremiahs had predicted, wage-rates began moving upwards early in the 1850s, and by 1865 they were on the average nearly 20 per cent above the level of 1848, and the price of necessaries had certainly not risen in anything like proportion. In fact there was a rather better distribution of the national dividend. And yet, 'with what serene conclusiveness', as Carlyle observed, 'a member of some Useful-Knowledge Society stops your mouth with a figure of arithmetic!' Statistical science could prove that the habit of saving had been increasing rapidly, yet the real misery of men was very great. For it had still to be asked: what constitutes the well-being of a man? His wages, and the bread he can buy, are no doubt preliminary to most else. But—can he enjoy hope, can he hope to rise to mastership, how is he treated by his masters?

Practically the whole of Carlyle's great essay, *Chartism* (1839), and his castigation of his own times in the light of an idealized Middle Ages, *Past and Present* (1843), was concerned to insist that the Condition-of-England Question was not political but social and, beyond that, religious. There was no revivalism about this teaching. 'Fancy a man, moreover, recommending his fellow men to believe in God, that Chartism might abate, and the Manchester operatives be got to spin peaceably!' Nor were Parliamentary Radicalism and Benthamite Utility anything but 'shadows of things...barren as the East wind'. Corn Law Repeal,

New Poor Law, and the rest of the popular specifics could be nothing but 'preliminary to some general charge to be taken of the lowest classes by the higher'. For this, Carlyle put no faith in the Tory Democracy of Lord John Manners and 'Young England'.[1] 'Partridge-preserving aristocracy' must give place to those whom he called (after the *chefs de l'industrie* of the Saint-Simonian Socialists) 'Captains of Industry', for he was sure that the problems of modern industry could only be solved by those who were actually engaged in it. Such men must learn from the responsibilities of the feudal lords of medieval society, a society of which he gained an imaginative picture from the *Chronicle of Jocelin of Brakelond*, recently brought out by the Camden Society (1840).

It is perhaps difficult today to form any idea of Carlyle's enormous influence in his own time. In the 1840s he was the author who exercised the most powerful charm upon the minds of young men who were beginning to think, men who were to be decisive in thought and action during the Victorian heyday. 'I am reading Carlyle vehemently', writes the young Bradford manufacturer W. E. Forster (Forster of the Education Act of 1870) in 1842, and urges his fellows to do the same, for he found in Carlyle 'the highest, or rather the deepest, mind of the age... the greatest modifying force of this century.' At no time in their history since the Cromwellian age had the English been so much in love with sermons, so voluptuously addicted to the rods of chastisement in the hands of preachers and prophets, as in the middle years of Queen Victoria.

The thunder-and-lightning preachments of Carlyle served the self-same cause of revived social responsibility to which some of the best energies of the religious denominations were directed as the century went on. The Methodists, who in the eighteenth century had often been politically indifferent or inclined to turn away from what seemed to be the inherent depravity of the

[1] A group of young men, of whom Lord John Manners and George Smythe are the best remembered, who subscribed with the young Benjamin Disraeli in the 1840s to the political and social principles of a romantic Tory Democracy, or an alliance of the aristocracy and the working class.

worldly order of things, steadily became allies of Radical movements for reform after the break-away of democratically inclined congregations like the New Methodist Connection (or the Kilhamites) after 1797, the Primitive Methodists (or the 'Cloweses') after 1812, and the Bible Christians after 1818. Older Nonconformist bodies like the Baptists and the Independents felt the impulse and underwent a plethoric reinvigoration. The Evangelicals within the Church of England gave birth to social reformers whose names are legion in the annals of 'practical Christianity', from Wilberforce and the anti-slavery movement to Shaftesbury and the cause of the chimney-climbing boys. The Broad Church Movement within the Church became the parent of Christian Socialism with F. D. Maurice and Charles Kingsley. The Oxford Movement not only encouraged parishioners to call their parson 'priest' but also 'father', and its revival of the pastoral care of the clergy greatly exceeded its enthusiasm for candles.

Care, conscience, concession, and in the end competition, all served to blunt the edges of social strife. And what of 'the state' and its statutes, all those compulsive agencies which later generations have come to regard as the sole effective organs of distributive justice? What of 'collectivism' and its famous battle with 'individualism', the overthrow of the philosophy of *laissez-faire* at the hands of state intervention, the triumph of 'social purpose' over private selfishness? It is a battle that has occupied the minds of academic historians and political scientists a good deal more than it ever occupied the minds of the men who actually governed Victorian England. If, for long enough, less was done by parliamentary intervention than a later generation may suppose to have been desirable, it has to be remembered that few people had faith in such a mode of activity in terms of either honesty or effectiveness. The '*let alone* doctrine, or the theory that governments can do no better than to do nothing', John Stuart Mill once said, was 'a doctrine generated by the manifest selfishness and incompetence of modern European governments...It was found that the State was a bad judge of the wants of society', and when it attempted anything beyond the minimal activities involved in the policing of crime it was soon seen to be the plaything of the 'sinister interests' of some class or individual, and did more harm than good to society as a whole. Mill's friend, Thomas Carlyle, was almost certainly right when he said that the demand for *laissez-faire* by a people from its governors at this time simply meant: 'Leave us alone of *your* guidance!'

When Matthew Arnold wrote his essay *Democracy* in 1861 (as a Preface to an inquiry into 'Popular Education on the Continent' which he undertook for the Newcastle Commission, set up in 1858 'to enquire into the present state of Popular Education in England'), he found it necessary to vindicate at some length his advocacy of state action on behalf of the education of the people. The obstacle to popular acceptance of this increased activity on the part of the state was the fact that to large numbers of people, and more especially to the middle classes, and 'the kernel of these classes, the Protestant Dissenters', the entity known as 'the state' was only another name for the Anglican and aristocratic monopoly from whose oppression they had suffered for several centuries. 'Having never known a beneficent and just State-power, they enlarged their hatred of a cruel and partial State-power...into a maxim that no State-power was to be trusted...' How true this was may be seen from the history of elementary education between the allocation of the first state grant in 1833 and the passing of the first Education Act in 1870. The brunt of that great task was borne by two voluntary societies[1] working on a financial basis of private subscriptions, and when the state began to grant funds (£20,000 in 1833; £484,000 by 1867), it was only able to intrude its authority in a gingerly fashion through the influence of inspectors and the imposition of certain minimal examination tests as a condition for a school's receiving a share of the grant: a principle which became notorious under the 'Revised Code' of 1861 as 'payment by results', during the administration of the fanatical free-trade individualist, Robert Lowe, who was responsible as Vice-President of the Council, for there was no Board of Education under a Secretary of State until 1899. The rigorous

[1] The National Society for the Education of the Poor in the Principles of the Established Church (1811), which was an Anglican body, and the non-denominational British and Foreign School Society (1814).

application of the 'payment by results' principle is said to have put the whole department in revolt, 'from the office-boy to Matthew Arnold'. Yet all that Robert Lowe was doing was to carry out the recommendations of the Newcastle Commission for the provision of 'sound and cheap' primary education. Unfortunately he was too fond of saying what he was doing, always a mistake in an educationist. He announced, very much in the words of the Newcastle Commission, that primary education hitherto had been neither cheap nor efficient. 'We have been living under a system of bounties and protection,' he said; 'now we prefer to have a little free trade.' It was Lowe who also said, not that we must educate our masters, but that 'it will be absolutely necessary to compel our masters to learn their letters'. Compulsion by statute began in 1876.

Competition was to prove the crucial factor in promoting state intervention in the vexed and tumultuous field of educational politics. It became fairly clear after the glories of the Great Exhibition had faded that the country was not maintaining its superiority in competition with its commercial rivals. This was revealed depressingly by Britain's inferior showing at the Paris Exhibition of 1867. In that year Parliament received from the Taunton Commission, which had been looking into secondary education for the past three years, a *Report Relative to Technical Education* which contained evidence supplied by both jurors and exhibitors at Paris. Opinion on the part of those best qualified to judge was coming to the view that France, Prussia, Austria, Belgium and Switzerland possessed the advantage of good systems of industrial education for employers and managers, while England had none. Indeed, within a short time, opinion was to take the form of advocacy not simply of better technical education but of more and better secondary education in general. The main obstacle for a long time was administrative, and only after the Local Government Act of 1888, establishing county councils on a basis of household suffrage, was this overcome. Only in the first year of the reign of Edward VII (1902), with the setting up of a Board of Education, was the country equipped with an authority to take charge of public education as a whole and a system of local education authorities to provide and augment primary, secondary and technical education on a rate-aided basis.

The confusion and delay in evolving a comprehensive educational system was partly the result of the fact that voluntary bodies promoted by a variety of religious denominations were from an early date in possession of the field, and that the schools run by these bodies had to be embodied in the slowly evolving public system, and not abolished, if only out of respect for voluntary agencies that had for so long borne the heat of the day. An old country with strong traditions of religious differentiation could not be put into a strait-waistcoat of state-provided and state-controlled 'public instruction' under some such alien and distrusted figure as a 'Minister of Public Instruction' after the style of Prussia or France or any other 'Continental' pattern. 'Tarrying for the congregation' was inevitable, and, of course, prolonged. Not only were the English of Victorian times intensely suspicious of state-inspired teaching and of the frightful notion of teachers as civil servants. They were for many years inclined, along with Mr Podsnap, to think they could get on very well, and a good deal better, without 'Europe' at all. For one thing, they still enjoyed a large and well-based sense of physical security. Like their descendants of the 1920s, but with a considerably greater substantial basis for their hopes, they trusted that the ages of war were past and gone. This basis consisted in the indisputable supremacy of the Royal Navy on all the seas of the world since Trafalgar. Upon this supremacy rested Europe's greatest, and most resented, debt to Great Britain for a hundred years: the *pax Britannica*.

From behind the bared teeth of the British man-o'-war Britannia cherished her favourite nineteenth-century image of herself as the land of liberty, teaching nations how to live, and the champion of small nations struggling to be free. The vision imported a flavour of chivalry into a scene so largely dominated, as Burke had complained long ago, by 'sophisters, economists, and calculators'. Burke had called chivalry 'the cheap defence of nations', and certainly Britain's patronage of libertarian movements in the age of George Canning and Palmerston and

Gladstone could hardly be accounted expensive, or even particularly dangerous. Sometimes, indeed, it was highly profitable. Both British trade and British security were well served by British sea-power in 1823 when Canning made it possible for President Monroe to promulgate his famous doctrine of 'hands off the New World', so that it was truly said that the American cockle-boat came in in the wake of the British man-o'-war. Again, when in these years the hare-brained British Admiral Cochrane won his laurels as 'Cochrane the liberator' in South American republics freeing themselves from Spain and in Greece winning her independence from Turkey, no one could deny that Britain's heart was in the right place. The peace of Europe, as well as Britain's oldest strategic interest across the Narrow Seas, was well served by certain British fleet movements which secured the independence and guaranteed the neutrality of Belgium in the 1830s. The same glad admixture of idealism and profit held good when Admiral Mundy's ships watched with benevolent neutrality while Garibaldi took his Thousand across the Straits of Messina to accomplish their great blow for the liberation and unification of Italy in 1860.

After the mid-century mark, however, when Lord Palmerston and Lord John Russell gave the positively last performance of John-Bull Whiggery in their Tweedledum and Tweedledee Administration of 1859–65, it began to appear that a world dominated by the giant shadows of Bismarck and Abraham Lincoln was becoming a dangerous place in which to indulge the passion for the game of 'backing the little 'n' against the big 'n''. Mr Gladstone, who served uneasily as Chancellor of the Exchequer in the government headed by 'the two bad boys', hated the bellicosity of Palmerston not only on moral grounds but on grounds of economy and sound public finance. But he outdid the old hands at the game in 1862 when he managed to discern another 'small nation' deserving of our enthusiasm in Jefferson Davis's slave-confederacy in rebellion against the Federal authority of the United States. Jeff Davis, he announced in a public speech at Newcastle, had made not only an army and a navy but was in the process of making a nation. It was promptly made clear that the Chancellor of the Exchequer had not spoken for the government, but the *faux pas* occurred at the most perilous moment for Anglo-American relations since the Treaty of Ghent had closed the sole armed conflict between Great Britain and the United States in 1814. In the last of his many good offices to a nation which had never loved him, the Prince Consort worked with Lord John Russell, the Foreign Secretary, to mollify the American government by conciliatory language before he gave up the ghost. The second case of brinkmanship in these years was in 1863-4 when Bismarck was at loggerheads with Denmark over the Schleswig-Holstein question. The Prince of Wales had recently espoused Princess Alexandra of Denmark, and Palmerston indulged in some loose remarks to the effect that if Denmark were attacked she would not have to fight alone—in other words, Great Britain would not stand idly by. This was not the kind of thing to deter Bismarck. Unfortunately it impressed Denmark. After having encouraged Denmark to assume an obdurate attitude over the disputed duchies, the British champions quietly withdrew from the arena. As usual, the British applauded Palmerston while it was a matter of strong words, but they were not in the least disposed to fight. The Queen herself took a firm line with Palmerston now, and in the following year the old rip joined the Prince Consort on another shore.

That 'gun-boat diplomacy' became a pejorative term in the twentieth century was a fortunate legacy of old 'Pam', but the Victorian Englishman never failed to applaud his antics. On close examination the faces of Sir Edwin Landseer's lions at the foot of Nelson's column in Trafalgar Square closely resemble the pacific and well-nourished faces of four £10 householders. They could earnestly proclaim that Great Britain's greatest interest was peace, even if the sentiment sounded equivocal in the mouth of a lion astride his prey. The Victorian paterfamilias astride the hearthrug brandishing his silver-mounted walking-stick while he reads the news of the Charge of the Light Brigade to his weeping women and cheering children is an authentic item in any collection of Victoriana. He was readily thrilled by the brave music of a distant drum. After all, a nation of shopkeepers may find a therapeutic value in foreign wars, providing they are a long way away. The paeans in praise of peace and progress which rang out at the Crystal Palace in 1851 had scarcely died away when Tennyson summoned his countrymen to 'wake to the higher aims of a land that has lost for a little her lust for gold', and to cry 'hail once more to the banner of battle unroll'd!' Rupert Brooke was a soldier under arms when he thanked God in 1914 for having 'matched us with His hour', but Tennyson had just moved into a comfortable house in the Isle of Wight when he rejoiced that again:

> ...a war would arise in defence of the right,
> That an iron tyranny now should bend or cease,
> The glory of manhood stand on his ancient height
> Nor Britain's one sole God be the millionaire...

In other words, he hailed the advent of the Crimean War in 1854.

Europe in general, however, did not find it easy to break the spell imposed by the unprecedented forty years of peace. The French had to be driven into the war by their emperor, Napoleon III, in pursuit of his vendetta with the Tsar. The English drove Lord Aberdeen's ministry into it on another wave of the Russophobia which had afflicted them in every generation since the days of the Holy Alliance, bringing back Palmerston to win it for them. When it was over, and it was settled that 'the Roosians shall not have Constantinople', Great Britain entered into a posture of splendid isolation with regard to the affairs of Europe, a kind of armed trance from which she was to awaken at the time of the South African War with a chill sense of being naked and unfriended in the dangerous world of the twentieth century.

The death of the Prince Consort, 'at his post', in 1861, left the Queen a desolate and sombre figure with half her life to live in what she chose to cherish as an unfriended isolation even greater. The nation, too, mourned the death of the Prince Consort for, as Disraeli said, 'we have buried our sovereign. This German Prince has governed England for twenty-one years with a wisdom and energy such as none of our kings have ever shown.' His sagacity and foresight had shown themselves especially at the time of the crisis over the American Civil War, and might, as Disraeli

VICTORIAN AGES

put it, have given us 'the blessings of absolute government'.
This, however, was not what the nation regretted to have missed,
but rather his guiding hand beside the Queen, his sober sense, his
indefatigable energy in the cause of social and domestic righteousness combined with progress in the useful arts and sciences, the
ideals which the nation had come to accept as specifically 'Victorian'. Public subscription raised £60,000 for the erection of the
Albert Memorial in Kensington Gardens, depicting the Prince
surrounded by symbolic figures to represent his labours for the
arts and sciences he had fostered, and holding in his hand what
may be assumed to be the catalogue of the Great Exhibition. The
Albert Hall, nearby, however, was raised by a joint-stock company.

The withdrawal of the Queen into the role of 'the widow of
Windsor' was in the course of time to arouse some misgivings,
even some criticism, on the part of people who cherished another
Victorian ideal, that of 'value for money'. The monarchy, it was
computed, cost the country nearly £400,000 a year. The Queen's
Civil List amounted to £60,000 for her private use. The rest
went on her household and the maintenance of the dignity of the
Crown, but the Queen was never backward in coming forward
with large requests for grants for the marriages and the maintenance of her numerous royal offspring. 'What does she do with
it?' was the title of an anonymous pamphlet, and the unspoken
comment was 'Is she worth it?' It seemed a great deal to pay for
an absentee monarchy. There was even a 'republican moment' in
the 1870s. It was perhaps fortunate that the greatest Liberal
statesman of the England of that day was Mr Gladstone, a man
deeply imbued with veneration for all that was ancient and long
established in Church and State. It was even more fortunate that
Mr Gladstone was succeeded in 1874 by a romantic Tory in the
person of Benjamin Disraeli, who wooed the widow with
oriental flattery, bringing her once more into the public gaze, and
identifying her with the destinies of an imperial people. In 1877
he succeeded in promoting her to the splendid title of 'Empress
of India'. In the previous year she had ennobled him as the Earl
of Beaconsfield. As Mr Punch put it, 'one good turn deserves
another'.

15

Imperial and Edwardian

The Crimean War was fought by Britain and France in alliance with the Turks to halt Russian advance towards Constantinople and the Straits. This was vital to Great Britain in order to safeguard the short route to India. The year after the Peace of Paris had registered the neutralizing of the Black Sea, the outbreak of the Indian Mutiny brought a complete reassessment of British policy in governing India. For nearly fifty years, British land policy in the subcontinent had been dominated by concern to protect the peasant and his traditional way of life at the expense of a native aristocracy and its servants. It was the annexation of Oudh in 1856, and the wholesale institution there of the village settlements and land tenures of the North-West Provinces, that sparked off the Mutiny. By the summer of 1859 not only Oudh but the whole of upper India, with the exception of the garrison at Lucknow, was aflame with rebellion. The peasant settlement of 1856 came to an end in a matter of weeks. 'It might have been expected that...the village occupants who had been so highly favoured by the British Government...would have come forward in support of the Government', wrote Lord Canning, the Governor-General. 'Such however was not the case.' Instead of arousing the gratitude and loyalty of the peasant by building up his proprietary rights it seemed that the policy had provoked him into hostility. Failing to grasp, or at least to acknowledge, that they had been reading the Indian mentality through liberalist Western spectacles, the British at first insisted that the revolt was simply military, arising from the Sepoys' abhorrence at having to use cartridges greased with fat of the sacred cow, and the distrust of the Brahmins at the introduction of railways and telegraphs, 'causes' which went promptly into Victorian text-books, and often remained there. In fact, the Mutiny was a costly and cruel lesson in the conservatism of the Indian peoples. Henceforth the supposition that they were incipient peasant proprietors or ten-pound householders, unfortunates who had been crushed for centuries by military despotisms and obscurantist religions, who could be raised up to the European level of 'enlightened self-interest' by experience of peace and liberal reform, was steadily discredited. Henceforth the aim was less to 'reform' India than to rule it, and to rule it in accordance with its traditional and deeply rooted customs. British policy from 1858 onwards was 'to enlist on our side, and to employ in our service, those natives who have, from their birth or position, a natural influence in the country'. In this she succeeded, and her solicitude for the interests and privileges of the landed classes was reciprocated by loyalty and affection. From this basis in the Indian aristocracy Great Britain was later to combat the growing nationalist movement.

The problem of Ireland, which became increasingly urgent in an age when nationalist movement flourished and triumphed all over Europe, was also at its grass-roots the problem of a peasant people, although it was also a good deal else. The Union of 1800, coming close on the heels of the Rebellion of 1798, had taken away Ireland's legislative independence. With the incorporation of Ireland into 'the United Kingdom of Great Britain and Ireland' and the addition of the Red Cross of St Patrick to the national flag (thus completing the Union Jack), Ireland was to be represented in the Parliament at Westminster by 4 bishops of the Protestant Church of Ireland and 28 temporal peers elected for life from the Irish peerage, and by 100 commoners elected by the Protestant minority of a Catholic country. Pitt had striven to couple Roman Catholic emancipation with the union, but George III had promised to go mad if he were required (as he saw it) to violate his coronation oath by permitting it. Quite apart from the fact that the Union had been put through the Irish Parliament by wholesale bribery (perhaps the most squalid example of *felo de se* on record), there could never be any prospect of a people whose first (and often last) loyalty was given to its priests coming to regard the Union of 1800 as anything but a standing monument to a crime. Required to support an alien Church and aristocracy in political subordination to England,

'John Bull's other island' continued to nourish its endless memories of cruel injustice with all, and more than all, the bitterness of a peasant people seemingly condemned to immemorial 'enemy occupation' by a power which elsewhere stood before mankind as 'the friend of small nations struggling to be free'.

Victorian statesmen, and most notably Mr Gladstone, were to concede Catholic emancipation and agrarian reform, but were unable to concede the rest, or even to understand quite what the Irish wanted or why. 'The Irish difficulty went deeper than the philosophy of the age could reach. The twin cell of English life, the squire administering what everybody recognizes as law and the parson preaching what everybody recognizes to be religion, had no meaning in a country where the squire was usually an invader and the parson always a heretic.' When it came to conceding Irish Home Rule, as it did with Gladstone in his successive legislative attempts in 1886 and 1893, the issue split both the Liberal and the Conservative parties, and still left the problem to be faced in the twentieth century. It was a *damnosa haereditas*, a child of time with its tale of old, unhappy, far-off things, and only time was to do away with it.

In the midst of distractions over Ireland, the accompanying dislocation of the parties, and the steady advance of 'demos' in the form of an extended franchise (represented by the Third Reform Act of 1885), the Victorians entered upon their imperial expansion in Africa. It was the Irish, not the African, question that held the centre of the stage in the very years of the British occupation of Egypt and the staking out of a huge tropical empire. How it came about is even now mysterious. The Victorians regarded India and the British Isles as the twin centres of their wealth and strength, and Africa as a huge unopened land mass between Great Britain and the Orient, not interesting as Africa but for its coastal stations *en route* to more distant lands. It was peripheral to the Mediterranean, the trade and trooping routes, and the Indian Empire: paramount influence over its coasts and (after 1869) the Suez Canal sufficed. Opinions about its value ranged from that of James Stephen of the Colonial Office in 1840, who simply summed it up by saying that 'if we could acquire the

Dominion of the whole of that Continent it would be but a worthless possession', to rather vague notions that it might at some distant date prove to be another Canada or Australia. When people talked like that they generally had in mind only the temperate southern subcontinent largely colonized by the Boer farmers. No one wanted another India-type empire. India itself was not properly 'Greater Britain' to Sir John Seeley. That was the title of territories inhabited 'either chiefly or to a large extent by Englishmen'. For long children were taught about 'Britain Overseas' rather than the British Empire. Of course India was the great exception, for India was (even if it was unpopular to say so) 'an English barrack in the Oriental seas', supplying the revenue and the manpower not only for its own defence but for the defence of all territories within its ambit, and for conquests beyond it. The sepoys and the Royal Navy guarded the commercial empire in the eastern seas and the Pacific. Africa's role could never be envisaged like that.

And yet in the 1880s an African empire was acquired; and, all things considered, it is not surprising that the year of publication of Seeley's *Expansion of England*, with its celebrated catch-phrase about 'absence of mind', was 1880. Perhaps 'presence of mind' was equally valid, since the African possessions were acquired in a European scramble by governments consisting of aristocrats and men of business who, over generations of estate-building and enclosure of commons, had developed an almost somnambulistic adroitness as pickers-up of unconsidered trifles. Yet, again, governments in later Victorian times were generally reluctant to undertake imperial expansion out of anxiety to avoid the over-taxing of Britain's financial strength, and they were very well aware that the people were wedded to peace and non-commitment. There was little instructed interest in Africa in either the electorate or their governors, and all through the equivocal story the official mind was concerned to clothe national interest in the garb of Christian endeavour towards the suppression of the slave-trade and the spreading of the gospel among the heathen. The Englishman's heroes in the story were Dr Livingstone and General Gordon. Victorian mothers taught their children the duty of taking up the white man's burden in terms of this hagiology, and the commonest gibe of the enemies of British expansion was always the conjunction of Bibles and muskets and brandy. The more sophisticated argument that would make the achievement of a new African empire in the 1880s the response to strong social and economic impulses generated by the saturation of existing markets and resources at the hands of a capitalist system beyond its peak is hardly borne out by the findings of the Royal Commission on the Depression of Trade and Industry in 1886. The evidence of the Chambers of Commerce received by the Commission shows in nearly all cases that the business community looked for relief to the established markets of America, Australasia, India and China. Only two made any reference to the possibility of developing tropical Africa. Neither 'the Imperialist phase of Capitalism' nor any other simple formula can account for the phenomenon of the African imperialism of the later Victorian Age.

When in 1897 the country celebrated the Queen Empress's Diamond Jubilee, London witnessed a pageant of empire worthy of an imperial capital, with marching contingents from the uttermost ends of the earth, while the guns of 165 warships sounded off in the great Naval Review at Spithead. In 1887 the toast had been 'The Queen'. In 1897 it was 'Our noble selves'. But the great catch in the throat and smarting behind the eyelids came with the verses of an Anglo-Indian journalist and bard of Tommy Atkins which *The Times* printed on 17 July, when the captains and the kings were on the point of departing. Kipling's *Recessional* was no gloat of imperial pride. It was a call to the future, to discipline and responsibility, to the humility proper to the successful, terms which later generations were soon to ridicule, but grateful to the ears of a people still famed for taking their pleasures sadly.

For there never was a less 'imperial' people. Every English schoolboy knows literally nothing about what used to be called the 'British Empire'. Every English schoolmaster knows that the least adequate pages in the text-book are those which profess to give the young some reluctant knowledge, and perhaps some shamefaced enthusiasm, for 'Britain Overseas', or the heritage of the Land of Hope and Glory. The truth is that the British never greatly cared about 'great' things until they were on their way to losing them. They love pomp and circumstance and brass bands, but they are allergic to size. Small nations, country cottages, small women, small dogs, these they adore. Hardy's lyric, 'Great Things', is typical. It celebrates cider, dancing, and sitting out in the garden to make love. The last Victorian Age put its great things—the navy, the Lord Chancellor, the House of Lords, the unarmed police force—on to the stage in the form of the comic operas of Gilbert and Sullivan, thereby preserving them in England's favourite pickle of warm-hearted laughter.

The death of Queen Victoria in no sense marked a turning-point in English history. She died in 1901, in the middle of the Boer War. Her son and successor was a fat and fashionable gentleman of fifty-nine, and as long as he lived England's fortunes were to be presided over by an eminent Victorian, even though his eminence was for the most part achieved in fields either neglected or unrecognized as pre-eminently Victorian. He had been Prince of Wales for nearly half a century, and his subjects continued to think of him under that title. A Prince of Wales was traditionally expected to enjoy himself, and King Edward more than maintained the tradition. He was the most widely popular Prince of Wales there had ever been. For the rest, he aspired to deserve the title of Edward the Peacemaker, which he was to enjoy for some years in the school-books. It was perhaps his sole claim to recognition as his father's son.

Politeness rather than actuality may vindicate the claim. He was certainly anxious that Lord Roberts and General Botha should reach an understanding in South Africa before his coronation. He was to show remarkable forbearance towards his posturing nephew, the German Kaiser, and he turned French jeers into cheers during his brief official visit to Paris in 1903. To accredit him with the Entente Cordiale which followed would certainly be a triumph of *politesse* over historical veracity. Only those who had forgotten the Irish passion for horse-racing were surprised at his enthusiastic reception in Ireland, and it was his death rather than his life which brought a short truce to hostilities

in the 'Peers versus the People'[1] contest of 1910. His death was
genuinely mourned, for he had brought the image of the monarchy back to the eyes of the people after the long withdrawal
of Queen Victoria, with his regular appearances at the theatre
and on the racecourse. The King died as he had lived. On the
morning of 6 May he tried to smoke one more cigar. In the
afternoon one of his horses won at Kempton Park. The Queen
herself brought his mistress, Mrs George Keppel, to his bedside
in the evening.

King Edward VII was not the last British sovereign to bear the
full title DEI GRATIA BRITT. OMN. REX FID. DEF. IND. IMP,[2] but he
was the last to look it. His bald and bearded head might have been
specially designed to adorn copper coins and penny stamps, and
he may well prove to have been the last to lend his name to a
distinctive style of British life. Edwardian—or as one of the
King's most typical lieges, Sir Max Beerbohm, preferred to call
it, 'Edvardian'—continued to elicit its image, if only as a colophon
to the last volume of the bound and boxed set of volumes marked
'Victorian'. The short reign of King Edward VII lingers on the
edge of subsequent darkness like a long summer afternoon,
quietly punctuated by the popping of champagne-corks, flav-
oured with cigar-smoke, and accompanied by the distant strains
of Elgar's *Pomp and Circumstance* march from the Guards Band
in the Park. The King and his age are certain of immortality from
the Second Symphony of Sir Edward Elgar, expensive and
expansive, full-blooded, over-dressed, in the best as well as the
worst sense a trifle vulgar.

When the King came to the throne the darkest hour of the
Boer War had passed; Kimberley, Mafeking and Ladysmith had
been relieved, and Cronje had surrendered to Lord Roberts. Both
the Orange Free State and the Transvaal had been annexed and
all that remained was to win the war against the guerrilla skill
and bravery of De Wet and the last Boer commandos. The war
had been a shamefaced business with many of the English. 'I

[1] See below, p. 276.
[2] By the Grace of God King of Great Britain, Defender of the Faith, Emperor
of India.

thought it was very sporting of the Boers to take on the whole British Empire', Winston Churchill had written early in the proceedings, and his attitude, as so often in his long and militant career, was very much that of the majority of his countrymen— not least, perhaps, when he added as a concession to principle that he was glad the Boers had put themselves in the wrong by making preparations. These preparations included the importation of masses of war material from Germany through Delagoa Bay. Many people held the war to be the blackest stain on British imperialism since the contest between George III and the American farmers led by George Washington. There was something irremediably squalid in the spectacle of a great empire bringing its military might to bear upon a small people at the behest of the City of London and the business empire of men like Cecil Rhodes. That was how it could be made to appear in the eyes of the man in the street, who never likes wars until they have begun, and the man in the chapel, to whom gold and diamonds are equated with sin. The discovery of the rich gold deposits on the Rand in the 1880s and the incursions of thousands of adventurers of all nations to swamp the simple, Bible-reading farmers of the Boer republics not only presented Paul Kruger with the problem of enfranchising the Uitlanders[1] but sharpened the conflict of two worlds, the pastoral, patriarchal, primitive world of the veldt, and the restless, godless, industrial world of the mining-camp symbolized by Johannesburg. It was never a contest between the powers of darkness and the children of light, for the Boers were possessed of the most benighted notions of the racial inferiority of their African brethren. The British pro-Boer was less impressed by the simple heroism of Paul Kruger than by the shady manœuvres of Rhodes and Joseph Chamberlain and Dr Jameson to despoil him and his Boers. He recognized that for all his bravery in defence of his land against the soldiers of the Queen, the Boer represented a backward civilization at odds with a progressive one, and nothing that has happened since in South Africa lends credence to the notion of the Boers as liberal communities

[1] The African's term for 'settlers'; that is, the adventurers who had come in to mine gold.

defending 'the higher values' against a money-grubbing tyranny. Boer sympathizers were moved by cherished memories of the righteous Mr Gladstone surrendering the Transvaal to the Boers after Majuba, and memories of the proud tradition of Great Britain in the nineteenth century as the champion of small nations. To the English of the mid-twentieth century, the imperialism of their grandfathers is apt to appear rather less as a concern to paint the map red than as a concern with the disintegration of Britain's position in the world, a willingness to promote a 'forward policy' of national self-assertion essential to the protection of British overseas interests. From the distant days when Julius Caesar crossed the Channel to safeguard Gaul against the Catuvellauni and when Suetonius Paulinus broke the Iceni under Queen Boudicca, imperialist expansion has been susceptible of excuse as a darker aspect of concentration. Extension of British influence beyond the limits of the empire, said the *Edinburgh Review* in 1884, was not positive but negative, justified by the necessity of averting greater dangers and calamities. 'Foreigners, newcomers, thieves and murderers', President Kruger concluded sadly. 'It is my country they want!' What Boudicca may have said has gone unrecorded. The death-mask of Cecil Rhodes is indistinguishable from that of a later Roman emperor, and the imperialist enthusiast paid a London bookseller some thousands of pounds to have translations made of the authorities for Gibbon's *Decline and Fall*.

The three-year war in a corner of the African continent cost Great Britain £270,000,000 and engaged little less than half a million men, about 22,000 of whom never returned. It dragged on for many months after the entry of Roberts into Pretoria. The guerrilla tactics of the Boers were only overcome by Kitchener's policy of blockhouses, scorched earth and concentration camps. The generous terms of the peace of Vereeniging in May 1902, including the promise of £3,000,000 for the rehabilitation of the Boer farms, reflect something of British self-hatred for the brutality of the final phases of the war, and when three months later the Boer generals came to London they were acclaimed with the customary three cheers for the losers at the end of the game:

'Our Friends the Enemy!' and 'Brave Soldiers All!' the banners ran. The South African War, however, inflicted wounds far deeper than the bruises suffered in a field-game. Indeed, the 'little war' marks a turning-point of greater magnitude than might be judged from its proportions as a military event. The trouble Great Britain had in winning it revealed to the world, and to herself, her military weaknesses and her friendless position among the powers of Europe. It left the country's conscience sufficiently shaken to shrink in future from full-blooded defence, in either word or deed, of her 'imperial destiny'. The reminder 'Lest we forget' really meant something, now, if only because there were a number of recent things that were best forgotten. There was reason for pride in the way that 'sons of the empire' had rallied to the mother country in her hour of need, but there was to be less boastfulness and more thankfulness about such things in future. Perhaps Jingo[1] was the chief and most fortunate casualty of the war.

The Liberals came into power on a landslide at the elections of 1906, and it was a Liberal government that made the Union of South Africa Act of 1909. The Act enshrined the liberal devotion to the principle of self-government for dependent peoples which had found expression in the British North America Act for the Dominion of Canada in 1867 and in the Commonwealth of Australia Constitution Act of 1900. It was inconceivable within the historic and ethnic situation that self-government in South Africa should have meant anything but self-government on a white man's franchise. Thus was displayed what was to prove the weakness of the liberal idea in this, its first encounter with the twentieth-century world of race antagonisms. The Bible-reading Boers' myth of their black brethren as descendants of Ham, the dusky son of Noah, destined by Divine Decree to wait upon his brethren, might have remained a charming domestic prejudice in the homesteads of the veldt had not Lord Milner, the High Commissioner at the Cape, insisted—despite Cape Colony's satisfactory experience of the Kaffir franchise—on the

---

[1] A slang version of 'Jesus', from the music hall song: 'We don't want to fight, but by Jingo if we *do*...'

impossibility of political equality between white and black. The Union of South Africa was brought into existence without reference to the black-skinned mass of the population. The British under a Liberal administration had unwittingly sold the pass to apartheid, inaugurating what Olive Schreiner called the 'long slide backward on the muddy road of time'. Afrikaner nationalism is the child of the annexation of the Transvaal in 1877, the Jameson Raid, and Alfred Milner. Liberal England suffered no greater eclipse anywhere than in what may be called the 'succession states' of the British Empire in the African continent.

Liberalism in England still lives on the memories of the great reforming era of Campbell-Bannerman and Asquith and David Lloyd George. There were manifold and strong connections between the leaders of the party, especially at a level somewhat below the top flight, and the intellectual aristocracy which distinguished English society in the last years of Victorian England and the early years of the twentieth century. Neither Campbell-Bannerman nor Lloyd George had much affiliation here, and Asquith was never more than an ardent amateur of scholarship. Rosebery alone among the top-ranking politicians was a distinguished scholar and man of letters, but slightly lower down the scale was a whole intellectual galaxy rarely equalled in British political life, such men as John Morley, Augustine Birrell, Viscount Haldane, C. F. G. Masterman, and (slightly later) H. A. L. Fisher. Never since the days of the Utilitarians had a political party been engaged so closely with an intellectual hegemony, excepting perhaps the Fabian Socialists, with whom from time to time the Liberals found themselves in uneasy alliance. For the Liberal intelligence remained shackled, in the last analysis, to the pure doctrine of nineteenth-century liberalism with its *laissez-faire* individualism in a new age which required a large degree of governmental agency for the solution of its problems, particularly those of state-provided education and socialized industry. From Gladstone to Asquith, the Liberal high command belonged to the pure liberal faction with its faith in a benevolent Providence, individualistic competition, and a self-righting economy.

'Organized labour' in the early years of the century was still a minority movement even among working men, although a powerful section had founded a 'Labour Representation Committee' in 1900 to secure the election of independent Labour candidates to Parliament. The independent Labour Party, set up in 1893, was already represented in the House of Commons by Keir Hardie, 'member for the unemployed', who had arrived at Westminster in a cloth cap and escorted by a brass-band. Nature, it seemed, could no longer be relied upon to contrive that every boy and every girl born into this world alive was either a little Liberal or else a little Conservative. 'The main reason for the existence of Liberals and Conservatives', the I.L.P. announced, 'is to protect the interests of the rich and keep you divided... Create and finance and control a party of your own, and thus prove democracy a reality.' But as long as Liberalism under Lloyd George could preside over the latest phase of that concessionism prescribed by Walter Bagehot[1] to the extent of initiating the welfare state with National Insurance, Labour Exchanges, and legislation to 'soak the rich' and draw the teeth of the House of Lords, Labour had to be content to serve the big guns of the Liberal party. Serve them it did, even while some might feel it necessary, like Bernard Shaw, to 'apologize to the Universe for any connection with such a party'. Another Fabian Socialist, Mrs Beatrice Webb, refused to deceive herself 'that this wave of liberalism is wholly progressive in character'. Liberals likewise suffered some *Schadenfreude* from the alliance. Winston Churchill, when offered the Local Government Board by Asquith, is said to have replied that he did not wish to be 'shut up in a soup-kitchen with Mrs Sidney Webb'. Only when Liberalism had shot its bolt, and after the configuration of the political landscape had been changed by the First World War, was Labour to rule as a party.

How little notion the 'concessionaires' of the comfortable classes had of the shape of things to come may be judged from their public demonstrations in 1911 to resist the tyranny of 'stamp-licking' involved in affixing stamps to the new state-insurance cards, those German-born harbingers of bureaucracy. Even when Lloyd George inflicted penal taxation on land in his

[1] See above, ch. 14, p. 243.

'people's budget' of 1909 in order to meet a deficit not wholly unconnected with the latest welfare schemes, he was met by contemptuous references to 'the robbing of hen-roosts' and other species of petty larceny. Only when the House of Lords, breaking with some three centuries of traditional abstention from interference with financial measures sent up by the Commons, threw out the Budget, were the Liberals faced with the call to heroic action. There was little or nothing heroic in Asquith's response. By indicating ('making it clear' would be much too strong a phrase) that the Government would ask the King to use his prerogative of creating new peers to overcome resistance by the House of Lords, he secured a hasty and muddle-headed measure known as 'the Parliament Act' of 1911, which began with the statement that 'whereas it is intended to substitute for the House of Lords as it at present exists a Second Chamber constituted on a popular instead of a hereditary basis, but such substitution cannot be immediately brought into operation' and went on to preserve the House of Lords by removing its powers over money bills and reducing its authority over other measures to a merely temporary, or suspensory, veto. 'The Peers versus the People' had for long been a contest in the minds of Radicals rather than a reality of political life, and the momentarily obstreperous patient's life was preserved in 1911 by a major operation. The House of Lords was saved as an institution. The peers had still to be deprived of equality of opportunity as individuals. The last member of the House of Lords to serve as prime minister was Lord Salisbury. When Stanley Baldwin instead of Lord Curzon replaced Bonar Law at his resignation in 1923, there were other reasons than his peerage to deprive Curzon of what he, at least, felt to be his rightful succession. When Harold Macmillan resigned forty years later, there was a stampede on the part of his possible noble successors to get rid of their peerages. It was not the Parliament Act that deprived peers of equality of opportunity, but the inverted snobbery of democracy.

The landed aristocracy which had ruled England for so long was fast losing its dominance in both politics and society in the reign of Edward VII. The process bears a close resemblance to the pattern of aristocratic decline in the seventeenth century. There is a similar permeation of peerage by new and vulgar wealth, a similar decline in aristocratic influence with the electorate. Peers have married actresses in every century of modern history. Under the leadership of society by Edward VII, 'Molly married the Marquess' better expresses the order of the procedure. W. S. Gilbert had put the peers on the stage, offering their coronets to a milkmaid, and at the same time commanding with ludicrous pomp:

Bow, bow, ye lower middle-classes,
Bow ye tradesmen, bow ye masses...

In the age of the Jersey Lily when Gaiety Girls were bought by the brace, the joke was becoming tedious.[1] The fact that within so short a time it was all to look like revels on the edge of a volcano does not prevent elderly survivors from describing Edwardian England as 'the last age of civilized living'. That is what a whole generation still means when it talks of 'before the War', the days when the cricketers C. B. Fry and 'Ranji' were making the sweetest of hay at Lord's cricket-ground while the sun shone; when Sherlock Holmes was back in *The Strand Magazine*; when tennis and golf were in full swing with a prime minister, Arthur Balfour, as Public Relations Officer; when the novel was entering upon its latest, and perhaps its greatest, period as middle-class entertainment undivorced from literature. It was the age of Conrad and Galsworthy, Wells and Kipling, Bennett, Henry James and Stevenson. The theatre which had been so wretchedly served in the old Queen's reign was producing such enduring work as the comedies of Oscar Wilde, the social criticism of Galsworthy, and the dialectical jesting of Bernard Shaw. Elgar, Sickert and Wilson Steer were surpassing the Victorians in music and painting. The barrel-organ, the music-hall and the dawn chorus of rag-time sound through these years like the veritable voices of departing ghosts before cockcrow on the Marne and at Mons.

[1] If by this time such names require elucidation, it may be said that Lily Langtry, or the 'Jersey Lily', was perhaps King Edward VII's favourite among the beauties of the stage; the young ladies of the chorus at the Gaiety Theatre were collectively known as 'Gaiety Girls'.

There were, too, ancestral voices prophesying, if not war, at least social revolution, presenting ominous alternatives as poet and prophet and playwright scanned the opening prospect of the new century. For those who had eyes to see, Kipling's *Puck of Pook's Hill*, though ostensibly a children's book, presented the historical allegory of a threatened culture. In 1910, the year of the King's death, E. M. Forster presented a quieter and more penetrating study in *Howards End*, embodying a novelist's vision of salvation through the culture of personal relationships and the education of the heart. 'Only connect...' is the epigraph. Only connect the prose and the passion of life. Margaret Schlegel, encountering the people of the 'outer world' of business, the Wilcox family, avows: 'If Wilcoxes hadn't worked and died in England for thousands of years, you and I couldn't sit here without having our throats cut....More and more do I refuse to draw my income and sneer at those who guarantee it', an avowal that sums up most of Kipling and dismisses much of Shaw. Shaw's *Heartbreak House* (begun in 1913, finished in 1916, staged in 1919) presented an oddly muddled Chekhovian comedy which affects to say more by ending with an air raid. Even more prophetic in a far-ranging sense was D. H. Lawrence's *Sons and Lovers*, which appeared in 1913, a novel which began a transformation of the relationship of literature to life after a fashion inconceivable to the Victorian Age and to its Edwardian Epilogue. It is difficult, now, to realize that D. H. Lawrence was an Edwardian.

The great Anglo-German war, which occupied so much of the first half of the twentieth century and involved the ruin of so much of Europe, was a single contest in two four-year bouts of blood-letting, separated by some twenty years of baffled fumbling after reconciliation. It was what Coleridge called its predecessor, a century earlier, 'a wanton, wicked civil war of a depraved knot of Co-Europeans against men of the same arts, sciences, and habits'. The preliminary sparring began when German industry armed the Boers and the Kaiser sent President Kruger congratulations on his rounding up Dr Jameson's troopers on their raid into the Transvaal. For generations the English had loved Germany as the land of *Gemütlichkeit*, of Christmas-trees, toy soldiers, fairy castles above the Rhine, street-bands, comic professors, and waiters (recognized in 1914 as German spies). After 1870 Germany assumed the grim face of Prussian militarism and industrial efficiency. The new Germany soon grew tired of the patronizing smile of their English 'cousins', a smile which seemed designed to divert attention while they collected the world's best colonies and built up an irresistible High Seas Fleet. For their part, the English came to admire and respect the new Germany. They paid the Germans the sincerest flattery by imitating their technical education, their state welfare schemes, their professional universities. Lloyd George went to Germany for his social-insurance scheme in 1908. Alfred Milner, too, was deeply impressed by Bismarckian state-socialism, and his conviction of Britain's role to unite South Africa after the Boer War was inspired by a Germanic conviction of the creative role of political power. Lord Haldane, Asquith's lord chancellor in 1914, was a convinced Hegelian and was dropped as a supposed 'pro-German' when the Liberals made their first coalition with the Unionists in 1915. When in 1899 Britain was beginning to look for allies to end her 'splendid isolation', Joseph Chamberlain had spoken publicly of the naturalness of alliance between the British and the German empires. An Anglo-German *entente* could have been achieved at the beginning of the century if the ruling powers in Germany, and especially the Kaiser, had been other than what they were. Instead, from 1906, Britain entered into the uncertain commitments of the Entente Cordiale with France, the old enemy. France was linked with Russia, and when Austria lighted the powder-train in 1914, bringing about the declaration of war by Germany on both France and Russia, Britain went to the defence of Belgium. The Britain that went to war in 1914 was far from being the united nation which drew the sword on Adolf Hitler's Reich twenty-five years later. Lord Morley was not the only Liberal who could not accept the irrefragable nature of Britain's commitment to France. The Labour Party, apart from its inherent pacificism *vis-à-vis* capitalist wars, was horrified at the prospect of fighting in alliance with the arch-despotism of Russia. Germany, however, soon made certain of British solidarity not only by her onslaught upon 'little

Belgium' but by Bethmann-Hollweg's imbecile reference to the treaty of guarantee of Belgian neutrality as a scrap of paper which stood between Europe and the preservation of peace. Within a few weeks, 'the scrap of paper' and the Kaiser's 'mailed fist', the German Emperor's turned-up moustache and his loving reference to his armies as 'the Huns', were plastered on every hoarding in England, along with the torn and bleeding lady Belgium holding up the banner of freedom. Thus was produced a war neurosis in England which Hitler was to achieve only after ten years of persecution and perfidy.

Little short of a million men from the United Kingdom and the Empire were killed in the first World War, and less than fifteen hundred civilians. Fewer fighting men but many more civilians were killed in the second. Figures, however, tell little of the casualty involved in either or both. Thomas Hardy thought that the chief casualty was bound to be Christianity, and that it might have been better to let Western civilization perish and the black and yellow races have a chance. Within a generation he was to be proved more prophetic than even he can have imagined or wished. Florence Hardy, in her *Life*, tells us that 'the war destroyed all Hardy's belief in the gradual ennoblement of man...He said he would probably not have ended *The Dynasts* as he did if he could have foreseen what was going to happen within a few years... the war gave the *coup de grâce* to any conception he may have nourished of a fundamental ultimate Wisdom at the back of things.' The great symbolic poem of the post-war years, however, was written by an American expatriate in *The Waste Land* (1922). Within a very few years, however, its author was to declare war on the modern history of his adopted country by avowing himself 'Royalist in politics, Catholic in religion, classical in art'. Such a credo went back at least to the 'crypto-Fascist' T. E. Hulme before 1914. If, as Montesquieu held, 'la corruption de chaque gouvernement commence presque toujours par celle des principes', the influence of T. S. Eliot could hold out little hope for the preservation of the English state. *Les principes* by which this ancient commonwealth was nourished to greatness in modern history were Aristocratic, Protestant, and Romantic.

Postscript

Large social changes had been brought about by the early 1920s:
the equalization of the status of women, the democratization of
the suffrage by the Franchise Act of 1928 (the 'Flapper Vote'),
the ubiquity of the state in all spheres of the citizen's life, the
replacement of the Liberal by the Labour Party as the self-
accredited party of progress. In 1926 a miners' strike culminated
in a General Strike, and four years later the Great Depression led
to the financial crisis which turned the second Labour Government
into the National Government of 1931, and the Tweedledum and
Tweedledee partnership of Ramsay MacDonald and Stanley
Baldwin which presided over Great Britain in the peculiarly un-
heroic years remembered as 'the Baldwin era'. While Mac-
Donald basked in the smiles of duchesses and kept his broad back
turned to the venom of his 'betrayed' party, Baldwin smoked
his pipe and earned the sobriquet of 'Old Sealed-Lips' concerning
the rearmament of the country in face of the mounting threat of
the dictators. These were, indeed, the 'Years of the Locust' when
the country was bedevilled by the antics of the Peace Pledge
Union, and of the Oxford Union and its notorious motion not
to fight for King and Country. Meanwhile Churchill was a voice
crying in the wilderness, and the Labour Party was led by George
Lansbury, a Christian Pacifist in his middle seventies who appears
to have believed that the peace of the world could best be saved
if only he could 'go and have a heart-to-heart talk with Hitler'.
Baldwin's successor, Neville Chamberlain, was to have the same
thought. The drivelling inanity of the popular song 'God bless
you, Mr Chamberlain' in 1938 was to be matched in 1939 by its
successor on the subject of hanging out our washing on the
Siegfried Line.

Great Britain entered the Second World War with far greater
unity of spirit than she had exhibited in 1914. The sickening
crimes of the German dictator and the poisonous doctrines of
National Socialism made it something nearer to a crusade than

any armed conflict in modern history. One by one the bulwarks crumbled before the Nazi hordes until the day when only a handful of young airmen stood between the people of the beleaguered island and annihilation. It would be both un-imaginative and graceless to describe them as ever really 'alone'. They had with them the hopes of free men everywhere and the invincible power of historic memory. They had the promise and, in time, the performance of brothers beyond the seas, in the British Dominions (more correctly known since the Statute of Westminster of 1931 as 'the British Commonwealth of Nations'), and the grown-up children of the first British Empire in the United States of America. And they had at their head, at last, a man and a historian.

When in 1926 Elie Halévy came to conclude his great *History of the English People in the Nineteenth Century* he rounded it off with an Epilogue embracing the period 1895–1914 which seemed to him to form no part of the British nineteenth century. A historian born under Edward VII whose more cursory narrative covers two thousand years may be forgiven for following his example, since in this long perspective 1914 might seem to mark not the end of an epilogue but the disappearance of Great Britain's *raison d'être* in the history of Western civilization. Identifying the phenomena of decadence, or as he preferred to call it 'senescence', Halévy thought to discover two leading examples: in 'the decline of that individualist form of Christianity in which Protestantism essentially consists—and a revival of Catholicism'—on the one hand and, on the other, the growth of Socialism with its opposi-tion to 'that zeal for production by which British industry had conquered the markets of the world'. He yet maintained a certain confidence in England's ability to preserve herself from the destructive effects of such forces by her ability to transform Neo-Catholicism into Anglo-Catholicism, and to transform Socialism into a moderate and constitutional form of 'Labour'. He did not live to see *A Passage to India* and the replacement of the British Empire by the British Commonwealth of Nations, the omission of 'Ind. Imp.' from the royal titles or the hauling down of the Union Jack by some royal relation all over Africa. The world of which he wrote had been a world to which Great Britain was essential, which she had indeed in large part built, which had for long depended upon her presence. Since that world has vanished in the twentieth century, Britain has been left, somewhat like the old Austro-Hungarian Empire after the disappearance of 'the Turkish menace to Europe' in the nineteenth, searching for a new *raison d'être*. That she will find it need not be doubted. What it will be is fortunately no part of a historian's task to discover, though he may well afford some assistance to such discovery by the strengthening of historic memory.

Further Reading

This is not a bibliography, but a selection of books accessible to the 'common reader' and, it is hoped, suited to his tastes and interests rather than to those of the specialist or scholar. Books mentioned in footnotes are generally included, but not always. All books are published in London, unless otherwise stated.

Two histories of England, each produced by a single hand in the present century, are those of G. M. Trevelyan (1926) and Winston Churchill (1956–8). Notwithstanding its title, *A History of the English-speaking Peoples*, Churchill's masterpiece, is no less a history of England than is Trevelyan's. Trevelyan also wrote his immensely popular one-volume *Social History* (published 1942 in the U.S.A. and 1944 in G.B.), a work which has met with great popularity in a 4-volume illustrated edition since it came out between 1949 and 1952. With the recent publication of A. J. P. Taylor's *English History, 1914–1945*, *The Oxford History of England* has been completed in 15 volumes. According to *The Times Literary Supplement*, 'the series has been accepted as the most authoritative general history of England'. These volumes supply bibliographical guidance for close reading on all periods of English history. For the history of Tudor, Stuart and eighteenth-century England, the general reader will find readier pasture in G. R. Elton's *England under the Tudors* (1955, 2nd imp. 1962), Trevelyan's *England under the Stuarts* (1904: University Paperbacks, 1965), and J. H. Plumb's *England in the Eighteenth Century* (Pelican History of England, 1950). He will also find much to interest him in the earlier volumes of the Pelican History, notably those on *Roman Britain* by Ian Richmond (1955) and *The Beginnings of English Society* by Dorothy Whitelock (1952). The best standard book on Romano-British history is the volume by Collingwood and Myres (vol. 1 in the *Oxford History of England*). There is an excellent short study, *Town and Country in Roman Britain*, by A. L. F. Rivett (1958 and 1966).

For the later Middle Ages, there is the volume by A. R. Myers in the Pelican series, and a useful short study by S. B. Chrimes called *Lancastrians, Yorkists, and Henry VII* (1964). The Wars of the Roses have recently been treated with valuable contemporary reference by J. R. Lander in a volume of that title (1965). Latest of all, of course, is A. L. Rowse's *Bosworth Field and the Wars of the Roses* (1966).

For the period of the Reformation, Professor A. G. Dickens has surpassed everything else in *The English Reformation* (1964). The Elizabethan age is splendidly served in A. L. Rowse's *The England of Elizabeth* (1967). The best biography of the Queen herself is J. E. Neale's *Queen Elizabeth* (1934). The same scholar's volumes on *Elizabeth I and Her Parliaments, 1559–1601* (1953 and 1957) and *The Elizabethan House of Commons* (1949) are of immense value and interest. Proceeding to the Stuart age, good introductory reading is to be found in Wallace Notestein's *The English People on the Eve of Colonization* (1954), and the revolutionary aspects of the period are amply revealed in Christopher Hill's volumes, *The Century of Revolution, 1603–1714* (1961), *Puritanism and Revolution* (1958) and *The Good Old Cause* (1949). The revolutionary story is carried further in A. S. P. Woodhouse's *Puritanism and Liberty, Being the Army Debates, 1647–9* (1938 and 1951). H. N. Brailsford's last book, *The Levellers and the English Revolution*, was edited for publication by Christopher Hill in 1961. The reader in search of narrative history, however, will find nothing to rival Miss C. V. Wedgwood's two volumes, *The King's Peace* (1955) and *The King's War* (1958), both of which are now in paperback (Fontana Library). The vexed question of the rise (and/or decline) of the gentry in this age may best be approached through Professor Lawrence Stone's *Social Change and Revolution in England 1540–1640* (Problems and Perspectives in History, ed. Hugh F. Kearney). Professor Stone's *The crisis of the aristocracy* (Oxford, 1965) is the latest and largest contribution to this debate. For later Stuart history there is Trevelyan's classic, *England under Queen Anne* (3 vols., London, 1930). Two short but invaluable studies for this great century are G. M. Young's *Charles I and Cromwell* (1935) and G. M. Trevelyan's essay *Cromwell Statue* (in his *Autobiography and Other Essays*, 1949).

Since the publication some thirty years ago of Sir Lewis Namier's classic, *The Structure of Politics at the Accession of George III*, most thoroughfares into English history in the eighteenth century should bear the notice 'Danger—men at work'. What has been going on here may be discovered from Professor Herbert Butterfield's *George III and the historians* (1957). Until the bulldozers and the reconstruction experts give place to another great historian, it may be better to read W. H. Lecky's *History of England in the eighteenth century*, in the assurance that in times like these the old books are the best books. A new edition of Lecky came out in 7 volumes in 1892. The reader who prefers history to historiography will find much delight in J. H. Plumb's *Sir*

Robert Walpole (1956). For the American crisis late in the century there is John C. Miller's *Origins of the American Revolution* (1946), and more immediately relevant to English political history, Bernard Donoghue's *British Politics and the American Revolution: the Path to War* (1964).

The transition from the eighteenth to the nineteenth century may be studied in Dorothy George's *England in Transition* (1931: Penguin Books, 1953), J. L. and B. Hammond's classic, *The Town Labourer, 1760–1832* (1917), Asa Brigg's *The Age of Improvement* (1959), and Harold Perkin's *The Origins of Modern English Society, 1780–1880* (forthcoming). The agricultural revolution may be studied in *The Agrarian Revolution, 1780–1880*, by J. D. Chambers and G. E. Mingay (1966). For the history of technological achievement in the age of industrial revolution, the best account may be gained from Samuel Smiles's *Industrial Biography*, and especially his *Lives of the Engineers* (Popular Edition in 5 volumes, 1904: or selections by T. P. Hughes, Cambridge, Mass., 1964). R. J. White's study in transition, *Waterloo to Peterloo* (1957), assumes no more than a minimal acquaintance with the history of the period.

For the Victorian Age, the general reader will find studies of its principal topics in *Early Victorian England* (2 volumes Oxford), edited by G. M. Young. The editor published his introductory essay in *Victorian England: Portrait of an Age*, in 1936, still the most attractive study of the subject. The B.B.C.s Third Programme series of talks, *Ideas and Beliefs of the Victorians*, was published in 1949 by The Sylvan Press (reprinted 1950). Two other studies of great value are *The Making of Victorian England*, by G. Kitson Clark (1962), and *The Age of Equipoise*, by W. L. Burn (1964). *Edwardian England*, edited by Simon Nowell Smith (Oxford, 1964), and A. J. P. Taylor's *English History 1914–1945* (Oxford, 1965) bring the story to within living memory. The classic modern English history, of course, is Elie Halévy's *History of the English People in the nineteenth century*, 6 volumes (2nd revised edition, 1949).

Index

Æthelbert, King of Kent, 32
Africa, British expansion in, 266–8
Agincourt, battle of (1415), 89
Agricola, Roman governor, 15, 20
Aidan, Celtic saint, 37
Albert, Prince Consort, 249, 261–3
Alcuin, Saxon scholar, 38
Alfred, King of Wessex, 33, 34, 36
American Colonies, 207–9
American War of Independence, 211, 213–16
Annates, 1st Act in Restraint of (1532), 117
Anne, Queen (1702–14), 180, 186–9
Anselm, Archbishop of Canterbury, 59
Antonine Wall, 21
Appeals, Act in Restraint of (1533), 116–17
Aquae Sulis (Roman town of Bath), 15, Map 1
Arkwright, Richard, 221–3, 227
Armada, Spanish, 125, 128–9, 139
Arne, Dr Thomas, 2, 180
Arnold, Matthew, 4, 160, 257
Arnold, Dr Thomas, 247
Arthur, the legendary British hero, 26, 34
Asquith, Herbert Henry, Earl of Oxford and Asquith (1852–1928), 276
Assizes, Possessory, 71, 74
Astley, Sir Jacob, 155
Augustine, Archbishop of Canterbury, 31
Augustine, Bishop of Hippo, 1, 23
Austen, Jane, 237, 247
Authorized Version of the Bible, 137–8

Bagehot, Walter, 188, 243, 250
Bakewell, Robert, 228, 229
Baldwin, Stanley (1867–1947), 281

Balfour, Arthur James (1848–1930), 277
Bank of England, 179, 225
Bannockburn, Battle of (1314), 87
Barbon, Nicholas, 169–70
baronage, 64
Bayeux Tapestry, 39, 58
Beauforts, 93, 110
Becket, Thomas, Archbishop of Canterbury, 60, 72, 74
Bede, the Venerable, 37
Bentham, Jeremy, 158, 195, 231–3, 240
Bible, see Authorized Version, 138
Bishops' Wars (1639–40), 148
Black Death (1348–9), 88
Black Prince, Edward Prince of Wales, d. 1376, 96
Blenheim, Battle of, 189–90
Boadicea, see Boudicca
Bodin, Jean, 135
Boers and Boer War, 267, 269–72
Boleyn, Anne, 114, 123
Bolingbroke, Henry, Duke of Lancaster (later Henry IV), 90
Bolingbroke, Henry St John, Viscount, 114, 187, 204
Boniface, Apostle of the Germans, 32, 38
Boswell, James, 140, 191, 222
Bosworth, battle of (1485), 91, 109
Boudicca (or Boadicea), Queen of Iceni, 14–15, 272
Boulton, Matthew, 222
Bowdler, Thomas, 248
Bracton, Henry, 71
Braddock, General, 200
Bretigny, Peace of (1360), 88
Brindley, James, 222
Browne, Sir Thomas, 170
Buckingham, George Villiers, Duke of, 146
Bull, John, 105, 205

287

Rosebery, Archibald Philip Primrose, Earl of, 274
Roses, Wars of, 91, 94–5, 100
Royal Society, 164, 165, 170, 171, 227
Rubens, Peter Paul, 142
Rupert, Prince, 154
Russell, Lord John, 260–1
Rutupiae (Roman town of Richborough), 14, 20, 31, Map 1

St Albans, battles of (1455, 1461), 94
Salisbury, Robert Cecil, Marquess of, 276
'Saxon Shore', 23
Scott, Sir Walter, 7, 95, 192, 247
Seeley, Sir John, 176, 267
Septennial Act (1716), 186
Settlement, Act of (1701), 175, 182–3, 184
Seven Years War (1756–63), 180, 200–1, 203
Shaftesbury, Antony Ashley Cooper, 7th Earl of, 245, 253
Shakespeare, William, 88–9, 90, 95, 137, 142
Shaw, George Bernard, 92, 275, 278
Sheriff's Aid, the, 60
Ship Money, 147 n., 149
Silchester (Roman town, and church), 16, 23
Simnel, Lambert, 109–10
Smith, Adam, 201, 238
Smith, Sir Thomas, 105
Smollett, Tobias, 202, 204
Somerset, Duke of, 'Protector', 122, 134
South Sea Company, 192–3
Southey, Robert, 190
Spanish Succession, War of, 169, 179–80, 190
Stamp Act (1765), 207, 208
Staple, Merchants of the, 98
Star Chamber, Court of, 104, 105 n., 111, 149
Stephen, King of England (1135–54), 59, 62, 63, 72
Stephen, James, of the Colonial Office (1840), 266–7

Strachey, G. Lytton, 249
Stuart, House of, 108, 142
Stubbs, William (historian), 76, 78, 91
Supremacy, Acts of, 118, 124, 125 n.

Tacitus, 15
Temple, Sir William, 168
Tennyson, Alfred, Lord, 4, 242, 253, 262
Tewkesbury, Battle of (1471), 97, 103
Thackeray, W. M., 188
Theodore of Tarsus, 32
Thirty Years War, 145, 152
Throgmorton Plot (1584), 128
Tithe (Saladin, 1188), 76
Toleration Act (1689), 167–8
Tories, 10, 172 n., 185, 192
Townshend, Charles, 2nd Viscount, 228, 229
Townshend, Hon. Charles, Chancellor of the Exchequer (1766), 212
Trevelyan, George Macaulay, 16, 91, 163, 188–9
Troyes, Treaty of (1420), 93
Tudor, House of, 96, 107, 108

Uniformity, Acts of, 122, 124
Union, Act of, with Scotland (1707), 180, 190–1
Utilitarians, 232
Utrecht, Peace of (1713), 169, 170, 190

Vermuyden, Cornelius, 147
Verney, Sir Edmund, 154
Versailles, Peace of (1783), 215
Verulamium (Roman town of St Albans), 15, Map 1
Victoria, Queen (1837–1901), 262–3
'Victorianism', 248–9, 269
Vikings, 34
villas, Roman, numbers and location, 17
villeinage, 9
Virginia, founding and settlement of, 106
Voltaire, 116, 168, 179
Vortigern, 26

way age really began on the day in September 1830 when the Duke of Wellington formally opened the Liverpool and Manchester Railway. In 1830 there were fewer than 100 miles of railway track in the country, but by the end of 1850 there were some 6,000. The building of the great London termini reflects most notably the robust self-confidence of the nation at that time. A terminus such as Euston was built (1838) by men who knew themselves to be building for eternity as surely as the men who built the medieval cathedrals or the pyramids. There were six of these monuments of permanence in London by the middle of the 'Hungry 'Forties', the very time when Europe at large was experiencing another spate of revolutions and certain British prophets of doom (like Thomas Carlyle) were giving our institutions another five years to live. Scarcely twelve months after the erection of the masterpiece in Euston Square, a railway train carried a hundred London constables to Birmingham to disperse a Chartist rally at the Bull Ring. The Chartist Convention called this 'a wanton, flagrant, and unjust outrage...by a bloodthirsty and unconstitutional force from London'. The arrival of the London reinforcement by railway gave notice that the twenty-four-hour start which provincial disorder had for so long enjoyed over the peace-keeping forces of the capital was at last coming to an end.

The Chartist Movement[1] and the 'Hungry 'Forties' coincided with a revolution in transport which revealed the country to itself by linking its various regions and bringing the physical facts of life under the passing gaze of thousands who in earlier times might have remained as distantly ignorant of them as the people of China or Peru. The actual manner of financing the railways also served to promote the development of what Carlyle called 'organic filaments', by spreading the network of property far and wide in the ramifying interests of a multitude of small investors. The 'railway share' brought the habit of investment to

---

[1] Chartism takes its name from the 'People's Charter', a six-point programme for a democratic franchise, all of which except the demand for annual parliaments was to be instituted over the next hundred years. But Chartism is more properly the name for the working-class movement for social justice in general over half a century.

men at every social level, to the trustees of the widow and the orphan, the chapel and the school and the co-operative stores. The growing dominance of the railway time-table in people's lives ('Bradshaw' first appeared in 1839) no doubt had something to do with the increasing regularity of life and habit which was overtaking the ways of an older and wilder England, a society in which the male sex—for so long resplendent in wigs and ruffles, brocaded coats and silken raiment—was encasing itself in the sombre, hideous, industrial uniform known as 'morning dress'.

The *annus mirabilis* of these far-reaching changes in life's tempo and rhythm came in 1851 when the excursion trains unloaded their thousands of ordinary folk at the doors of the Great Exhibition in Hyde Park. The pundits had prophesied disorder, riot, even revolution in the capital with the arrival of these hordes of country cousins, not to mention international crooks and anarchists, in the city whose streets were paved with gold; but all passed off peacefully in a fume of ginger beer and a crumble of penny buns. It was more than an exhibition of the arts and industries of the new age. It was an exhibition of the growing respectability of the working-class world at whose hands these wonders had come. The 'swinish multitude', the 'great unwashed', the 'mobility': such terms were henceforth to become myths of historic memory, best forgotten. The future was to lie with the 'respectable artisan'. The year of the Great Exhibition saw the foundation of the Amalgamated Society of Engineers, that aristocracy of labour which Disraeli had dreamt of including as a 'Praetorian Guard' among the 'fancy franchises'[1] which appeared in the Conservative Reform Bill of 1867. What was happening was an early phase of that 'universalizing of the middle class' which in the end may prove to have been the greatest single social fact, if not the best description of English social history, in the nineteenth century: the pride and joy of lower middle-class

---

[1] 'Fancy franchises', or the admission of the more educated and skilled members of the working class, but not the working class *en masse*, to the suffrage, had figured in Disraeli's thinking and speaking on parliamentary reform as early as 1848, although he rejected, even ridiculed, the idea in his speech on the third reading of the Conservative Reform Bill of 1867.

poets and prophets like Martin Tupper (*Proverbial Philosophy*, 1838) and Samuel Smiles (*Self Help*, 1859) and the disdain of revolutionaries like Karl Marx, already at work in that hot-bed of revolution, the Reading-room of the British Museum. The first volume of *Das Kapital* appeared in 1867.

It was a long and painful process, fraught with many an hour of danger and dismay for the owners of property. Tennyson's *Locksley Hall* in 1842 contained the lines:

Slowly comes a hungry people, as a lion creeping nigher
Glares at one that nods and winks behind a slowly-dying fire.

Such images of civilization under siege, of beasts advancing out of the darkness upon the camp-fires of the guardians of man's inheritance, were part of that apocalyptic view of history as a great succession of catastrophes which dominated men's minds long into modern times. 'Remember the proud fabric of the French monarchy...supported by the triple aristocracy of the church, the nobility and the parliament', Gibbon had written in 1792. 'They are crumbled into dust; they are vanished from the earth.' Burke's fearful prognostications on the French Revolution had embodied the belief that one mighty blow could overturn the world, a horrid vision which could trigger off the malevolent imagination of a desperado like Arthur Thistlewood of Cato Street fame.[1] Even Macaulay conjured up the vision of a future visitor from New Zealand sitting beside the Thames to sketch the ruins of St Paul's. In *Coningsby* (1844), Disraeli expressed the view that the English social system was in infinitely greater danger than that of France, and in the previous year Lord Shaftesbury had warned the House of Commons that 'no one who knew the facts could hope that twenty years could pass without some mighty convulsion, some displacement of the whole system of society'. How a society thus racked and haunted by premonitions of catastrophe, social revolution, even race suicide, was able to pass peacefully into the humdrum but hopeful world of the Parliamentary Labour Party and the Trades Union Congress

[1] The Cato Street conspiracy (1820) was a plot for the wholesale assassination of the Liverpool Cabinet.

is a question only to be answered by the total history of that society over the greater part of a century.

A crucial factor in the story must be the general downward trend of prices in the 1830s together with an unmistakable upward trend in the general standard of living immediately after the bitter years remembered as the Hungry 'Forties. Sir John Clapham's famous dismissal of the notion that everything was getting worse for the working man between the Great Reform Bill and the Great Exhibition as 'a myth that dies hard' is unlikely to solace anyone who chooses to look at all closely at conditions of life and labour in any one industry. Cheaper bread after the repeal of the Corn Laws in 1846 certainly helped. So far from wages being reduced as the price of bread fell, as the Jeremiahs had predicted, wage-rates began moving upwards early in the 1850s, and by 1865 they were on the average nearly 20 per cent above the level of 1848, and the price of necessaries had certainly not risen in anything like proportion. In fact there was a rather better distribution of the national dividend. And yet, 'with what serene conclusiveness', as Carlyle observed, 'a member of some Useful-Knowledge Society stops your mouth with a figure of arithmetic!' Statistical science could prove that the habit of saving had been increasing rapidly, yet the real misery of men was very great. For it had still to be asked: what constitutes the well-being of a man? His wages, and the bread he can buy, are no doubt preliminary to most else. But—can he enjoy hope, can he hope to rise to mastership, how is he treated by his masters?

Practically the whole of Carlyle's great essay, *Chartism* (1839), and his castigation of his own times in the light of an idealized Middle Ages, *Past and Present* (1843), was concerned to insist that the Condition-of-England Question was not political but social and, beyond that, religious. There was no revivalism about this teaching. 'Fancy a man, moreover, recommending his fellow men to believe in God, that Chartism might abate, and the Manchester operatives be got to spin peaceably!' Nor were Parliamentary Radicalism and Benthamite Utility anything but 'shadows of things...barren as the East wind'. Corn Law Repeal,